HANDCRAFTING BAMBOO FLY RODS

HANDCRAFTING BAMBOO FLY RODS

Wayne Cattanach

THE LYONS PRESS
Guilford, Connecticut
An imprint of The Globe Pequot Press

Copyright © 2000 by Wayne Cattanach
Illustrations © Wayne Cattanach

First Lyons Press paperback edition, 2005

The Lyons Press is an imprint of The Globe Pequot Press.

10 9 8 7 6 5 4 3 2 1

Printed in the United States of America

ISBN 1-59228-837-5

The Library of Congress has previously cataloged an earlier (hardcover) edition as follows:

Cattanach, Wayne.
        Handcrafting bamboo fly rods/Wayne Cattanach.—[Rev. ed].
p. cm.
ISBN 1-55821-769-X (hc.)
1. Fishing rods—Design and construction. 2. Fly fishing. 3. Bamboo. I. Title

    SH452.C28 2000
    688.7'91221—de21   99-04485

CONTENTS

Appendices

PREFACE

In the years since the first edition of this book appeared, the craft of bamboo rodmaking has given birth to a social subculture. Many of us feel that the makers of the past were linked in some fashion. Today connection to other rodmakers is as close as an e-mail on the information super-highway or a face-to-face conversation at one of the many organized and unorganized gatherings that occur throughout the year (see appendix E).

The result of this linkage is a growing cottage industry of hobbyist artisans — of individuals who momentarily break away from the "golden hand-cuffs" of their day jobs to craft bamboo. Some of the best bamboo fly rods ever made are being crafted today by these dedicated folks. And because of their genuine interest in advancing their craft, they aren't afraid of sharing the methods and techniques they've learned along the way.

But behind the skills of each maker you'll also discover unique and varied personalities. These fine folks make the world more enjoyable,

and I feel fortunate to know so many of them. I've shared some space at the "Clubhouse" with them, as well as a trout stream or two. A rare blend of bamboo, trout, and just hanging out with a coffee or a microbrew — these are the kinds of activities on which true friendships are built.

On a personal note, it seems that you can brush away certain signs of the passage of time, but you can't do so with others. I have always shared the fly-fishing adventure with my family. Over the years both Matt and Lyndi have learned the craft of bamboo rodmaking. (And yes, there is a purple fly rod, and even a purple reel or two to go with it; see appendix D.)

Together we have shared the special times in the basement workshop as well as on the magical stream, deep in the enchanted forest. But a few years ago Matt went away to college. Now it's Lyndi's turn, before she too soon heads off on a new adventure in her education. The workshop will be a different place.

ACKNOWLEDGMENTS

It's a challenging task to make a bamboo fly rod — but it's just as big a challenge to write a book. Although I've given many seminars on the subject, the transformation from spoken word to printed text has been a learning experience. Fortunately, several friends have helped and encouraged me along the way. One person in particular has made this book possible — Carlos Santos.

I met Carlos through our mutual interest in making fly rods. He dreamed of making his own bamboo fly rod, but he was struggling with the details and looking for advice. Through our conversations we discovered that we had many common interests, and over the years we have built a bond of friendship. Although we did not actually meet face-to-face until a year ago, I consider Carlos an old friend.

Other individuals who gave me valuable assistance and support in completing this project were Ron Barch, Glen Blackwood, Bob Hoekstra, and Joe Loverti. And at the Lyons Press I am indebted to Nick and Tony Lyons, Don Sedgwick, and Jay McCullough for their encouragement and editorial assistance.

Finally, I must thank my wife, "Ben," and our children, Matt and Lyndi, for all their patience, understanding, and help.

INTRODUCTION

A simple definition of a fly rod's function is that it transmits energy from the fisherman directly to a fly line. The line, in turn, extends to full length and comes to rest, carrying with it the fly of choice. I hardly need to add that a fly rod needs to be made with strong yet flexible materials: It must be able to withstand the forces needed to create the cast, yet still not sustain any damage. Finally, an ideal rod should have a character suited to the individual fly caster.

Of course, we all have our own style of fly fishing. A particular kind of trout or salmon, for example, piques your interest. Or maybe you have a passion for small, clear mountain streams that require featherweight rods and delicate presentations. As a result, many factors contribute to our vision of the ideal rod, some real and some imaginary. And these characteristics of the perfect rod are as varied as the individuals who use them.

As a rodmaker, I've been led by my own preferences in rod performance — and you'll see them evolve in the pages of this how-to manual. But I also want to share what I've learned from my own work over the years, and from my rodmaking peers. I hope it may help other makers find new ways to approach old tasks, and to discover new techniques and designs in their search for the ultimate rod.

Before I begin, let me offer the first of many suggestions on how to organize your rodmaking projects. I have included as appendix A a detailed list of the steps involved in making a bamboo fly rod. You might want to photocopy these pages and tack them to a wall or bulletin board in your work area. This checklist should keep you organized, and may even help you schedule your time.

The checklist of tools in appendix B is equally important. It's your shopping list before you begin working, and a handy reference list as you make your way through the projects. Once again, you may wish to post a copy of it in a convenient place. Details about particular manufacturers of these tools, as well as their preparation and maintenance, are included in the text.

The next few pages will help get you started by depicting the basic anatomy of a rod and its parts. Take a moment to read over these terms. Once you understand the language of the parts and processes, you should find that the instructions are relatively easy to follow.

Finally, I hope that this revised edition of my book provides hours of pleasure as you explore the craft of rodmaking. It's a detailed road map to the ultimate destination — your own handcrafted bamboo fly rod.

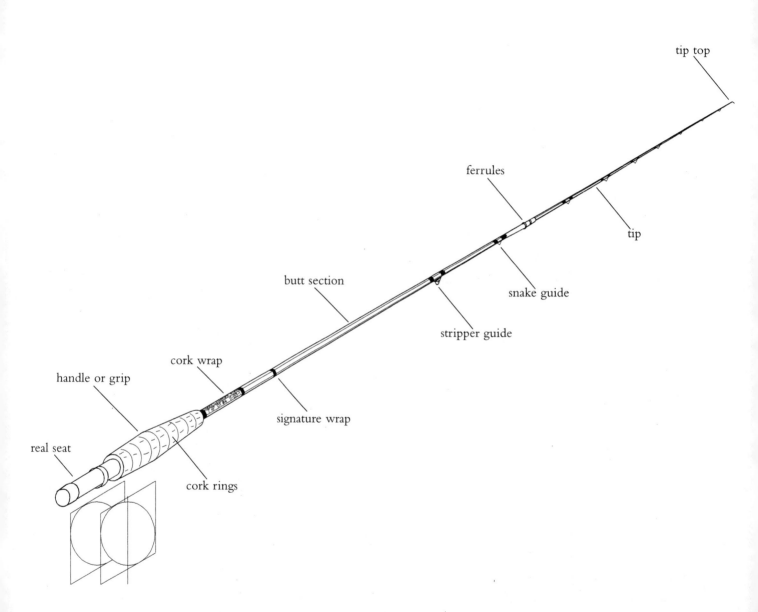

tip top

ferrules

tip

butt section

snake guide

stripper guide

cork wrap

handle or grip

signature wrap

real seat

cork rings

ROD BASICS

The rod (7′6″, 2/2, #4-weight, fast action)

Length: The overall length of a rod when assembled. In the United States length is given in feet and inches.

Pieces: Refers to the number of sections that are needed to assemble the rod to its full length. This number appears after the length and to the left of the slash.

Section: One element or part of a rod. It may be further described as a butt section, midsection, or tip section.

Tips: Traditionally bamboo fly rods are made with two tips. Occasionally each of the tips is made to a different design (one WF or wet fly, the other DF or dry fly). The designation of the number of tips follows the indicated number of pieces and is placed to the right of the slash.

Line weight: The line weight that the given rod was designed to cast, preceded by the # sign. Today the American Fishing Tackle Manufacturer's Association (AFTMA) standard is used, represented by a number. Previously the line weight was indicated by a multi-letter nomenclature, each letter representing a specific diameter of part of the line (*HDH*, for instance).

Action: A word or words used to subjectively describe the character of a rod and the way it casts. Examples are fast, medium, slow, nymph, parabolic, and semi-parabolic.

Strip: A rod subsection or basic triangle. Six strips (triangles) are glued together to make a hexagonal section.

Bamboo: Also known as *Arundinaria amabilis,* "the lovely reed," or by the trade name *Tonkin.* The word *Tonkin* is said to have originated with the Montague Rod Company, which first used this type of bamboo in 1898.

Handle or grip: Constructed from rings of cork, the grip usually varies in length according to the rod's intended use. Its shape or profile will be one of many traditional varieties (cigar, half Wells, and more), or a unique and nameless design.

Cork ring: Called "specie" (coin) because of its round shape, it is available in $1/4$- and $1/2$-inch thickness and is graded by its pores or lack thereof. Flor, Super Flor, Champagne, and 5-star are a few of the classifications. Some names are used by the industry; others are added by local suppliers.

Reel seat: The device that holds the reel to the rod. It may come in a variety of sizes and operating types: dual slide band, downlock slide band, downlock threaded, uplock slide band, and uplock threaded.

Reel-seat stamping: Added by the rodmaker, a stamping is used to personalize a rod. Usually a name is featured, with the word *maker* underneath.

Ferrules: The male and female parts used to mate or join the sections. Inexpensive production rods used ferrules that were extruded from copper and then plated. Better examples are machined from 18 percent nickel silver.

Tiptop: The line guide at the very tip of the fly rod. It is constructed of a barrel with a wire loop soldered into it. The barrel is sized to slide over the end of the bamboo section. This sizing is in sixty-fourths of an inch, and further defined by half numbers (x. 5/64's) for half sizes.

Snake guide: Light-wire line guides fashioned in the long, open loop of a snake. When viewed from above, the traditional American guide usually rises to the right, while the English version rises to the left. Finishes vary from painted (Japanned) to hard-chrome-plated. The latter guides hold up better against the wear of the fly line.

Stripper guide: This is the first guide up the rod from the handle. It's constructed of a "doughnut" mounted in a bifooted wire frame. The doughnut can be of agate or of wear-resistant metal. Today's space-age plastic guides offer less friction in casting, but they detract from the traditional look of a bamboo fly rod.

Wraps and tipping: *Wraps* of thread are used to secure mounted items to the rod. *Tipping* refers to the decorative wraps at the end of the main wrap, usually only five threads in width. Of special note are the following examples:

> **Ferrule:** The wraps reinforce or secure the tabs of the ferrule to the shaft.
> **Cork:** The wraps are placed tight to the end of the cork handle and extend outward. They add a transitional element to the change from cork to bamboo.
> **Signature:** This is the wrap that is outboard on the shaft of the written information or maker's signature. It acts as an accent or block to the writing.
> **Client:** Similar to the signature wrap, this wrap accents the client's name (if present) on the rod shaft.
> **Intermediate:** Additional thin wraps added along the rod between the ferrules. They add both an aesthetic touch and extra strength.

Cork check: A metal disk or cone placed at the transition between the cork handle and the rod shaft. The inner opening should ideally be of the same shape as the cross section of the rod. It's often viewed as simply another part that can come loose later in a rod's life.

Hook keep (keeper): A functional decoration that's normally mounted just above the handle. The common design is a ring held in place with a strap wrapped at each end to the rod shaft. It safely holds the fly when it isn't being cast.

Inscriptions: A rod shaft that has been custom-made may include the client's name, in addition to technical information (length, line weight, number of sections, number of tips, and the like).

1
ORIGINS

Tonkin Bamboo

The splitting and binding of bamboo to make fishing rods can be traced back to China before the time of Christ. The evolution from these ancient rods to the bamboo instruments of today, however, has been a slow process.

In England — a nation steeped in fly-fishing history — early rodmakers experimented widely with the many exotic materials available from the vast outreaches of the British Empire. The list included lancewood, greenheart, ash, and basswood. Each species enjoyed a period of popularity when it was considered the correct material for rod assembly.

It wasn't until the mid-1800s that bamboo was first used by American and British rodmakers. Initially, only tip sections were constructed of bamboo — and the bamboo came from Calcutta. By the turn of the century, complete rods assembled from Calcutta bamboo had moved to the forefront of the industry.

Tonkin bamboo (as it is labeled by many importers), or *ch'a kon chuk* or "tea stick bamboo" (as it is known to growers), wasn't discovered as a rodmaking material until the 1930s. Professor F. A. McClure, who traveled to China in 1927 to join Lignan University as an assistant professor of botany, classified several of the unnamed species

of Chinese bamboo. Among them was Tonkin bamboo, which he gave the Latin name *Arundinaria amabilis*, or "lovely reed."

A. amabilis is cultivated in the rising hills along the Sui River in the adjoining provinces of

The enlarged area shows the region on either side of the Sui River where high-quality Tonkin bamboo flourishes.

Kwangsi and Kwantung. The total growing area is merely 20 to 30 square miles. This is the only region in the world where this species attains the characteristics demanded by rodmakers. Grown on plantations (much as Christmas trees are in North America), stalks of Tonkin cane can reach heights of 40 feet.

Once harvested, the stalks are cut into several pieces and transported to the Sui River for cleaning and straightening. The stalks, called culms by rodmakers, are then graded, bundled, and barged downriver for export throughout the world.

The lower, larger-diameter culms are used for making fly rods as well as furniture. The upper or smaller sections are sometimes used to make the cane fishing poles for kids. In Europe these sections are made into tomato stakes and ski poles — although I've heard of some finished fly rods being referred to by this term.

The Tonkin bamboo that was imported into the United States before the 1950 Truman embargo ranged from 46 inches to as much as 8 or 9 feet in length. The embargo, aimed at halting the spread of communism, prevented the importation of bamboo, as well as all other Chinese imports, from 1950 to 1970. When the bamboo trade was restored after 1970, the culms were cut to 12-foot lengths and came in bundles of 25. Recently the packaging has changed from 25 culms per bundle to 20. The embargo, combined with the advent of fiberglass and its suitability for mass production, brought an end to the golden age of bamboo.

Tonkin bamboo now is available in two grades, depending on the diameter of the butt end. The smaller is 1¾ to 2 inches in diameter. The larger, which is becoming more difficult to obtain, is 2 to 2½ inches. Quantities of less than a complete bundle are usually shipped by United Parcel Service. Because of the company's length restrictions, the 12-foot culms are cut in two when shipped.

Notice in the lower row of the opened bundle that there is a smaller piece of bamboo inside a larger culm. It was used as a handle for carrying the bundle and then driven out of sight as the bundle was loaded into a shipping container.

The one remaining importer of Tonkin bamboo is Charles H. Demarest, Inc. This multigeneration business has seen the transformation from the golden age of bamboo rodmaking earlier this century, through the Truman embargo, to the reduced production of today. (For further information on ordering Tonkin bamboo, see appendix F.)

Size versus Quality

With Tonkin bamboo available in more than one size, how do you know which one to choose? If you're considering the purchase of an entire bundle or more — a large investment — this decision becomes even more agonizing. Our society is ingrained with the idea that bigger is better, which isn't always the case. Each size of bamboo has its advantages and disadvantages; knowing these characteristics will help you make an informed decision.

The larger size (2 to 2½ inches) is at the upper end of Tonkin bamboo's growth limit. Only rarely do you see larger culms; over the years I have collected just a couple of examples that measure 3 inches. This size usually has greater power-fiber depth, which is important if you're consistently making rods heavier than #5 line weight. With the larger circumference of this size of bamboo, you can also alter a splitting pattern to get more strips for those times when you want

Before and after: On the left is an end view of raw bamboo, and on the right a section of cane rod.

to make a dual line-weight rod (four tips) or a braced set of rods. And a larger circumference means that the enamel surface will initially be a little flatter.

But these benefits come with a price. In general, large-size bamboo has more defects — which you may or may not be able to work around. If you're intent on making blond rods, you'll also be faced with some special challenges. Finally, the larger size is more expensive per culm.

It's strictly a numbers issue. To provide the quantities of larger-size bamboo that have been ordered, Chinese producers may at times have to lessen their standards. Because a greater percentage

of the harvested culms are in the 1¾- to 2-inch range, producers can maintain a more rigid standard for this size.

Make, Not Build

This is a terminology distinction that we can trace back to one of the rodmaking pioneers, H. L. Leonard. Stamped on his reel seats below his name was the word *maker*. Today a commonly accepted definition would be that a person who makes the main component of a rod — the shaft — is a *maker*. A *builder* is someone who purchases components (shaft included) and from them assembles a rod.

A butt cap from a 1920s-era Leonard rod showing the use of the term *makers*.

Hexagonal Shape

Most modern bamboo fly rods are made from six strips or splines fashioned into a tapering hexagon. Rodmakers have experimented with 3-, 4-, 5-, and even 12-strip rods with varying degrees of success. The six-strip rod is considered the best and most practical.

Parts and Pieces

The wall of Tonkin bamboo is composed of a hard outer surface, or enamel, that protects the stalk from insects and disease. Immediately below the enamel is a gradually diminishing layer of parallel

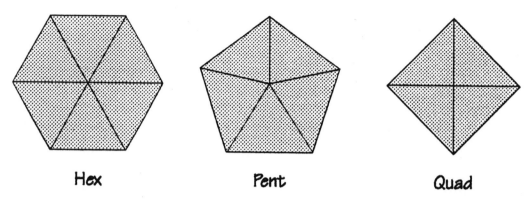

Hex   Pent   Quad

Three cross sections showing the different shapes of traditional cane rods.

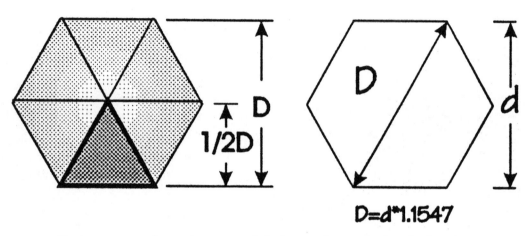

$D = d * 1.1547$

Precise geometry plays an important role in the complex mechanics of a fly rod.

celluloid strings called power fibers by rodmakers. The power fibers run from node (ring) to node in alternately stacked rings that encircle the culm and give strength to the cylindrical structure. The power fibers are bonded together by a substance called lignin. As the rows of power fibers stack inward, they gradually become sparser and no longer touch one another. At this point a light chalky substance called pith starts to develop, which grows inward to a depth of about $3/16$-inch.

At a ring or node (which you will quickly learn to hate), the power fibers from one cell meet with the power fibers of the adjoining cell, crossing and entwining much like interlocked fingers. Also at the node and inside the culm, the pith closes off to form a diaphragm that both gives the stalk strength against an inward collapse and helps the plant reach its tremendous heights.

Bamboo Quality

Culms of Tonkin bamboo are normally harvested with a machete. Because the harvesters don't want to bend over for each culm, they cut the culm at whatever height they can comfortably reach when standing up, usually 24 inches from the ground. At this point the internodal spacing is 10 to 12 inches, but it gradually increases throughout the length of the culm. At the end of 12 feet, the internodal space has increased to 18 to 20 inches; there is little if any dimensional increase past this point.

An inspection of power-fiber depth would indicate solid fibers to 0.200 inch at the lower level, decreasing to 0.080 inch or so at the tip of the 12 feet. The average weight of a 2-inch-diameter culm is 7 to 9 pounds. Lighter culms indicate less power-fiber depth.

Currently Tonkin bamboo is harvested in its eighth growth year. Of the harvested culms, only one out of every five is selected for shipment. The culms that are culled aren't discarded: They're used locally for a variety of projects ranging from fences to construction materials.

A workable goal is to make one fly rod from one culm. Trying to increase this number can be counterproductive. And even with such a 1:1 ratio, the bamboo itself is still the cheapest major component of a bamboo fly rod.

Personal Protection

Throughout this book I'll be referring to how sharp the edges of the bamboo strips are, and the importance of maintaining sharp edges on such tools as plane blades and splitting knives. Rodmakers, especially novices, should practice caution and protect themselves against the inevitable cuts.

Initially you may choose to wear leather gloves when working with these tools. However, you'll soon realize that delicate parts require manual dexterity. The gloves will probably have to be set aside at some point between the coarse and fine work.

I can vividly remember the night I sharpened the blade on my model 212 scraper. I was testing the depth of cut, so I had purposely left the blade lock-down screw less than tight. I picked up the scraper to start a test pass on the edge of my workbench, only to have the blade fall from the unit. On the way to the floor the blade glanced off my right knee, leaving a very nasty slice not only in my jeans but in my flesh as well.

Another hazard for many rodmakers is caused by the time of day they reserve for rod construction. Most amateur makers head for the shop after work or late at night. Indeed, much of my own rod-making time is available only after my wife and children are in bed. When you're tired, things are more apt to go wrong. You then increase your chances of injury and of setbacks due to ruined rod parts. The work can be exciting and enjoyable, but you have to know when to quit.

Use common sense and know the safety rules for all of your equipment.

Splitting Knife

Recently I began using a bamboo froe — a knife meant to be struck with a mallet. In North America froes are used to split cedar shakes for roofs. A bamboo froe is used by Japanese crafters to split and cut bamboo for traditional Japanese construction. Mine is 8½ inches long, which is comfortable for striking with a mallet or for twisting to split the culms. The tool is made of three layers of laminated metal. Each layer is tempered to a different hardness to maximize its usefulness and includes a soft body to absorb the energy of the striking mallet and a hard edge to hold a sharp cutting edge.

A modified bamboo froe used to split bamboo.

In the past I've used several types of knives and chisels to split bamboo, but I must caution you about this: Hunting knives and other hard steel blades can shatter when struck with a mallet. I once broke a very expensive hunting knife with the first blow from a wooden mallet. Be extremely careful to select the proper knife or froe when making bamboo rods.

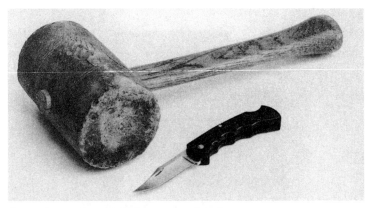

A wooden mallet and knife — my original splitting tools.

Making a Froe

It's not difficult to build a splitting froe. All you need is a piece of cold roll steel flat stock (commonly known as CRS). A piece that's ³⁄₁₆ to ¼ inch by 1¼ inches by 10 inches would work well. For the knife part, the first 3 inches of one side should be sharpened. Even though the steel isn't hardened, the edge will be quite lasting. Once you've initiated a split, it's the width of the froe and not the edge making contact that causes the bamboo to continue splitting. A twisting action of the froe is used in the more critical steps of splitting.

The Modified Froe

Whether you buy or build your froe, you might consider a modification: adding a cushion to the handle. On all the froes I own, I've wrapped the handles with a few layers of cardboard followed by an overwrap of either electrical or duct tape. This is a rather crude method, perhaps, but it works. The cardboard cushions my hand when I strike the froe with a mallet and provides extra grip when I twist the froe. I could have mounted wooden handles on the froes to give them a more proper look, but occasionally I'm more the duct-tape type.

Rubber Mallet

You can use virtually any hammer you like to drive the splitting froe. However, a rubber mallet offers a couple of advantages. First, it has a larger face area for striking the froe. Also, you'll feel the shock of contact less in your hand. And a rubber mallet usually costs less than other types of hammers.

Drying Split

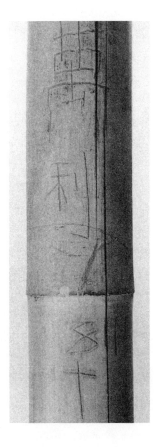

When you receive an order of bamboo, your first step in preparing the culms for storage or use is to start a drying split. This allows the bamboo to season properly: Unless you use a drying split, a drying culm has a tendency to crack in multiple places. Such a split also allows the inner pith to dry properly.

A side view of a drying split, which should always start from the butt end.

On arrival the culms may already have some splits or cracks. These splits may be at the butt end, at the tip end, or even midculm. The drying split should start from the butt end, which has the highest concentration of power fibers and so is under more tension than any other part of the culm. As a properly split culm dries and unrolls, it will split neatly to its tip and pass its energy forward. (This is similar to the way a taper leader passes energy from the large end to the small.)

If a split already exists in the butt end, use your splitting knife and mallet to simply extend this split slightly past the second or third node (ring).

If there are no splits, you must start one. Starting at the butt end, place your splitting knife on the culm and lightly tap it with the mallet. Once the split is initiated, continue tapping lightly until the split has extended through the second or third node.

A warm, dry area in the house makes an ideal bamboo-storage location. A quiet corner or closet away from a damp basement or garage is best for proper seasoning. I should warn you, however, that as the culms dry and split to adjoining nodes, they make a loud popping noise. In the middle of the night the crack of splitting bamboo can be quite unsettling.

2
PRELIMINARY STEPS

Evaluation

I once heard a story about an old bamboo-rod company that created the means to run its plant machinery entirely from scrap and rejected bamboo. When the company received a rail car full of bamboo, 50 percent of the shipment was rejected and sent off to the boiler room for fuel. I am not suggesting that you should reject half of all the bamboo you receive, but there will be defects that pose definite problems. Some culms require so much effort to sort and fix that they aren't worth the trouble.

Any obvious physical defects, of course, should be avoided. These include leaf nodes, worm holes, graffiti (grower marks), and sections burned during the straightening process. Leaf nodes are scars on the bamboo where a branch or outshoot once grew. The growers remove these branches as part of their regular pruning, but the branch growth leaves a crease in the surface of the culm. These valleys are normally $\frac{1}{4}$ to $\frac{3}{8}$ inch in width, but you can usually split around them.

Worm holes are caused by small insects that bore into the stalk of bamboo as it grows. Similar to corn and pine borers, these insects see the stalk of bamboo as a home with a built-in food supply. Their bore holes, which look like the craters of a volcano, normally show up on the surface of the enamel. However, the insects can go undetected if they enter the stalk of bamboo at an early stage. Hidden worm pockets will show up internally as blackened areas. When I find a volcano on the surface, I normally drill it with a $\frac{3}{16}$-inch bit, leaving the hole so that I'm aware of it when I use the culm. Hidden worms can only be found by careful inspection of the freshly split strips. You can work around one or two worm holes, but if you do find even one be sure to inspect *all* the strips from that culm for further infestation.

Tonkin bamboo is grown on plantations, all in the same geographical area but by many growers. To distinguish his stalks from the adjoining plots', each grower carves an identifying mark in Chinese characters in the enamel of some of his stalks. In pre-embargo days these markings were much smaller than they are today. Pre-embargo marks were inscribed in an area approximately $1\frac{1}{4}$ by 8 inches; now fewer characters still take up as much as $2\frac{1}{2}$ by 24 inches of culm. The marks are inscribed on the lower portion of the culms, and should be split around. (They do make interesting conversation items, by the way; I have accumulated several from both the modern and pre-embargo periods with the hope of having them translated.)

Tonkin bamboo, like most plants and trees, can grow crooked at times. Strong winds, poor rooting, and shading from taller stalks may all

A leaf node or outshoot scar is a common physical defect in bamboo culms.

A grower's mark will deface the enamel in that section.

A section that has collapsed from heat straightening is unusable.

power fibers and renders the straightened area of the culm useless. Anytime you see a culm with a heat-discolored, concentrated brownish area, that section of the culm has been straightened and should not be used.

Another defect that doesn't physically damage blond rods but may be considered unsightly is a water mark or stain. Because these small brownish spots show through the enamel, using water-marked bamboo is a personal choice. Most careful makers avoid using such strips, believing it shows a lack of concern for detail. On the other hand, if the culm is going to be flamed, then the water marks may actually add character.

Proper Power Fiber

Perhaps the most crucial step in rodmaking is

Tips

Tips

Butt (2pc)

Butt & Mid (3 pc)

Each rod section should ideally come from a corresponding part of the culm.

result in the occasional crooked or bent stalk. Growers, eager to maximize their harvest yet stay within standard shipping dimensions, will straighten any severely crooked culms. The growers warm the crooked areas of the culm over a small fire, then lash the culm to a straightening bench that resembles a sawhorse. Pressure is applied until the bend straightens. This crude method does tremendous damage to the valuable

determining the depth of power fibers necessary to make a particular rod. Yet there seems to be quite a bit of misunderstanding about this subject.

To keep this discussion simple, I'll examine the taper of a common trout rod — a 7-foot, 6-inch two-piece for a #4-weight line. Each section is about 45 inches in length. Assuming you have a 12-foot culm, the 6-foot butt section should be used for the butt of your rod; use the

7'6" DT#4

TIP

00	0.070
05	0.081
10	0.094
15	0.115
20	0.134
25	0.146
30	0.155
35	0.170
40	0.192
45	0.203

BUTT

45	0.203
50	0.214
55	0.225
60	0.237
65	0.246
70	0.257
75	0.268
80	0.275
85	0.275
90	0.275

One example of a taper listing.

6-foot tip of the culm for your rod's tips. For three-piece rods, the tips come from the upper half of the culm and the butt and mid from the lower half. This is especially true if the culm was cut into two pieces for shipping.

To highlight the power fibers, sand the end of each half with 100-grit sandpaper mounted on a sanding block. The sanding block I recommend is made of hard rubber by 3M and commonly used in body shops. The heavier weight — as compared to plastic versions — will make sanding easier.

Dial Caliper versus Micrometer

In the course of making a bamboo fly rod you'll be taking hundreds of precise measurements.

There are several advantages to using a dial caliper for this, rather than a micrometer. Operated with a simple thumb movement, the dial caliper offers the efficiency of speed. It also allows you to read dimensions directly. If you already have a micrometer, by all means use it. But if you need to buy a measuring device, spend the extra money and buy a good dial caliper with a 4-inch range.

Measuring Power Fibers

Now take a close look at the end section of the culm. You're searching for a white line that delineates where the dark brown power fibers make the transition from being interconnected to being encircled with pith. Make a light mark with a sharpened pencil at this point on each end of the

An end view of a finished rod section that highlights the solid power fibers.

A comparison of a finished #4-weight tip and the O on the back of a quarter.

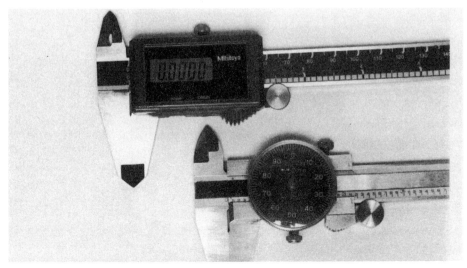

Two choices of calipers for making precise measurements.

two pieces of bamboo. Then measure these depths with your dial caliper and compare them with the half dimensions of the rod taper you plan to use.

Remember to compare the butt power-fiber depth to the butt taper, and the tip power-fiber depth to the tip taper. If the power-fiber depth is greater than the half dimensions of the taper, then the culm can be used for your planned rod. If the power fibers are too shallow, set the culm aside for possible use on a lighter-action rod.

Keep in mind that a rodmaker is seeking to put only the densest power fibers in the finished product. If a rod were made with shallow power fibers and later judged to be a weak casting tool, it would be impossible to judge which element was the cause: the taper design or the quality of the bamboo.

Eventually, you'll be able to judge fiber content merely by hefting a culm. It's not magic, just common sense. The density of compacted power fibers is far greater than that of pith — the more weight, the more power fibers.

Testing Bamboo

Although Tonkin bamboo has been in continuous use for making fly rods since the turn of the century, there is precious little published data on its material strength. Perhaps no one has ever felt the need for such information, or perhaps it never got shared. (Everett Garrison assigned to the material allowable values that worked hand-in-hand with his mathematics for rod design. But that was apparently the end of his investigation.)

Because Tonkin bamboo is a natural material, a window of variation can be assumed. But how broad is the value range?

And how is the material affected by external variables such as long-term storage, or (if improperly stored) mold?

In the process of trying to find answers to these questions, I devised a device I affectionately dubbed the "Cane-O-Tine." The purpose of this testing unit is to monitor the breaking of specific sizes of bamboo strips. The Cane-O-Tine consists of two support arms spaced 6 inches apart with Vs cut into their top edges. Centered between the support arms is a slide device constructed of ½-inch-thick material. Atop the slide is a flat surface to accept weight. (In my own case, I use barbell rings.)

The test samples were 12-inch strips of bamboo that I heat-treated and planed to triangles

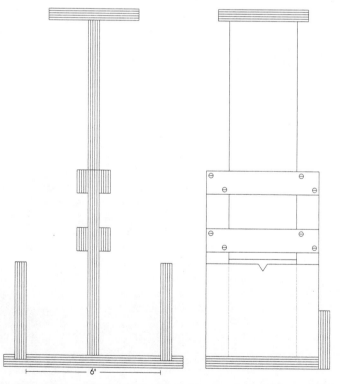

The custom-built "Cane-O-Tine," used to test the breaking point of bamboo strips.

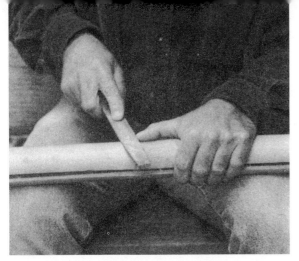

The author sitting on his deck, patiently filing a node.

measuring 0.150 inch (solid power fiber) from flat to apex. The samples were placed into the support arms, enamel-side up, with equal overhang. Then I lowered the slide and added various weights at timed intervals until the strips broke. The results of this primitive

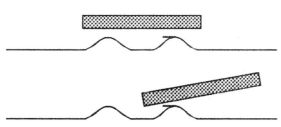

The different angles of the file used to dress a node.

test mechanism revealed 7 to 8 pounds of weight was needed to break the sample pieces.

I should add that I'd been making rods for many years without questioning the ultimate strength of my materials before I devised this test method.

Sanders

The use of a vibrating sander can speed your initial prepping of the nodal areas. Modern high-speed pad sanders work best, particularly if you add a piece of Plexiglas over the sander's felt pad. This gives the sandpaper a rigid backing, since the nodes are to be

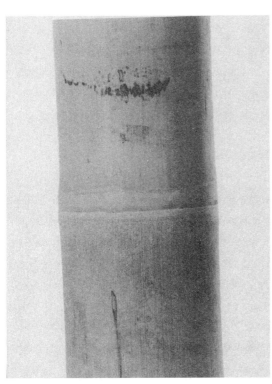

A node before filing.

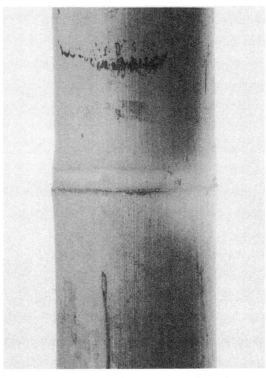

Careful filing has now reduced the node without damaging the power fibers.

sanded flat. Without the Plexiglas, the felt pad would follow the contour of the node and yield poor results.

Nodes

Node areas recieve special attention, because one mark of a quality bamboo rod is nodes that have been flattened without cutting any power fibers. Examine sample rods through history and you'll see that the more respectable rodmakers have always addressed flattening nodes. Production-oriented companies didn't bother; their method was simply to sand nodes away, leaving in their path several layers of cut power fibers. When viewed carefully, the cut fibers look like fingers above and below the nodes.

Preparing Nodes

Your first step in preparing the culm of bamboo is to reduce the depth of enamel at the nodes. This is done initially with a mill file and then with a pad sander.

Use the mill file sparingly and then only with a pulling or drawing action. First, place the culm on a solid work surface. Grasp the culm with your left hand and hold the file in your right. If you are left-handed, hold the culm in your right hand and file with your left hand. As you pull the file across the node, slowly roll the culm forward. The file must be kept parallel with the surface of the culm. Keeping the file centered on the highest area of the node will help keep the file traveling flat.

Only a moderate pressure should be used; too much wrist pressure will cause you to lose control of the file. Scraping the edges of the file across the flats of the culm can damage the outer power fibers. I normally file until I've removed a ¼-inch-wide path of enamel from the nodal ridge.

After you've dressed all the nodes with the file, switch to the pad sander. This is essential in order to keep from leaving deep gouges in the surface of the bamboo. Such gouges would be noticeable in later stages, and they'd be hard for you to remove without sanding through layers of the valuable power fibers.

Use a pad sander with 100-grit and begin sanding in the same manner in which you used the file. Keep the pad parallel to the culm surface, and use the identical rolling action on the culm. If the nodal area is so flat that you're sanding adjoining areas other than just the nodes, try using only the corners of the sander.

As you sand, the nodal valley will slowly disappear. Stop sanding when there's still a ¹⁄₁₆-inch-wide strip of enamel left in the valley. At this width the enamel will start to look greenish in color.

Using the rolling action is important in order to remove material uniformly — a difficult trick on the round surface of the culm. If the enamel ring left from sanding isn't uniform in width, concentrate your sanding effort on the wider areas. Avoid creating segments of flat spots as you sand.

File in Hand

One of the rodmaking methods that has changed for me over the years involves the sander. I don't use it any more. Shortly after my son, Matt, started making rods, he chose to prepare a node area entirely with a file. By careful work, he was able to remove the entire node lip with a file without damaging the enamel surface or leaving excess file marks. This is a time-saving method that eliminates the expense of the sander. And with practice you can increase the coarseness of your file from a mill file to a more aggressive bastard type.

There's one caution that I should add about using a file on the node lip: If you apply too much pressure you can lose control of the file. If the file were to fall off the node lip, for example, its sharp corner could cut the surrounding enamel surface that it contacts. This could damage the surface and the power fibers.

Additionally, you should slowly roll the culm as you file the node lip. This will prevent segmenting and allow the file to remove a more uniform amount from the circumference of the culm.

In most cases the two mounds that form the node area will both show evidence of filing. However, there are exceptions. Occasionally an entire node area or part of one will be flush or submerged in comparison with the surrounding bamboo. This will make it very difficult to file the node lip without doing damage to the surrounding area.

An alternate method in such cases is to tilt your file and address only the lipped ridge. Another trick is to choose a file with a smooth side edge and use the thumb of your culm-holding hand as a guide point. Place the thumb next to the node valley, then touch the file to the thumb. When done properly, your thumb will keep the corner of the file from contacting the surface of the node valley, avoiding file damage to this area.

You'll know that you're done preparing the node area when you've removed enough of the lip that you can't catch it with a fingernail. A good indicator is the dirt that settled under the lip as the bamboo grew. As the last of the dirt disappears, so should the last of the lip. Here again, practicing with different files and file pressure might be advisable. Using a practice culm for your first attempts is a good idea as well.

Splitting the Culm

I prefer working with split strips that are between $3/16$ and $1/4$ inch in width. And because I most frequently work with a culm 2 inches in diameter or $6\frac{1}{4}$ inches in circumference, I ended up with 24 strips per culm.

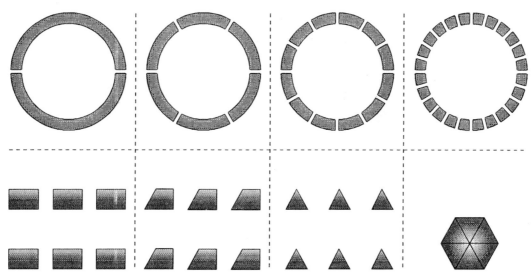

An end-view schematic of the various steps from culm to assembled section.

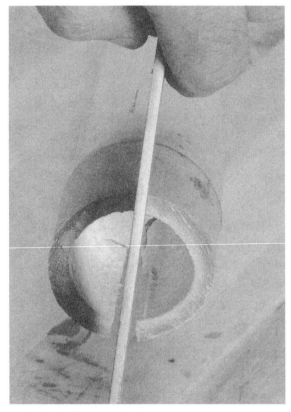

Initiating the split with the froe.

Starting with a whole culm with a drying split, first split the culm into two pieces. Using the drying split as a guide, halve the culm along a line exactly opposite the drying split. This will give you two pieces with a 3⅛-inch circumference.

Splitting from the butt of the culm to the tip works best. Place the splitting knife in the drying split and on the unsplit side. Initiate the split by tapping with a mallet. Once the split starts, you can extend it through the culm by twisting the blade of your splitting knife. As the split extends, follow it down the culm with your knife. If you come to a spot where the splitting knife hangs up, twist its blade again or give it a light tap with the mallet.

Once the culm is opened up into two pieces, you'll see little shelves that bridge the inside of the culm at the node levels. These diaphragms add strength to the bamboo, allowing it to grow tall. The bulk of these diaphragms can be removed by tapping them with a carpenter's hammer. Later, you'll plane away the remaining ridge.

After the culm is split in half, each half is split into thirds. Using a flexible rule to guide you, place pencil marks to indicate the split points on the outside rim of the butt end. To start the split, place your splitting knife on a pencil mark and on an imaginary point that would be the center of the culm. This will give you uniform angles on the split strips. Then run the splitting knife down the length of the culm either by taping it with

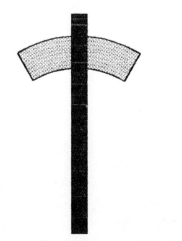 

An end-view of how the froe should (left) and should not (right) correspond to the culm.

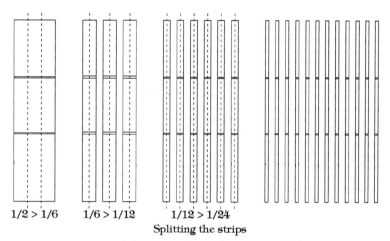

1/2 > 1/6   1/6 > 1/12   1/12 > 1/24

Splitting the strips

A top view of the stages from culm to assembled section.

your mallet or by twisting it. When you're finished, you'll have six pieces of equal width.

Up to this point the splitting has been more or less straightforward, done either by driving your knife (or froe) or by twisting the froe the length of the culm. For the next two series, you'll advance the split by a twisting action of the knife. For safety's sake once you've initiated the split with the sharp edge forward, it's best to reverse it so the knife's blunt edge is forward. Holding the strip in your left hand and the knife in your right, twist the knife and advance the split, then feed the strip to the knife for the next twisting.

The splitting continues as each of the six pieces is split in half. Again mark the pieces, using this mark and the imaginary center point to keep the angle of your split correct. This will give you 12 pieces that are each about ½ inch wide. To finish, you'll split each of these strips in half for a total of 24 pieces, all of them about ¼ inch wide.

I use this method for both the butt and tip sections. Ideally, the tip sections would be split narrower, but I've never been successful at doing this. Any gain I make in the number of strips is usually negated by those that I ruin.

A Safety Issue

During the earlier stages of splitting the culm (those that involve driving the froe the length of the culm), you must exercise special caution. Work in such a manner that if the froe does come free of the culm, you can still avoid an accident. A natural approach might be to work with the culm directly in front of you, with your arm holding the froe straight ahead of your body. In this position your arm acts to guide the froe toward your leg area if it comes free of the culm.

An even safer position is to bring the culm a bit closer to you and hold the froe with your elbow bent at 90 degrees. In other words, when your forearm is viewed it should be seen as horizontal and not vertical. In this position, if the froe were to dislodge it would swing off to the side, away from your body rather than toward it.

Walking

Just when this rodmaking exercise is beginning to seem easy, you may be in for an unpleasant surprise. Splitting the culm in half may go smoothly, and even splitting the halves to create six pieces might not seem too challenging. The problems begin, however, when you try to create 12 pieces, and they'll certainly hit when you attempt 24 pieces. The challenge is that in some culms, the

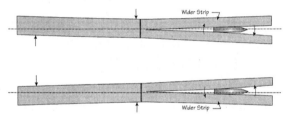

The taper in the strip illustrates an uncontrolled split.

split runs to one side. In fact, the split may even "walk" right to the edge, leaving you with a fat wedge strip and a long slivered strip instead of the neat 1/4-inchers you intended.

The way to control the path of a split is to flex the wider side against your splitting knife. This creates a slight bow in the strip. At the same time you might want to twist the blade so that its

Using this technique, the split can be controlled to center.

leading edge pushes against the wider piece. And it doesn't hurt to slow down a bit and carefully watch what's happening.

To illustrate how the strips should flex, try this exercise with a 1/4-inch dowel rod. Hold the

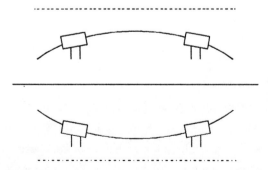

The upper view is an outward flex; the bottom is an inward flex.

rod with your hands about 12 inches apart. Now pivot your wrists so that your thumbs move outward. This will force the dowel to flex away from you. Likewise, pivoting your wrists so the thumbs move inward will force the dowel to flex toward you.

Imagine that I'm splitting a strip with the bamboo held in my left hand and the splitting knife in my right. At this point the split has walked from the center and left the strip closer to me wider than the piece farther from me. To correct this problem, I twist my left hand, moving the thumb away from and bringing the pinkie closer to me. This puts pressure against the splitting knife, pushing it away. But by resisting this pressure with the froe in my right hand, the bamboo is flexed outward with pressure. It doesn't take much pressure or flexing to make this work successfully.

Now with the strip flexed, twist your splitting knife so that you push its leading edge against the wider strip. In this case I would twist the splitting knife; now the leading edge comes toward me.

If you're midway between nodes, you may gain nothing until you split through these nodes. Once you split through one of them, however, stop to see if you've moved the split back to the center. If so, you can once again split without flex-

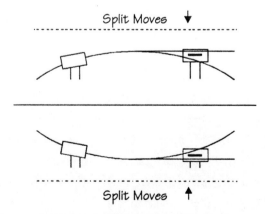

A more defined and detailed view of the flexing control.

ing the bamboo. But if you're still off center, maintain the flexure until the split is back on the centerline.

A common splitting error is to try to *push* the knife through the bamboo. This is a mistake because the split is best advanced by slowly *twisting* the splitting knife. After each twist, reposition your splitting knife to within approximately 6 inches of the connected V, then repeat the twist. Use this technique for the entire length of the split.

It's also a mistake not to keep your splitting knife perpendicular to the crown of the strip that you're splitting. An improper position leads to incorrect edge angles and will affect how the strips fit into your first planing form.

Another Splitting Method

I have come to learn that the splitting method outlined above doesn't work for everyone. My daughter, Lyndi, for example, has problems with this technique, as do some other rodmakers. At 13, Lyndi didn't have the wrist muscles to make the strips flex correctly. As an alternative, a firmly mounted vise will help provide a steadier support for the splitting knife.

The split is initiated with the froe. However, instead of holding this tool in your hand to do the splitting, mount the froe in a vise with the blunt edge facing you. Then place the strip against the mounted froe at the initiated split and push the strip forward. This forward push should make the split advance. If the split starts to go off center, you can force it back to center by using a bit of body English. The strip still needs to flex on the wider side, as illustrated earlier, but now you can use your entire body to help with this effort, and not just your wrists. As the strip flexes in the proper direction, push forward to advance the split.

This procedure requires a little more time than the froe-in-hand method, but it works quite well. As for Lyndi, she can also enlist Dad's help if she gets stuck. Four hands are usually better than two.

Backcuts

One of the problems that can arise during splitting of the culm is *backcuts*. I use this term to describe those times when the froe goes off the desired angle. Remember, the froe should always be perpendicular to the surface of the culm at the split.

Correcting a backcut once it starts is a simple matter of holding the bamboo and forcing the froe back on track. When you're splitting the half culms into sixths, you can watch the path of the froe fairly easily. Once you start splitting the next series and holding the bamboo in your hand, though, it's easy to let the froe wander and vary the angle of its cut.

The problem with backcut angles is that they won't fit into the angle-starting form correctly, and you may then have problems getting correct 60-degree angles. To fit the first form, at least one side angle must be correct: 7½ degrees.

Fortunately, the problem of backcuts can be reduced later. When you choose the six strips to create each section, you'll have to stagger them and cut them to a working length. At that point you can attempt to cull out backcuts and other flaws. Once the strips are staggered (but before they're cut), their ranking can be changed and you can eliminate the unwanted sections.

If the strips are staggered and cut to length but not all of the backcut is removed, then some preliminary planing will be required. To plane a backcut to a proper angle, set the strip on edge and cut a new angle freehand. The new angle can be tested for a proper fit in the first form and adjusted as needed.

Gouging the Diaphragms

Some rodmaking manuals suggest that when the culm is split in half, the diaphragms should be removed by chiseling them away with a gouge. It seems to make sense: The more you remove in

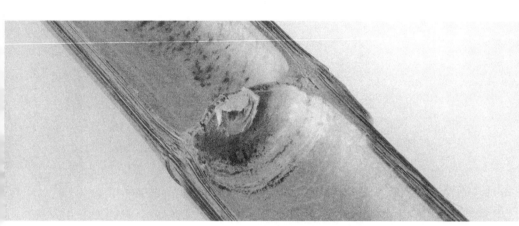

A view of the diaphragm inside the culm.

these areas before splitting, the easier the next stage will become. When I used this technique, however, my chiseling didn't go well. I managed to get the diaphragms removed, but it didn't leave a nice surface on the pith, and it didn't make the splitting any easier.

The Ideal Strip

As you practice the art of splitting bamboo, you'll know when you're mastering the technique. The split strips will be of uniform width, and the split edges will reflect an angle that consistently fits into the first planing form correctly. But like other life skills, practice is needed. Today, after many years of trial and error; I split only the strips that

I need to make a rod. But if you're a beginner, my recommendation is to split all the bamboo at hand — and enjoy the practice.

Flaming

To some rod aficionados, there's nothing as exciting as the mottled appearance of a bamboo fly rod that has been flamed. With its multitones of brown, even water spots — the bane of blond rods — become interesting little highlights. Many of the classic rods of the past were flame-toned in some fashion, and sooner or later most rodmakers try flaming at least once. (When attempting new techniques, I always use sample pieces first. This allows me to test my equipment and skills without committing large amounts of time and materials to failed projects.)

Flaming the bamboo produces a burned-marshmallow look.

As a mechanical contractor, I have a variety of torches for different tasks. I've found two of these to work well for flaming. The first is a propane torch I use for soldering large (up to

The commercial Turbo Torch.

6-inch) copper tubing. It's a Turbo Torch with a T-7 head and an output of about 150,000 BTUs. The next time you're in the basement, walk over to your furnace and check out it's output. It will probably be less than this torch.

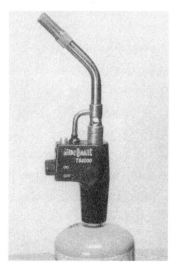

The readily available BernzOmatic torch.

The other propane torch I use has about a tenth the BTU output of the first. It is a SureFire model T-550 (now known as a model TS4000) manufactured by BernzOmatic. This unit screws to the top of a 14-ounce propane cylinder and is self-igniting:

The flame can be started or stopped with one finger. You should be able to find one locally at a larger hardware store or wholesale plumbing supply outlet.

The feature that makes both these torches excellent for flaming is that their flame is defused into a wide, flat pattern. There isn't just one distinct point of flame; instead, the flame is spread to cover a larger area with the same heat intensity.

For flaming I've found it best to split the culm into two halves and place the halves on the barbecue. This should only be done, of course, outside in the fresh air. This will give you better freedom of movement, making the job easier and safer since you won't have to hold the hot, steamy cane. If you choose to flame the culm whole, it must have one split that runs the length of the entire culm. This will prevent the culm from cracking during the severe expansion and contraction caused by the rapid application of heat.

There are two basic types of flaming: a solid, uniform toning, and a mottled or tiger-striped flaming. Each requires a different torch method. For a more solid toning, run the torch parallel to the culm. For a mottling effect, run the torch perpendicular to the culm while maintaining a uniform distance from the tip of the flame to the cane's surface. Indexing on each pass by about $1\frac{1}{2}$ inches gives good results.

Using the T-550 torch, the tips of the flame should just touch the surface of the cane and be moving at all times (about 2 to 4 inches per second). Always start at one end of the culm and work toward the other, either in straight passes or spirals. This pushes the moisture out of the culm. Other patterns may trap moisture and leave dead spots in a finished rod.

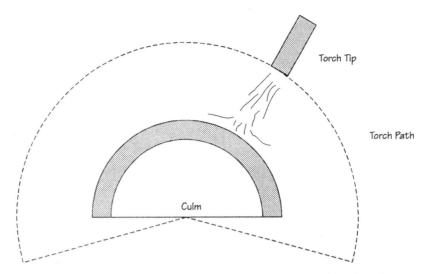

The torch tip and the positioning and path, as viewed from the end of the culm.

When you come to a node area, treat it as you do the rest of the culm, wielding the torch at the same speed and distance. As you run the torch over the surface of the cane, you'll notice that the enamel has a tendency to "explode" or flake up as the torch passes over it. Don't panic: Flattening and final dessing will come later.

How much flaming is enough? This is a matter of trial and error, as well as personal taste. The surface may look black, but you're looking for proper toning at the top of the power fibers that are a few thousandths of an inch below. As I suggested, try this flaming technique on sample pieces first. Flame a piece and then block-sand it with 220-grit sandpaper to check your results, noting the correct speed and distance of the torch. This is where having seen a properly flamed rod comes in handy. Try to attend some shows or meetings of other rodmakers to see samples of their work. You will soon start to notice other areas of detail and begin to develop your own sense of an ideal bamboo rod.

Flaming Advantages

Besides the benefit of masking water marks in the bamboo, flaming the culm also helps reduce the resident moisture. This will work to your advantage later when you're splitting and completing the preliminarily planing of the strips.

Avoid the Cheapie

Some of life's lessons can be disheartening. The least-expensive and most readily available propane torch is the single-pointed flame unit found at most hardware stores. Don't fall for the temptation. By the time you get the outer enamel as you might want, the low heat output from these torches will carbonize the power fibers beyond use.

The best analogy I've found is that of searing a steak. Over low heat, the steak will cook through before the surface browns. But over high heat, the surface can be browned while the core is still unaffected. This is important if you like your steak rare — or your bamboo usable.

3
WORKING WITH PLANES

Planes

The tool that epitomizes the rodmaking craft is the hand plane, the most basic and commonly used implement for all makers. And of the many hand planes available, the Stanley 9½ is by far the most popular. After trying a variety of hand planes for

The old and the new: Grandfather's 9½ and the recent G12-020.

the different stages of cane removal, I settled on the Stanley 9½ block plane for all my cane work.

When I use the generic term 9½, I'm referring to a group of block planes modeled after the original Stanley 9½ block plane. This was a fully adjustable block plane with a mouth (forward sole) adjustment, a fine blade adjustment, and a lateral blade adjustment. It also featured a quick-release locking lever for fast blade removal. All these features made the model 9½ ideal for delicate finish work, which is essential for the precision of rodmaking.

The original model 9½ is easily identified by the stamping on the left side of the body. This plane also features a brass adjustment wheel and guide knob. The model 9a is a copy of the 9½, except that the brass parts have been replaced with steel. The Record Company of England still

makes a model 9a, which is available in the United States through selected outlets.

The latest version of this tool is the Stanley model G12-020. The left rear side of the plane's

Note that the plane is stamped "G12-020," but the box is labeled "12-920."

body is stamped "12-020." However, if you look for this plane at a local hardware store, note that the box is now marked with the stock number "G12-920." This is the new stock number for the plane and reflects the ISO 9000 quality-assurance guidelines. It has been refitted with a direct pressure turn-bolt system for adjusting the blade exposure. (Models 9½ and 9a used a turn wheel that drove a leverage arm to force changes in the blade exposure.)

A comparison of the new and old blade-adjustment systems.

Until recently, your choice of fine adjustment plane was limited to a Stanley or Record. Now Lie-Nielsen Toolworks has also introduced a 9½ version to its line. (Later I will mention the model 212 scraper that this company has produced for several years.) Tom Lie-Nielsen and his company have established an excellent reputation for fine woodworking planes and scrapers, carrying on the legend of the 9½.

The main body of the Lie-Nielsen plane is made of cast iron, with the forward foot-adjustment knob and blade lock-down fashioned of bronze. The fit and finish are exacting, with no major tuning required. I found that after a simple sharpening of the blade, the plane was ready for use. Not intended for the budget conscious, the Lie-Nielsen Toolworks plane costs about twice as much as a Stanley or Record after adding a proper blade.

No Low Angle

Throughout the many chronicles of rodmaking, there are several references to the use of the Stanley 60½ plane. This is very similar to the model 9½ in function (adjustable front foot and lateral blade adjustment), except the blade angle is set lower, at 12 degrees.

Like many other rodmakers, I bought one as a necessary tool for my rod-making arsenal. But when I tried to use it, I had problems. Because of the low blade angle, the bamboo would split ahead of the blade cut — resulting in a loss of control. My 60½ now sits on the "tried but failed" shelf in my basement.

In fairness I should mention that some makers have been able to use low-angle planes for rodmaking. In my conversation with these individuals, I recently learned the key to their success: They changed the blade angle from a

The Lie-Nielsen version of the 9½.

standard 30 degrees to a steeper 40 degrees (approximately). By changing the blade pitch, you end up with an angle of attack that's the same as that of a 9½ with its blade angle at 30 degrees.

Tuning a Plane

Even if you've purchased a new hand plane, you'll want to properly tune it before using it on your rod projects. The most critical area to check is the flatness of the sole. If the sole has a concave shape to it (and most will), you'll have problems planing the strips correctly. The problem in using a sole that isn't flat is that the bamboo can be pulled up from the form. And once it's pulled up, you may remove more material than you intended and end up with undersize strips.

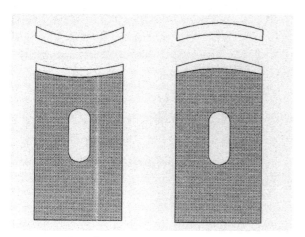

Two examples of problems that can arise if a blade isn't flat.

To check your plane, you first need to adjust it to a cut of 0.005 inch with a throat opening of 0.014 inch to 0.020 inch. Apply the same pressure to the blade and throat lock that you intend to use later. Moderate pressure is all you need to hold the throat and blade properly. Once you have the adjustments correct, back the blade into the body until you can no longer feel it when you run your thumb over it.

Next you need a flat surface. A piece of ¼-inch Plexiglas or a table-saw top will work well. Lay a sheet of 400-grit (wet or dry) sandpaper on your flat surface with the abrasive side up. Using a light pressure, set the plane on the sandpaper and move it in a back-and-forth motion. A few passes are all you need. Now flip the plane over for a visual inspection. If the surface of the sole doesn't give evidence of the sandpaper immediately in front of and in back of the blade, then the sole needs attention.

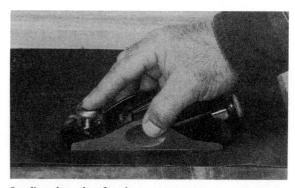

Sanding the sole of a plane.

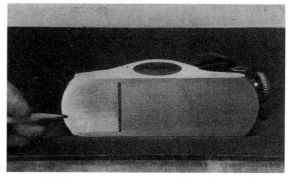

A view of the initial contact, indicating a crowned sole.

Upon inspection, you may either decide that the sole is flat or choose to continue sanding. If you continue, you'll gradually see the polished areas grow together until the entire sole has a uniform sheen. Go even farther by using 1,500-grit sandpaper after the 400-grit. The 1,500-grit will give the sole a mirrorlike finish. This finer finish doesn't make the plane slide any easier, but it will impress your friends when they come over to see your shop.

A properly surfaced sole.

A word of caution. You may think that the sole can be flattened on a surface grinder. I tried this once. When you chuck the plane up in a holding vise, the pressure on the sides of the plane will pop the sole up. You grind the surface flat, but when you remove the pressure of the vise from the sides of the plane, the sole pops back into place and you still have a concave sole.

Recently I tried another trick. Before I sanded the sole, I placed a 0.0005-inch piece of shim stock between the tongue and the surfaces that it seats against. Then I sanded the surfaces as before. When I removed the shims I had a slight recess, which seems to keep me from planing as much metal from the forms as I once did.

Blade Slide

For years I could never get as fine a cut with a current-model Stanley plane as I could with my grandfather's original. Before I am misunderstood, however, I need to explain that the new Stanley would consistently adjust to a 0.001-inch removal. However, Grandfather's would consistently adjust down to 0.0005-inch. That's a mere half thousandth of an inch viewed one way, or only half as fine viewed another. With either plane, a human hair could be split several times.

The problem was something I had overlooked. When I first purchased and tuned my current-model Stanley, the blade-rest area (the surface that the lower part of the blade touches) was machined to a reasonable smoothness. So I chose not to do any resurfacing of that part of the plane.

As time passed, I had added several more new versions of the Stanley to my collection of rod-making tools.

One night as I was sharpening the blade of the plane, I looked down to see that the blade rest had been poorly machined. Not having named all my planes, I didn't know how long I'd been using this particular one. My discovery started a quest of sorts. Before long I had all the planes I owned lined up on the workbench with their blades removed. I decided that the best thing to do was resurface the blade-rest area on all of them.

To accomplish this I first removed the blade, then the blade tensioner, and finally the front adjusting foot. With 220-grit sandpaper wrapped around a plane blade, I sanded the seating surface to remove all evidence of machining. I switched sandpaper in progression to 400-grit, then 1,000-grit, until I had a mirror surface.

A plane with its blade removed, ready to have the blade-rest area resurfaced.

While doing this I reflected on how I had cleaned up Grandfather's plane. It had become quite rusted by just sitting around, so to brighten it up — but not remove the patina — I rubbed the entire plane down with 0000 steel wool and Vaseline. This was a conditioning tip that an antique-tool dealer had passed along to me. Then, using 0000 steel wool and a Teflon-based grease, I polished the seating surface of the planes. My thought was to work the lubricant into the pores of the cast-iron body for a slicker surface.

In the end I was able to increase the fineness of the cut of the new-version planes. Deep down, however, I still feel that Grandfather's can kick butt on the others. Or perhaps that's just a matter of emotional loyalty.

Tension Screw

One of the weak points of the Stanley design is the lock-down adjustment screw. It's supposed to control the tension placed on the blade by the lock-down cam. However, it turns so easily that it constantly goes out of adjustment. Having put up with this frustration for several years, I finally took some action and used thread sealant to halt its random movement.

But I had to make a few decisions. The first was the amount of tension that should be placed on the blade. Because of the fine amount of control needed, this tension should be held to a minimum. You want to allow the blade to slide reasonably freely. Excess tension will cause the blade to skip or move erratically, making it difficult to obtain minute setting adjustments.

Second, because there can be slight dimensional variations from blade to blade, I dedicated a single blade to the plane. This meant that I wouldn't have a sharp blade in waiting and would need to interrupt planing when sharpening was required. (This might be a nonissue if you order a couple of blades at a time. Within each batch the thickness is very consistent, with only slight variations from batch to batch. But there are other drawbacks in trying to use more than one blade with a plane.)

Then there is the choice of thread-sealant strength. Thinking ahead, I chose to use the softer set of Loctite 242 to allow for a later blade change. I avoided the stronger sealant (Loctite 721), which may not allow the screw to turn again. My suggestion to the designers at Stanley would be to add a nylon insert to this screw to dampen unwanted movement.

Applying Loctite to the blade tension screw.

Cut Adjustment

Each time you remove the blade from a hand plane and return it, a slight amount of readjustment is required. The impact of this can be reduced by following a few simple steps.

The first is to remove all debris. In almost every instance when you remove a blade, you will find underneath it some bamboo shavings. To ensure properly seated surfaces, whisk the shavings from the body cavity and hold-down lever cap with a paintbrush.

Another tip is to reassemble the plane with the body setting on a flat surface. Then you can be fairly assured that the point of the blade and the surface of the sole are in proper alignment, and that the blade is correctly seated against the adjusting stop. But before you start working again, check all of the parts carefully.

The blade point and sole alignment require a visual inspection. With the plane in your hand, flip it over and hold it in a position such that you can see the two against each other. Looking from the back of the plane and at a low angle will visually place the blade edge and the back edge of the front foot against each other. If necessary, use the lateral adjustment to bring the two into alignment.

Finally, inspect the blade seating by checking the depth of the cut on something other than work-in-progress strips. One suggestion is to screw a 12-inch piece of wood to the edge of the workbench for just this purpose. Always check the cut and make adjustments before proceeding. In most cases the blade will need to be backed up for a shallower cut. It's hard to get the blade fully seated to the stop and tight enough to retain the previous setting.

Here's where I appreciate the direct-bolt system of the newer model G12-020. To back the blade involves only a quick counterclockwise twist of your wrist. Follow with a clockwise twist, stopping short of the original starting point. This will leave the blade just shy of where you need it. But the blade will now be fully butting against the stop. A test and a quick adjustment and you'll be back to the work at hand.

Dueling Blades

The idea of having several blades sharpened ahead of time, ready for use, has some merit. But there is a downside: the extra time you'll spend readjusting the amount of the cut. This variation is a result of the adjustment indent versus the blade-point distance being different with each blade. Even if two blades start out identical, over time they'll wear differently as a result of sharpening.

Plane Blades

Over the years the edge-holding quality of the blades supplied with hand planes has lessened. The blade in my grandfather's original 9½, for example, holds a sharp edge for a fair amount of time. But the blade that came with the G12-020 I purchased recently didn't hold a good edge.

The reason may be that the features many carpenters are looking for in a blade have changed. In my grandfather's day everything was done by hand and it was crucial to carpenters that tools held a sharp edge. Today, as a result of power tools, a carpenter may only be concerned that the blade on his hand plane doesn't rust while it rides around in the back of his pickup truck.

This rust resistance is achieved by adding chromium to the iron mixture. However, chromium crystals are larger in size than high-carbon steel molecules, resulting in a compromise on how keenly a blade can be sharpened. Think of a blade as akin to a concrete sidewalk, with the finer portion representing the high-carbon steel and the chromium being the stones that show through the surface. Chromium-mixture blades can be a big source of grief for the unknowing rodmaker.

Fortunately, the solution is simple. Merely replace the blade with a Hock blade. Ron Hock, a knife-maker from Fort Bragg, California, makes his plane irons from high-carbon steel tempered to produce long-lasting sharp edges. All the budding rod-

Hock, the symbol of quality in a plane blade.

makers to whom I've recommended the Hock brand have commented on how much easier it is to plane strips with these high-quality blades.

Like Planing Concrete

It may be news to some readers that Tonkin bamboo has been found to contain high amounts of silica (sand), perhaps blown into the growing plants by strong winds. Combine this with the fine tolerances required in our craft and you can understand the need for sharp planes and scraper blades. This is an area that I cannot stress too much: Many of the frustrating problems that arise in bamboo rodmaking arise directly from the use of dull blades. When in doubt, resharpen. The few minutes it takes may save you hours of grief.

Sharpening Stones

Another area that most potential makers know little about is sharpening stones. I once asked a finish carpenter to show me how he sharpened his plane blades. He walked over to his power belt sander, flipped it over, and began grinding away on the blade of his hand plane. "There," he said. "Nothing to it." And the blade certainly would cut the soft pine he used in his carpentry. But the surface of the cutting edge had several gouges in it, which I knew would be disastrous for working on bamboo.

It wasn't until I spoke to a woodcarver that I understood the value of sharpening stones. The smoother the cutting edge, he insisted, the smoother the cut. A coarsely sharpened blade tears fibers, while a finely sharpened blade slices them. The surface smoothness of the edge is all-important.

If you walk into a local hardware store, the stones it's most likely to carry are Coarse Crystolon or possibly an India Combination. The grit equivalent of these stones is 100 to 220, and they produce an edge that is sufficient for coarse woodwork. But for the fine cane removal a rodmaker desires, a 6,000- to 8,000-grit stone is essential. This caliber of smoothness is obtainable only with waterstones.

Nevertheless, a 6,000- to 8,000-grit waterstone only polishes. For actual sharpening, I recommend waterstone in the 1,000- to 1,500-grit range. The solution I've found is a King 1,000-6,000 combination stone. It has a 1,000-grit side for sharpening and a 6,000 side for polishing — all for about $20.

Most fine waterstones require soaking prior to use, usually for about 20 minutes. However, there's a simple way to have your waterstone available at a moment's notice: Store it in water. I found a Rubbermaid storage tub that's just the right size for my stone, and with its snap-on lid there's no chance of water spillage. If your workshop is subject to freezing conditions, waterstones can even be stored in an automotive antifreeze solution without damage.

Flattening a Waterstone

One of the drawbacks of using waterstones is that they can wear rapidly. Depending on the stone, "dishing out" or "glazing" may occur after just a few sharpenings. Dishing out occurs when the center of the stone wears away more than the edges. Glazing is the stage when a stone loses its abrasion. If it isn't addressed, the dishing out will blend with crowning of the blade. This effect can be lessened to an extent by constantly moving around on the surface of the stone while using it. But sooner or later the problem will need to be addressed.

Flattening or deglazing a waterstone can be accomplished by sanding it. A Plexiglas sheet with 220-grit wet or dry sandpaper works well for this task. With the stone wet, simply sand the needed side until the entire surface shows signs of abrasion.

Diamonds Are Forever

One of the new entrants to the sharpening market is the diamond stone, a mixture of a nickel plate and a plastic base. The size-graded monocrystalline diamond particles are bonded to the precision-ground nickel plate. This is only possible because the plate is honeycombed with small circular voids to accept the metal fines from sharpening.

Diamond stones can be used dry or with a light water wetting. As with other stones, a lubricant speeds sharpening by flushing away the metal waste. The diamond particles do load up with metal debris, but they're easily refreshed with a toothbrush and Soft Scrub cleanser.

A distinct advantage of the diamond stones is their nonwear surface; in comparison, traditional waterstones have a soft one. The diamond stone's assured surface is ideal for maintaining a constant level of blade flatness. The obvious drawback of diamond stones is their expense.

Stone Comparison

Given the wide array of different sharpening stones available today, it might be helpful to compare how they rank in terms of their abrasion qualities. I have adapted these details about the micron sizing and grit equivalents from manufacturers' catalogs.

	U.S.	Japan
Medium diamond (blue)	320	500
Soft Arkansas	500	1,000
Hard Arkansas (white)	700	2,000
Fine diamond (DMT-red, 30 micron)	600	2,000
Fine diamond (3M-white, 20 micron)	800	3,000
Hard Arkansas (black)	900	4,000
Extra-fine diamond (DMT-green, 9 micron)	1,200	6,000
Extra-fine (3M-blue, 10 micron)	1,800	8,000

Nagura Stone

Another option is to use a Nagura stone. This is a water-soluble sandstone abrasive that will speed the polishing process. The stone is dipped in water and then rubbed on a 6,000-grit surface until a light paste is formed.

Sharpening Guides

To maintain a consistent angle while sharpening plane blades, I recommend the use of a sharpening guide. There are people who believe they can handhold a blade while sharpening it. This sounds good in theory, but a plane blade is difficult to hold at a consistent angle. Any inconsistencies in the angle will cause a bow in the blade surface, resulting in little or no sharpening of the edge.

The Veritas "on-the-stone" blade holder.

The General "off-the-stone" blade holder.

There are two basic types of sharpening guides. I call the first an on-the-stone guide, because it travels with the blade on the surface of the stone itself. The second is an off-the-stone guide. This has an outboard caster or wheel that rides on the same surface on which the stone rests.

If you use individual stones for sharpening and polishing, you should use an on-the-stone guide. In this way the blade angle won't change between stones. The only drawback is that the guide is also wearing away the stone where the two surfaces meet.

If you use a double-sided stone (one side for sharpening, the other for polishing), then I recommend an off-the-stone sharpening guide. It will maintain consistent blade angle and does not wear the stone prematurely.

Stop Block

A stop block is a setting fixture that I fabricated myself out of wood. It consists of a small piece of plywood (4 inches by 6½ inches by ½ inch) with a lattice piece nailed to it about 1 inch from the long edge. I use it to consistently set the

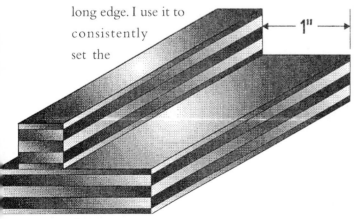

A schematic of a blade-adjustment stop block.

blade in the sharpening guide. This keeps the amount of metal that I remove during sharpening to a minimum. Without a stop block you may be changing the amount of exposed blade, which in turn changes the angle of the blade slightly.

Altered Stop Block

Ken Rongey, a local rodmaker and friend, showed me a different style of stop block when I bor-

Ken Rongey designed this stop block for the author.

rowed his diamond stone. His stop block was constructed for a Veritas on-the-stone sharpening guide. Not only does it have a stop to set the blade to the correct exposure (1⅛ inches) for a 30-degree blade

The stop block being used to set the blade in the holder.

angle, but it also has a side stop that butts and guides this edge of the blade. Because of the sharpness of the blade edge, the single-stop block can occasionally allow the blade to be mounted crooked in the holder. But with the addition of the side-stop block, the blade is always mounted squarely in the sharpening guide.

Flattening the Blade

The edge of the blade won't perform properly if the back of the plane blade is not flat. Although some makers advocate using a piece of steel and graphite dust to wear the blade flat, I prefer to use a waterstone, starting with the 1,000-grit side.

Place the blade perpendicular to the stone so that you're dressing the first ½ inch of the blade. Then, with light pressure, start a back-and-forth motion. Watch closely to verify your progress. Gradually, you'll see the worn surfaces grow together into one uniform sheen. Flip the stone to the 6,000-grit side and repeat the process to polish the blade. Repeat the back-and-forth motion, and gradually the back of the plane blade will yield a bright mirrorlike surface. Unless the blade is sprung, it will remain perfectly flat.

Blade Sharpening

Because I sharpen at the workbench where I also plane, I decided that I needed a waterproof surface on which to place my sharpening stone. Otherwise the wood surface might hold moisture and eventually come in contact with the steel planing forms — creating a rust problem. I ended up with a piece of nylon sheeting that's 6 inches by 24 inches by ½ inch thick, which I bought from a local plastics supplier. An alternative is to buy a piece of Plexiglas from your local hardware store. In either case you end up with a waterproof, smooth surface on which to work.

My General sharpening guide works best with the blade extended 1 inch from the holder. This leaves the base of the holder about ¼ inch off the stone when the blade is sharpened to 30 degrees. When this is mounted in a Stanley 9½ plane, it gives a 51-degree angle of attack to the surface of the cane. This is where the stop block is very important in getting the blade set consistently at 1 inch. If the blade changes, so does the angle, which will lengthen sharpening time because of the additional metal removed to form a new angle.

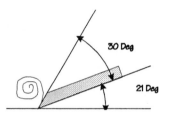

The correct blade angle for planing bamboo.

Before sharpening begins, you must decide on the blade angle you prefer. I use a 30-degree angle, which can be set with a protractor. On the General guide, for example, set the index arrow to 1. Remember, you're looking for this angle when the blade rests on the sharpening stone.

Sharpening should be done with the 1,000-grit side of the stone; work the blade back and

The burr being developed on a fine diamond stone.

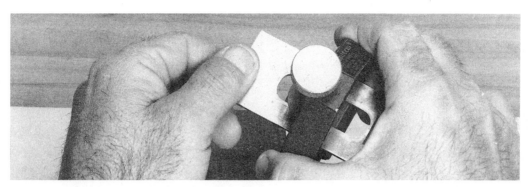

Inspecting the progress of the formed burr.

forth on the stone with light pressure for best results. The surface of the stone should also be kept wet at all times. This washes away the metal particles, preventing them from being embedded in the surface of the stone. After several passes, inspect the sharpened surface. You'll see where the metal is being removed. Feel the back of the blade at the edge to detect the start of a burr. Sharpening should continue until a burr is present across the entire width of the cutting edge and all nicks have disappeared.

Without removing the blade from the holder, flip it so that its back is on the stone — the same position you used to flatten the blade. Using light pressure, make two or three back-and-forth passes. Then

feel for the burr. Continue doing this until the entire burr has disappeared.

Polishing the blade is your next task. Using the 6,000-grit side of the Nagura, wet it and rub it on the polishing surface until a light

After the burr is formed, the surface quality of the face is increased on a waterstone.

paste forms. Now repeat the same procedure as before, using back-and-forth motions until a burr develops at the edge. Then flip and polish the burr away.

Sharpening and polishing take just a few minutes. If you're using a Hock blade, they may take a little longer. However, a Hock blade doesn't break down at the edge as quickly as the standard Stanley blade.

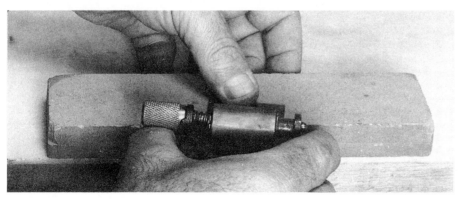

The burr is then removed.

There are those who advocate the use of a compound angle or double-tapered cutting edge. The first cut is sharpened in at a 25-degree angle, then a second angle of 30 degrees is added. The 30-degree angle is sharpened only to the very tip of the blade (about $1/16$ inch). This method lessens

which is basically the same as the double-tapered method. I just haven't had good performance with either technique.

Once you have a sharp blade, you'll want to protect it with a light coat of oil. I use a general-purpose household oil (3 in 1). If I'm storing a

Here's the face surface of a freshly sharpened blade. Notice the high quality of the reflection.

resharpening time and gives the same angle of attack to the cane surface.

I've tried both methods, and it seems to me that the single angle works best. First, the double-cut angle doesn't appear to last as long as a single one; the double angle doesn't have the backing to absorb the pressure of planing. Second, with the smaller (25-degree) secondary angle, the cane isn't rolled off as easily. But this is certainly an area where you can experiment. Try different angles and combinations to see what works best for you. I've even tried hollow-grinding of plane blades,

spare blade, I also wrap it in a rag lightly sprinkled with oil to prevent rusting.

Alternative Method

For years I was locked into my sharpening routine. Then a weekend trip to the Catskills pried me from my rut. Miles Tiernan, a rodmaker and trout bum buddy, rode with me through the night across Ohio and New York. At three o'clock in the morning, with a strong coffee buzz, what better topic of discussion could there be than sharpening?

A coarse diamond stone will quickly remove any nicks in the blade.

Miles had been using a (red) diamond stone for what he termed his "grinder." He used it to take out nicks in the edge, or anytime he needed to remove excess metal from the blade. Then he switched and used the 1,000–6,000 waterstone for finishing up the job. If a light brightening up of the blade was needed, then he used just the waterstone. Because of the change in sharpening-stone height, he used a Veritas on-the-stone blade holder.

After trying this method for a few weeklong classes, I found that it is a definite time saver. This method also extends the time period between reflattening of the waterstones, because they're being used less frequently.

Power Waterstones

Although you might think that motorized sharpening units would save you time, they don't. I had an opportunity to try one a few years ago, and I couldn't see any time savings. They're also a little expensive: The unit I used cost several hundred dollars. To be fair, I'm told that these units are especially helpful when you're sharpening the long blades commonly found in the popular 12-inch power planers.

4
CUTTING AND PLANING

Sacrificial Culm

Some rodmakers are overly concerned with the number of rods they can make from each culm of bamboo. Others attempt to make rods from questionable culms with shallow power fibers or other major defects. Even if the rods are for your own use, some discretion is advisable. As I suggested earlier, it's a good idea to be selective in choosing your bamboo. Leave a few culms or parts of culms for your experiments. I mentioned this earlier in connection with flaming, but rodmakers can always find new techniques that require a bit of practice.

I remember one new rodmaker who should have taken this advice when I sold him some special select cork. I finally saw the rod for which the cork was intended, and I noticed that the handle had been formed from some mediocre stock. Instead of using "practice" cork, he had burned up all of the 100 select cork rings that I sent him in designing handles by trial and error.

A similar mistake is for a first-time rodmaker to use the best culm for his initial rod. Just the opposite should hold true. Start with what you judge as the worst culm in the bunch. Practice splitting, straightening, and planing a few strips. Then set it aside and start your first rod from a second culm. There is a tremendous learning curve when you start to make bamboo fly rods.

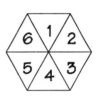

Staggering Methods

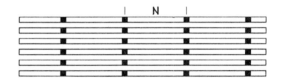

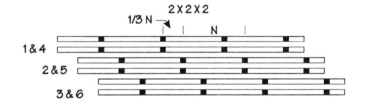

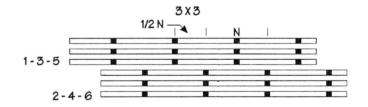

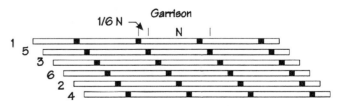

A schematic of various staggering methods.

I've given several culms to fledgling makers, telling them to practice with these before actually starting on a more serious effort. This is common sense and it applies to each stage of rodmaking — from splitting to planing to varnishing.

Staggering Methods

There are four common methods used to stagger bamboo nodes. The first is a 2 x 2 x 2. Each node level has two nodes 180 degrees apart on opposite flats. The second method is a 3 x 3, in which each node level has three nodes, one on every other flat. The third is the Garrison staggering method, which aligns the nodes in the same sequence as the firing order of a six-cylinder engine as the rod is rotated: 1–5–3–6–2–4. Finally, many production makers use a "mismatch," intermixing the strips of many different culms into one rod. Just make sure the completed sections don't have adjacent nodes.

Neutralized Tensions

If a culm of bamboo has any twists, sweeps (light bends), or offsets in it, the entire diameter at that level is usually affected. This should be evident after you've split all the strips and laid them side by side. An additional advantage of the 2 x 2 x 2 stagger is that similar strips on opposite sides have a tendency to neutralize each other.

For a visual example of this effect, place two identical slash marks on a sheet of paper spaced to divide it into thirds. Then roll the paper into a cylinder with the base of the slash marks opposite each other. If you were to now plot a line that was the average of the two slashes, you'd get a straight line running parallel with the cylinder. The same holds true with the natural tensions within the strips in a 2 x 2 x 2 staggering. When you later bind the strips for heat treatment, then glue them into sections, the opposites tend to neutralize themselves. This is definitely the staggering method I recommend.

Staggering

Once you have chosen your own staggering preference, the next step is to implement it. A good visual technique is to lay all six strips out on your workbench along with a carpenter's ruler. Using a

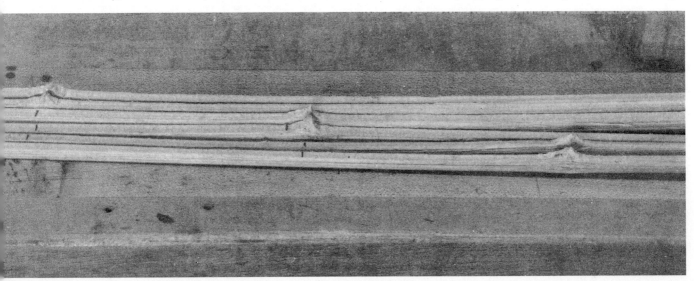

This is a traditional 2 x 2 x 2 stagger.

piece of masking tape, mark a 4-foot rule at the length you'll need for your strips. Then measure the distance between the first and second nodes, starting from the tip end. Use this measurement to determine the offset of each strip or set of strips, depending on your staggering method. Then, moving from strip 1 to strip 6, slide each strip accordingly.

Finding the optimum start and end point for the six strips is your next task. Use the 4-foot rule as a guide and choose your points so they're spaced evenly from the adjoining nodes. If the space from the tip start point and the first node is less than 2 inches, then slide the 4-foot rule toward the butt until you have a free area to the node of at least 2 inches. (Remember that the butt end of the strips will get encased in a ferrule or in the handle of the rod.)

This illustrates why I prefer the 2 x 2 x 2 staggering method. I would rather have two nodes across from each other than a single node in the first part of the tip section of a rod, which sees the maximum amount of flexure in casting. With the 2 x 2 x 2 staggering, you usually have at least 5 inches of space from the tip of the rod to the first node.

After you're satisfied with the start and end points, mark the strips: Simply lay a straightedge perpendicular across them, aligning it to the 4-foot rule. Then use a pencil to make a light mark on each strip, marking both the start and end points.

Matched Tips

One of the subtle details of a good bamboo fly rod is that the tip sections are matched or butterflied according to the nodes. When the nodes of the sections are matched (twinned), they both appear to rise to the left or right as you turn the sections. When the nodes are butterflied, those of one section will rise to the right and those of the other to the left as the sections are turned. In either case the nodes match locations over the length of the sections. These details show that the rod was custom-made and set it apart from any mass-produced product.

If you want to incorporate matching nodes into your work, start now with the staggering and cutting of your start and end points. Intermix both sections as one. Instead of working with 6 strips, work with 12. If you chose a 2 x 2 x 2 staggering, this would mean that instead of two strips per stagger there would be four.

Switch to Maximize

Once the strips are staggered and marked for length, it might be wise to take a close look at them. If necessary, you can switch the positions of different strips to eliminate any possible flaws. If you do switch strips to different positions, however, don't forget to re-mark them so that you'll cut them correctly.

Cutting to Length

Once the six strips are staggered and you've marked the lengths on each strip, your next step is to cut off the excess. I strongly recommend that you add at least 2 to 5 inches of length to each end of your planned start and end points. This will provide a safety factor and make it easier to work with the strips.

When cutting the strips, use a fine-toothed blade hacksaw or coping saw. And always cut from the enamel side toward the pith side. This way, if the last cut stroke tears fibers, it won't be from the needed power-fiber side — which could ruin the strips.

Painting Ends

After the strips are cut to length, I suggest that you paint the butt ends. You'll soon find yourself flipping the strips during the straightening and preliminary planing processes; if you're like me, you'll get involved with the work at hand and forget which end went where. By painting the ends of the strips, you'll know at a glance which end is the butt. Before I started painting the butt ends of each section, sooner or later I'd have to stop construction of each rod and sort out the orientation of the strips. I ended up measuring the different node spacings to determine direction — a problem that can be easily avoided.

you might also want to redeem yourself by spending some time with your spouse and children. Making fly rods — and fly fishing in general — can become an obsession, and it's relatively easy to forget that not everyone shares your passion for this activity.

Planing Diaphragm Ridges

Your first planing on the strips is meant to remove the diaphragm ridges on the pith side. Set your plane for removal of approximately 0.006 inch. Place a strip, pith-side up, on your work surface. Working from right to left, hold the plane with your right hand and the strip with your left. Hold

Planing a diaphragm ridge.

For paint, I use regular enamel purchased in the small 4-ounce cans. (Sometimes I even use a red permanent marker, which dries in seconds.) Having a color scheme can be helpful as well: Always paint the butt ends of each bundle of strips the same color. I merely shake the can of paint, pry the lid off, and then touch just the ends of the group of six strips into the film of paint on the lid.

While you wait for the paint to dry you can make use of your extra time by sharpening plane blades or polishing the glue off the binder. If you've been working overtime on rod projects,

the strip upstream of the plane.

The ridge is now removed with a series of short strokes. When the surface of the ridge is blended with the pith surface, it's time to quit. Flipping the strips end-for-end will make it easier to hold them as you work past their centers. What you're trying to create is a smooth, flat area on the pith side of the strip that's about 3 or 4 inches long and centered on the node. Later, when you vise the node area, this will be the index surface.

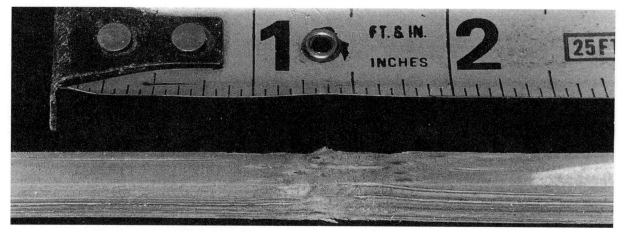

The prepared diaphragm after careful planing.

Heat Gun versus Alcohol Lamp

Traditionally, an alcohol lamp was used to heat the strips of bamboo during the straightening process.

Speed 2 is the author's recommendation when using a Black & Decker heat gun.

But alcohol lamps or candles can scorch the enamel of the strips, and a flame can actually add moisture to them. Dry heat from a heat gun doesn't scorch the enamel as readily. And most heat guns apply their heat over a larger area. I use my old Black & Decker Heat 'N Strip with a rectangular diffuser attachment. The discharge temperature at ¾ inch from the diffuser is 550 degrees F. (Later I'll describe why the rectangular diffusion becomes such an important feature.)

Heat Guns

The Black & Decker heat gun available today is a bit different from the model I own. Today it's simply called the Heat Gun, model 9756, and the nozzle kit with the rectangler diffuser is part 284589. This tool now has a dual range: For your purposes, you want to use the higher output setting, or 2 on the selector switch.

Another tool that I've used successfully is a similar unit made by Easypower. Its model 72102 heat unit, with accessory pack 79214, is seen quite often at building supply chain stores. Again, use the higher output setting.

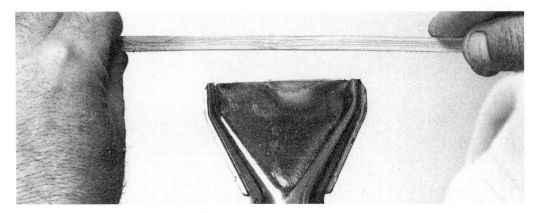

Heating the node area approximately ³⁄₄ inch above the diffuser.

Exhaust Fan

Anytime bamboo is heated, during either straightening or tempering, fumes are released. These can be annoying, if not to you then certainly to other members of the household. When I ran into this problem, I installed an exhaust fan.

The unit I installed was the type normally used for bathrooms. It moves 75 cubic feet of air per minute (cfm) and is vented to the outside of the house. To help collect the fumes at the source, I added a three-sided curtain to the fan unit. The fan and curtain are located so they're immediately above the heat gun when I straighten strips.

Vising Nodes

When I first started making rods, I straightened the strips of bamboo one kink at a time. For a heat

source I used an alcohol lamp, which supplied heat to the strips in a concentrated area. Leafing through Martin Keane's *Classic Rods and Rodmakers*, though, I came across two pictures that started me thinking about my technique. The pictures of Jim Payne on page 70 and Charlie Doane on page 88 show these gentlemen pressing nodes on cane strips. In the text the author mentions charcoal heat boxes.

This gave me the idea of using a vise to flatten my nodes. At that time I was using an electric heat gun to soften some plastic tubing on a floor-heating unit. (It magically removed some kinks by "resetting the tubing's memory.") One night I experimented in my workshop by using the heat gun on strips of bamboo, then squeezing the strips in a smooth-jawed vise that I'd bought as a kid. It

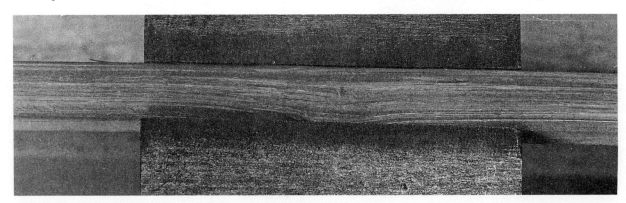

A vised node. Notice the contact along the entire jaw surface.

worked, and since that night I haven't used an alcohol lamp for straightening. And using a vise to flatten nodes certainly makes quick work of a formerly time-consuming job.

The keys to properly vising nodes are first to have smooth jaws on the vise, and second to make sure the cane is heated enough to make it soft. The vise I use is an inexpensive unit I picked up cheaply at a flea market. It's cast aluminum with 2-inch jaws that had been marked up heavily. To correct this flaw, I set a mill file between the jaws and slowly added pressure as I filed. This cleaned up the marks and insured that the jaws were parallel.

To soften the cane, first prop the heat gun on the workbench and lock the trigger down. Hold the strip of cane about ¾ inch above the diffuser. To evenly heat the strip, slowly rock it through three-quarters of a turn. Start the turn with a split edge toward the heat, and then roll past the pith and to the other split edge. Flex the strip occasionally until you feel it "melt" and lose its springiness — approximately 1½ to 2 minutes. Once the strip can be flexed and it stays in an offset position, it's time to vise the strip.

Simply place the strip in the vise and apply pressure until the enamel on each side of the node is flat-

tened to the jaws. To speed the process, start heating the next strip while the first one is cooling in the vise. After you've flattened the node, a light block-sanding with 360-grit sandpaper will finish removing any light ripples that might remain. If everything has gone to form, the node area will be perfectly flat and there will be no cut power fibers.

If the node has been flattened properly, the block-sanding should remove the last of the

Sanding the last of the enamel at the node area.

enamel valley that was left from earlier filing. To have better control and vision of the area, use the corners of the sanding block. Sand in a manner

The before (bottom) and after pictures.

that allows between ¾ inch and 1¼ inches of the block to be in contact with the strip. When you're finished, the strip should appear flat and uniform in thickness when viewed from the side. If a bump still appears at the node, this is a sign that the node area wasn't softened enough to form parallel lines in the vise. It's time to repeat the process.

Notice how the cap fibers overlay the power fibers at the nodes.

Node Fibers

As you sand the node area after vising, you may see the end sections (fingers) of power fibers immediately under the enamel of what was the nodal valley. Your first thought might be that the area was oversanded to the point of cutting power fibers. Fortunately, the fiber ends you see here are actually cap fibers. They lie immediately over the intertwined power fibers, acting as a bridge. The cap fibers are normally ³⁄₁₆ inch in total length, in what appear to be two staggered layers. They can be sanded away and will normally disappear with the last of the enamel's outer surface.

About Block-Sanding

As wasteful as it may sound, try to use only the corners of your block sander. This will give you a better view of the area you're actually sanding. The "sweet spot" on a block sander starts ½ inch from the corner and extends inward to 1¼ inches. By using this cautious approach, you'll be able to follow the surface better and avoid sanding errors. To get the best possible results from your sandpaper, keep it as fresh as possible. Give the block an

occasional flat tap on the side of the workbench to knock loose the excess bamboo.

The Vise

In lieu of a 2-inch smooth-jawed vise, you can also modify a common Pony 3-inch clamp-on vise to suit your needs. First, use a hacksaw to cut ½ to ⅝ inch from each side of the jaws. Because the Pony vise is cast iron, filing away the knurling is also an easy task.

The reason you cut down the jaws is so they are about ½ inch narrower than the width of the rectangular diffuser used on the heat gun. If you left them full width, you'd be trying to compress unsoftened bamboo. And by reducing the surface area, you also reduce the amount of pressure applied to the handle while still accomplishing the flattening.

The author's modified 3-inch Pony vise.

To remove the knurling, very slowly close the jaws while filing them with a mill file. This becomes a matter of finding the balance between the filing pressure and the amount of pressure you apply to the handle closing the jaws. Continue filing until the last of the knurls are removed and the jaws are smooth.

Bubble Buster

On flamed bamboo strips I sometimes sand a node area too much, or for some reason leave an area too light. To fix this, I cosmetically touch up these areas with what I call a "bubble buster" — an alcohol lamp used to work the air out of epoxy wrap finishes. Mount an alcohol lamp head on a plastic squeeze bottle

A bubble buster alcohol lamp can be used to perform cosmetic touch-ups on bamboo.

filled with denatured alcohol. When the bottle is squeezed, it pushes the flame to the side and sharpens the flame intensity to a point. The bubble buster can be used like an airbrush to retouch flaming highlights.

Use the bubble buster only *before* you begin planing the strips; you could burn the edges of the strips or glue if you use this technique later. Also on the subject of safety, the unit I bought includes a few marbles inside the plastic bottle to add ballast. This prevents the unit from tipping over, which could potentially cause a serious fire.

Finally, never leave a burning alcohol lamp unattended or anywhere near rodmaking solvents.

Reflame

To redarken any "golden" nodes, you can use your original torch — but be careful. The corners of the strips are very vulnerable to burning, so you must use quick and light passes. The technique that I use is to start with the torch off to the side of the strip and a bit away from the lightened node area. I then move the torch parallel to the strip, jogging the flame onto the strip and then off while the torch is in motion.

Flick the Bic

Another reflaming method that I will mention here and later involves a butane pocket lighter. With a pocket lighter, the idea is not so much to reflame the area as to soot it. With the lighter burning in one hand, place the strip into the flame low enough so the flame rolls around the strip. The flame isn't actually burning the strip, but rather depositing soot on it. With this soot in place, you can then blend it into the previous flaming by rubbing it with your finger. Here again, short bursts are better than lengthy ones.

Later, when you glue the strips into sections, this method can be valuable for highlighting any light areas where you might want a darker tone.

A final word of caution about pocket butane lighters is in order: Do not allow the flame to burn for long periods of time. The burning area of these lighters can become very hot — and even create a small explosion.

Other Kinks and Bends

In addition to flattening the nodes, you'll need to remove any sharp kinks in the strips. These can be eliminated by heating the strips perpendicularly across the rectangular diffuser. As with flattening, wait until you feel the bamboo relax, then slightly overflex the strip in the opposite direction of the kink. Hold the overflex until the bamboo cools and sets. This will take about one minute.

Between the node areas you may have long sweeps. These will relax for the most part later, when the sections are heat-treated. And, even if heat treatment does not relax the sweeps totally, the weight of your hand plane will flatten them into the forms for planing.

5
FIRST FORMS

Angle-Starting Form

The first of the three sets of planing forms that you'll need to make bamboo fly rods is the one used to create the initial 60-degree angle. This set of forms is easy to make. Because no accuracy in depth is required, the forms can be fabricated from wood with a table saw and a hand drill. I recommend using a straight-grained, kiln-dried hardwood. Having the form as straight as possible is important for maintaining accurate angles.

To begin, cut a piece of ¾-inch wood 24 inches long. For the width, cut the board to the finished width plus the kerf, or saw cut. Before you cut the piece in half, predrill the screw holes. By drilling the holes now, the two pieces will reassemble in perfect alignment. And to remind yourself which end goes where, mark an X at one end across the width of the board. Now cut the board into two pieces.

If you've read other books on bamboo rod-

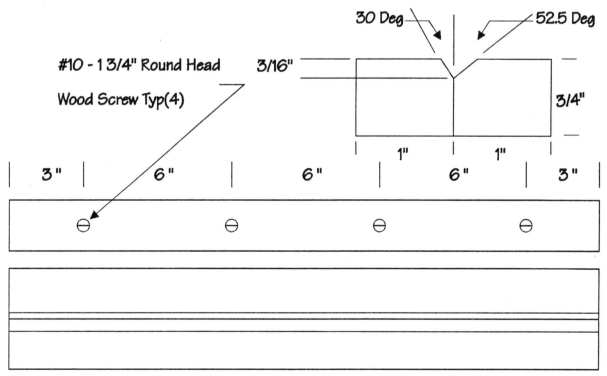

A basic form used to create the initial 60-degree angles in the bamboo.

making, you may notice here that the angle supporting your side of the strips has been modified slightly. Using an angle of 53 degrees, as specified by other authors, you'll have to tilt your hand plane to get a true 60-degree angle on the strips. Because I normally split 24 strips from every culm half, each strip is a wedge of 15 degrees. (There are 360 degrees in a circle, divided into 24 equal angles.) The 15 degrees create a pie-shaped wedge. But because there are two equal sloping sides, each split side is 7½ degrees from perpendicular to the center point of the enamel surface.

You can alter the depth of the V to accommodate the size of the strips with which you commonly work. My normal strip width is approximately ¼ inch. With a 3/16-inch-deep V, 75 percent of the strip is supported. This 3/16-inch depth should work well for most trout-weight rods. However, if you intend to make heavier salmon and steelhead rods, then you may need a set of forms with a deeper V to support the wider strips you'll need in the butt sections.

Remember that the form is intended to act only as a holder. If you plane until you contact the surface, you'll shave away the form as easily as the bamboo.

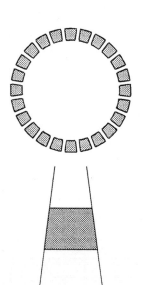

An inward slope created when the strips are split from the culm.

Which Edge First?

You're now ready to start planing the first 60-degree angle. Using either of the split edges as your guide edge, place this side in the angle form. Here I recommend testing to see which side fits tightest to the angle of the form. This side will obviously get you off to your best start.

Remember that the enamel side of the bamboo is the base for forming and checking the angles. Due to the arch in the enamel surface, the correct point of contact for either the forms or the checking gauge is the midpoint (widthwise) of the enamel surface.

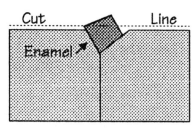

When the enamel side is placed correctly, the bamboo fits the form.

Correcting Backcuts

If neither side of the strip seems to fit the form correctly, then you can do

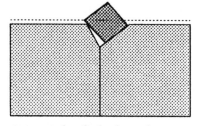

An example of a backcut, demonstrating how an improperly split strip does not fit the form.

some initial planing to correct the split angle. This can be done freehand by setting the strip on edge on your workbench and planing it to a "best fit" level. After you've made a couple of passes with the plane, check to see how the strip fits into the form. If more altering is required, replane the strip

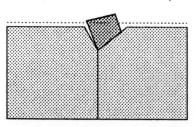

Here's another view with the strip also not fitting into the form correctly.

surface by tilting the plane as needed, and then check the fit again after a few passes.

Anytime that you're changing angles, remember to plane with a light touch. The plane's forward foot has a tendency to follow the flat left by previous passes. Any amount of pressure will cause the strip to twist, joining its original surface and the sole of the plane. Too much downward pressure will make an angle change virtually impossible.

Center Gauge

A center gauge is a tool with three 60-degree notched angles. Normally it's used for setting

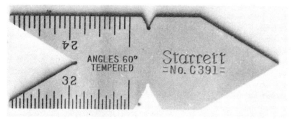

The 60-degree center gauge is used to check and correct the angles.

thread-cutting tools, but to the rodmaker it's invaluable for checking the 60-degree angles required to make hexagonal rod sections. Center

Confirming the first 60-degree angle. Note that the enamel should touch the gauge leg at the center of the crown.

gauges are readily available from most industrial hardware suppliers and machine tool outlets.

First Angle

Plane the initial 60-degree angle with the enamel side of the strips placed against the steeper angle of the form. *Never plane the enamel side,* under which lie the critical power fibers. Only the split

Planing the first 60-degree angle.

sides may be planed. You'll also find planing easier if you place the split side that's smoother down in the form.

The body position I recommend using in all phases of planing may seem a bit awkward at first, but it will quickly become comfortable and workable. If you're a right-hander, hold the hand plane in your right hand and the strip in your left, but to the right of or behind your right hand with the plane. (As I warned earlier, this is where an unprotected left hand can get sliced quite badly if you don't wear a glove.) By the time you get to the finishing stages of planing, you'll need only a light pressure to hold the strips. Initially, though, a firm hold is required.

The plane (Stanley Model 9½) should be set to 0.005 to 0.008 inch. The simplest way to check its setting is by making a pass with it and then measuring the shaved curl. Adjust the throat opening so the shaving has just enough room to pass through comfortably.

If you're beginning to wonder how to work the long strips of bamboo in the short form, it's really quite simple. Place the front tip of the strip even with the front edge of the form. Now, with the sole of the plane parallel to the surface of the form, start at the front of the strip and gradually work farther and farther back with each pass of the plane.

Because the grain in the strips is parallel, the edge of the strip should come to a sharp point at the same depth of cut. You can watch this in the surface that you're planing. To confirm that you're planing the correct angle, occasionally check the strip with the center gauge. Place the strip in the gauge with the planed edge tight against one leg of the angle. The other leg of the center-gauge angle should touch the enamel side of the strip in the center of the enamel crown. If it doesn't, you need to adjust the tilt of the plane to accommodate the change needed in the angle of the strip.

Plane the angle until you're past the center point of the strip. You'll notice that the unsupported portion of the strip that overhangs the form is unaffected by the plane as it passes over. Once you're there, then flip the form and the strip end-for-end and repeat the process. Again, start from the front and work farther back into the strip with each successive pass.

Holding the Plane

Remember that you'll be using the hand plane for countless hours, so it's important to hold it with a comfortable grasp. You don't want to tire your wrist from overuse. The Stanley plane was designed so that it could be used with the roundness of the blade lock-down fitted into the palm of your hand. Your thumb then rests on one side, with the first two fingers of your hand on the opposite side. With this grasp it only takes a light amount of pressure from your thumb and fingers to secure the plane for lifting. To maximize your efforts, apply just enough pressure to push the plane parallel to the work surface.

The only downward pressure is created by the weight of the plane itself. Many times I've seen new rodmakers using what could be described as a white-knuckled death grip on the plane. Usually this is accompanied by the facial expression of someone who is seeking forced submission. All this effort is uncomfortable and counterproductive. In fact, such overuse of force suggests that the planing system isn't working properly. At these times it's best to stop and sort out the problems.

Holding the Strip

A second key to proper technique is how the strips are secured while you're planing or scraping. Here your concerns are with the way you're holding the strips themselves, and with where you're holding them with respect to the plane or scraper.

I've found it best to use the first three fingers of my left hand to hold the strips. With the forms close to the edge of the workbench, my thumb hangs over the edge and my fingers then fall onto the strips. This position allows me to pinch the strips if needed, but it also allows me to quickly raise my fingers in an emergency.

As you plane the strips from roughly split pieces into the needed triangles, the corners or points will become razor sharp. Your concern here is to avoid getting cut by these corners. Taking too deep a cut or using a dull blade can cause the cut to stall. And with the forward momentum of the plane, the strip may slide in the forms. If you sense this and are quick enough, you can lift your fingers before they are injured.

Now it's always best to plane or scrape *away* from the anchor point created by your holding finger. But when you start to make full-length passes, you'll find that it isn't possible to use this technique. The problem arises when you go to initiate the pass. At this point you'll need to hold the strip downstream of your plane or scraper. To lessen the chance of the strip buckling up from the forms, keep the anchor point close to the plane or scraper and switch to an upstream holding position as quickly as possible.

When I'm planing the strips for tip sections, I start the cut with my fingers only an inch from the plane or scraper. I work this short distance, and then reposition my fingers only an inch or so farther down the strip. Once again I plane or scrape up to my fingers. I repeat this jogging until there's enough of the strip exposed behind the plane or scraper to hold with my fingers. Then I change positions to hold the strip there and complete a full-length pass.

Proper Stroke

Bad habits can be difficult to change. I once spent an entire summer correcting the improper casting style I'd used on small trout creeks for many years. In the same way, bad planing and scraping habits that may not hurt your work in the earlier stages of rodmaking can haunt you in the more critical later stages. And it's just as difficult to unlearn these techniques. Try to start with the correct strokes and continue them throughout your work.

The plane or scraper should be lifted clear of the strips at the end of each pass. Then hold it suspended as you bring it back to initiate the next pass. Too often I see new rodmakers drag the plane or scraper back on the strips to initiate the next pass. You'll get away with this sloppy technique when the strips are large, but when you come to the more delicate tip-section strips, you'll be flirting with danger. More than once I've seen strips snapped in two when they buckled up because of this dragging action.

Can't Cut It

One of the most important lessons of rodmaking is learning when you need to resharpen the plane or scraper blade — or just give the unit some attention. Both tools should be able to remove material with just the forward downward pressure coming from the weight of the plane or scraper itself. If you find yourself bearing down on a plane or scraper to force it to cut, then something's wrong. And simply pushing harder is not going to make the tool work better or the task more enjoyable.

Here are some explanations for the problems you'll run into when you use a planer or scaper blade:

1. A dull blade, which usually has visible nicks or a blunt surface. Try resharpening the blade.
2. A flipped burr, which you can feel along the blade edge. The burr should have been removed as the last step of sharpening.

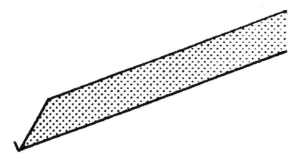

A flipped burr on a plane or scraper blade will cause serious problems at this stage.

3. The forward foot of the plane is closed against the blade, not allowing a cut.
4. The blade is mounted crooked and is not exposed correctly.
5. The blade has slid inward and is too tight against the adjustment stop. This often happens just after reassembling the plane following a sharpening.
6. There is debris lodged against the blade, not allowing it to cut.
7. You are caught up in the excitement and expecting the work to progress too quickly.

The hand-planing of the strips for a bamboo fly rod takes time. You'll be spending hour after hour at this task. The secret to making it enjoyable is to develop an almost effortless technique. The magic is in knowing how to correct the problems as they arise.

Bad Angles

The angles that you're creating in the initial stages will follow through to the end of the project. If they aren't a true 60 degrees, then you don't have an equilateral triangle, and the three sets of point-

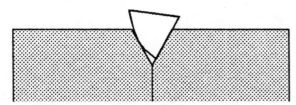

An end view of an incorrectly shaped triangle.

to-flat dimensions won't be equal. If this is the case, it will haunt you later when you're trying to meet the final dimensions.

It's best to have the correct angles early in the work, but of course this isn't always possible. The sweeps and twists in the strips can make it frustrating to keep them in the first angle form as you plane. Later, as the mass of the strips is reduced, they'll become more flexible and more workable. And later still, once they've been heat-treated, many of these haunting sweeps and twists disappear altogether.

Some Causes

Although it's frustrating to discover that your angles aren't correct, it's also a challenge to find out what has gone wrong. The following list might help you to sort out the problems.

1. **Plane positioning:** The plane needs to pass parallel to the forms throughout the length of the cut, time after time. (To confirm this visually you can set a mirror at the end of your workbench and angle it in a manner that allows you to watch as you plane.) To shore up the plane position, touch your third and little finger against the corner of the form. Using your finger as an outrig can stabilize the plane, but you might consider softening the corners of the forms so that you don't cut your fingers.
2. **Blade setting:** The cutting edge of the blade needs to be parallel to the front foot surface at all times. The front foot and the planed surface of the strip will then seat to each other. If the blade is canted in the plane, it will cut an uneven amount of material. Even though this inaccuracy may be slight, the accumulated difference can be dramatic after several passes.
3. **Nodes:** Any of the areas that aren't flat can rock in the forms and cause a shift in the angle. Test each strip before you start to plane. It should sit tight against the form at the nodes. If not, then you need to correct this error by re-pressing before you start to plane.

4. **Debris:** A never-ending source of problems is the debris that you're constantly creating. Unchecked, it will surely cause something to go wrong. Always keep the forms and the surrounding area clean of shavings and sanding dust. Not only can debris end up in the forms, but it can also get wedged between the plane's front foot and its seating surfaces.

5. **Backcut strips:** This problem is unique to the first-angle form because the holding angles of the two form sides are not symmetrical. If the enamel side is placed into the form against (what is viewed from above as) the wider surface, it's in the wrong position. Then an angle of 37 degrees will be formed, instead of the required 60 degrees. Writing the word *enamel* on the correct side of the first form will prevent this problem.

6. **Form fit problem:** Once again, this error is most common with the first form and is generally an indication that the angles of the split edge are not the needed incline of 7½ degrees. You can check the fit of the first form to the strip visually by viewing from one end as you pull the strip lengthwise through the form.

7. **Severe twists:** It isn't a common occurrence, but a strip may have a natural twist in it. A hard twist along the enamel side can cause the strip not to fit the forms correctly. If you spot this flaw, bring out the heat gun and take corrective action.

Correcting Bad Angles

Of all the times to use a dull plane, this is the worst! You absolutely must use a sharp plane to change the angles of a strip. Here's why: As your blade dulls, you'll need more downward pressure to create the cut. When an angle change is required, any downward pressure beyond the weight of the plane itself will simply cause the surfaces of the previously planed bamboo to mate with the sole of the plane. This is clearly not the way to fix the incorrect strip.

Regardless of when the bad angle or angles appear, you first have to determine what caused the error. And then you have to decide if there's enough material left for the needed correction. If there isn't, a new strip is your best alternative.

If the strip appears to be of sufficient size, your next step is to plan for the angle correction. This involves moving the plane inward far enough on the proper side that you can pitch it to achieve the correcting angle. Your initial pass at the new angle will yield only a very light shaving. As you make subsequent passes, the shavings will grow wider until they once again reach the full width of the strip. At this point the angle correction has been completed.

Second Form

The second set of forms is used for planing the strips into nontapering equilateral triangles. Because the planed dimensions of the strips still aren't critical, this second set of forms can also be made of wood and fixed to one dimension. As with the first set of forms, choose a straight-grained hardwood — but this time make the forms at least 48 inches long. The angles on both halves are now identical at 60 degrees.

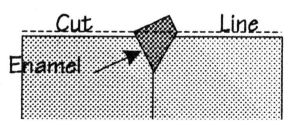

An end view of a correctly shaped triangle.

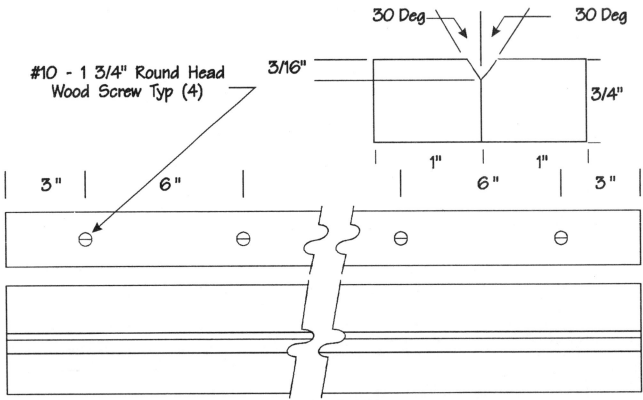

The second set of forms, used to create the nontapering equilateral triangles.

Triangles

Planing the second split edge of the strips to form an equilateral triangle is essentially the same process as planing the first split edge to an angle. The blade setting is also the same: 0.005 to 0.008 inch. With the strip set in the form, the appearance of the unplaned surface is the same. And the planing technique is identical, too.

With the strips bedded in the longer forms, you'll notice that it takes less pressure to hold the bamboo in place with your left hand. And with some material removed, the long sweeps will now flatten to the forms with less downward pressure on the plane. Again, the actual dimensions are not critical. Getting true 60-degree angles, and following the grain to keep the strips uniform, are your two important tasks.

Planing the second 60-degree angle.

Let me put these issues into perspective. Once the strips are heat-treated, they plane and handle easier because the bamboo is tempered and the long sweeps are relaxed. Spending the extra time heating and straightening the strips is simply a waste — and the strips can be damaged by over-working as well. Second, spending extra time measuring strips and fine-tuning their dimensions doesn't make sense. When you become proficient, you'll be able to go from a fresh culm to heat-treating the untapered strips in only an hour per section.

6
THE BINDING PROCESS

Binder

Among professional rodmakers there are varying opinions about the binder design recommended by Everett Garrison. I built his binder pretty much true to form and have had great success with it. But I've had even more success by using lighter loading weights and adding guide-troughs to both the incoming and exiting side. Other than wrap-

ping the shaft by hand, however, your options are fairly limited.

The Garrison binders that work poorly seem to have simply been built poorly. Some rodmakers demand quality for their final forms, but deem the quality of accessory tooling unimportant. This is a mistake. The binder parts should be made from brass or aluminum. These metals will resist the

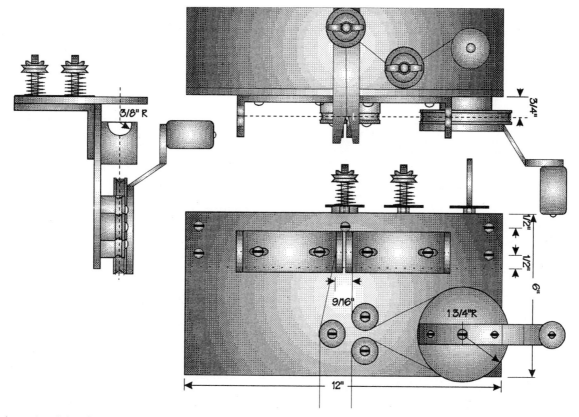

A schematic of the classic binder design by Everett Garrison.

adhesion of the glues you use to assemble the rod and will make cleanup less difficult. I did, however, build one all-steel binder (except for a wooden drive pulley), and it has worked fine for many years.

The assembly of the binder begins by drilling and tapping the main plate and mounting angle, and then bolting the two parts together. If you have a doweling jig, you can drill a hole in a piece of wood as large as the tap that you're using. This will act as a guide to keep the tap in perpendicular alignment with the surface being tapped.

Perhaps the most difficult parts to make are the two guide arms. Start with a piece of square tubing and drill the larger holes with a 1¼-inch holesaw. Then the tubing needs to be cut in half and the ends cut off. After the parts are cut, the edges should be rounded and polished. The important areas are the radii in which the rod will ride. Any sharp edges on these half circles could cut the binding thread or, worse yet, nick the strips of cane.

A good way to polish the arms is to mount them individually on the main plate and then

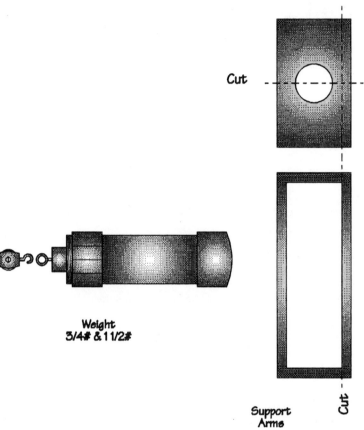

Cutting directions for the support arms.

smooth the edges with narrow strips (⅜ inch) of emery cloth, starting with a coarse grit and working to finer grades. Like the guide arms, the string guide needs any part of its surface that touches the string to be polished in order to prevent the string from being cut.

I made the drive wheel from ½-inch (nine-ply) Baltic birch,

A close-up of the binder arms.

The author's binder, showing the effects of years of epoxy glue application.

which I precut to a circle on a bandsaw and then trued and grooved on a wood lathe. The tensioning devices are available from rodmaking supply houses. Using two units gives you better tension control of the binding thread.

For weights, I recommend building them from schedule-40 PVC tubing (marked "Sch-40 PVC"). By using lead shot in the plastic tubing, you can fine-tune the desired weights. However, I must caution you never to melt lead, especially not indoors. The fumes emitted by lead can be toxic.

Drive Belt

If you choose to use epoxy glue to assemble your rods, your binder's drive belts need to be disposable, because the strength of cleaners needed to remove the glue will destroy them. The best cord that I've found for this job is the 75-pound-test braided kite string that my son, Matt, once used on his acrobatic kite. To make the drive belts, I simply cut a 54-inch length and tie a tight square knot to form the continuous drive belt. To secure the knot, I add a single drop of superglue. Once the glue is dry, I trim the tag ends back to the knot so they won't get inner-wrapped in the binding cord as it is applied to the rod.

The only special attention required when you're using a knotted drive belt is during the two or three times when the knot passes over the rod section. As the knot approaches the rod section,

A PVC weight container helps to maintain steady tension.

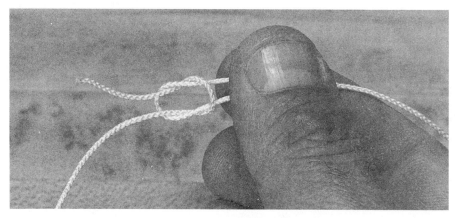

Forming the familiar square knot in the binder drive belt.

The author seals the square knot with superglue.

I slow the through speed to a crawl just to make sure the knot passes safely through this crucial area. Once the knot has passed, I increase the speed again. Even with these slow-ups, a single pass through the binder will take only about one minute. To gain traction on the drive wheel, you might want to put two wraps of the drive belt around it. You can also wrap a rubber band around the drive pulley.

Binder Feed Guides

When I first considered building guides for my binder, I thought about splitting a piece of 1¼-

Guide Arms

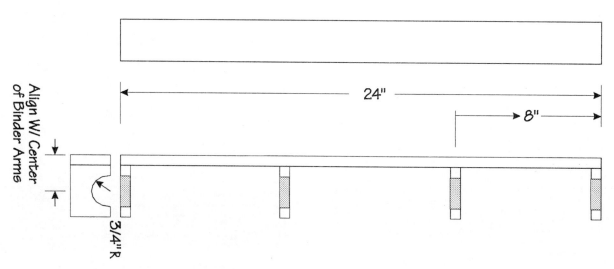

A recommended design for guide arms on a binder.

inch PVC pipe. When I couldn't come up with a method of effectively cleaning the dried glue from the pipe, I squelched that idea. And as more surface area comes in contact with the rod shaft, it can become more twisted. By using only a few arms to support the shaft, cleanup time is reduced; the reduced drag also lessens the possibility of twisting in the rod shaft.

The construction of guides is fairly simple. Cut the rectangles and then create a hole with a holesaw. Now cut the rectangles in half and mount them to the rail. The key is to use a long straightedge when mounting the arms to the rail. Also, make sure the arms are properly aligned.

If the binder and the guides are going to be positioned permanently on your workbench, they can be mounted separately. If you want them to be removable, they should be mounted together on a solid board. Having the guide arms and the supports on the binder in a straight line is essential.

To help in your alignment, use a 3- or 4-foot straightedge or a yardstick. Set the straightedge in the binder supports and mount the guides with the cradle of the arms butted to the straightedge. Taking the time now to get the alignment correct will pay dividends later in straighter and flatter glued sections.

Binding Thread

Twice during the construction of a bamboo fly rod, the six strips that form each section are bound together. First you bind them for the heat-treating process. The second binding comes when the six strips are glued. Each process requires a different cord or thread.

For heat treatment, an obvious requirement of the thread is its ability to withstand temperatures up to 375 degrees F. The thread also needs

Examples of various threads used with the binder.

enough strength to hold the strips firmly together without stretching. A good choice is a glazed cotton upholstery thread in size 10/4. This term denotes that the thread has been polished to remove any fuzziness. Glazed thread will pass smoothly through the tensioning disk and feed arm. This kind of thread is also easier to remove from the glued strips.

For glue-binding, I use two different sizes of thread in two different colors. I use size 16/4 for glue-binding the butt sections, and 24/4 for binding the tips. These sizes ensure that I have enough thread strength to adequately pressurize the glue bond while still using the smallest-possible-diameter thread. The diameter of the thread becomes particularly important during the straightening and flattening done before the glue sets.

You can choose the different thread colors to match the tone of your rod. I use a dark (red) thread on a blond shaft and a light (white) thread on flamed shafts. This contrast of colors makes it easier to see the glue seams and flats when I look down the shafts to check for straightness.

I've seen and experimented with an array of shaft-binding cords and threads — everything from the cord a butcher would use to wrap meat, to fly-line backing, to old-style cotton baitcasting line. I once watched a fellow bind a rod shaft; after his two passes through the binder, I couldn't see the shaft at all.

An upholstery supply house is a good source for glazed cotton thread. I walked into one shop here in Grand Rapids and found racks of the three sizes I wanted. The yardage per spool varies by its size — from 100 to 500 yards per spool. Each time you bind a section, you'll need about 20 feet of thread for each wrap. A single spool should last several rods.

Tuning the Binder

Once you've assembled the parts and pieces and acquired the correct thread, you should tune up and test your binder before you actually run strips of bamboo through it.

The thread tension is the first item to set. If this is too taut, you'll find yourself breaking the string midway into a wrap, which can be very frustrating. I adjust the tension to size 24/4 thread at 1½ pounds. To make this adjustment, tie the thread to the ¾-pound weight suspended from the guide arm of your binder. Run the thread through only the tension disk that's closest to the guide arm. When the tension is correct, the weight will drop with a slight pressure. Then change to the 1½-pound weight and run the thread through both tension disks. This time adjust only the second tension disk until the weight will drop with light pressure. This is the tension that I use for all sizes of thread; I do not readjust for each size.

Now place a ⅜-inch dowel in the binder arms with the right end of the dowel ½ inch to

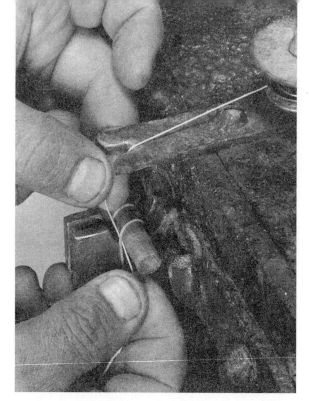

Feeding the binding thread behind the drive belt.

the right of the middle arms. Wrap the drive belt around the dowel twice in a clockwise rotation. Then run the binding thread in back of the drive belt and around the bottom of the dowel rod and

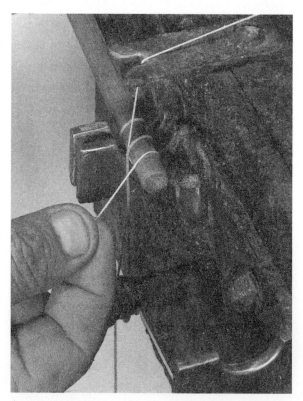

The binding thread is then looped over the bundle.

make two half-hitch knots on the open part of the dowel. Pull any slack thread back through the tension disks.

Slowly turn the handle on the binder drive. The dowel should begin to rotate with the thread wrapping to the dowel. A good rate to turn the drive handle is one turn every two or three seconds. In a matter of a few turns of the drive handle, the entire dowel shaft should be wound with thread spaced at ⅜ inch per wrap.

Continue turning the drive handle until the dowel has cleared the drive belt and dropped off the shaft. Then pinch the thread to the dowel with your finger and pull it away from the binder until there's 6 to 8 inches of free thread. Cut the thread and half-hitch its free end tightly to the dowel. That's all there is to it.

To finish the test bind, place the dowel back at the start point. This time, wrap the drive belt in a counterclockwise direction and follow with the

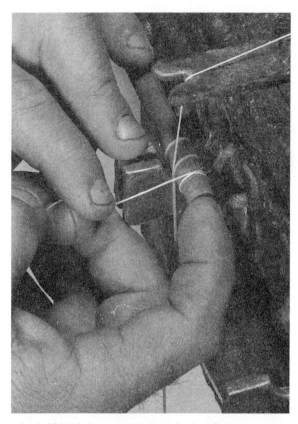

The half-hitch knot is slid onto the bundle.

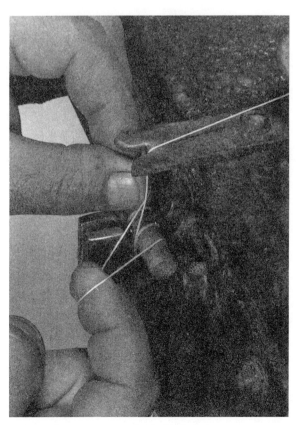

Using a finger to create the half-hitch knot.

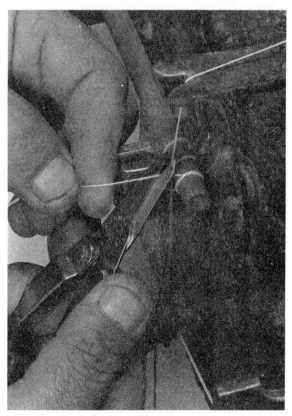

After a few half-hitch knots are in place, the free end of the thread is cut.

The first layer of binding in progress.

The drive belt is wound onto the bundle in the reverse direction of the first pass.

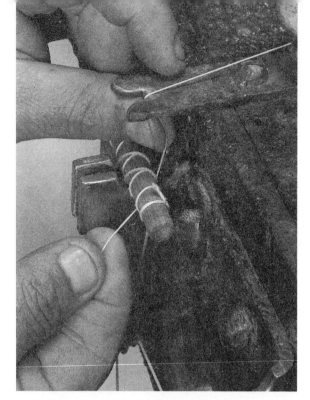

Once again, the binding string is drawn under the drive belt.

binding thread, also counterclockwise. Make the second run through the binder and tie the thread off.

Now look closely at the dowel. Are there any cut marks or nicks caused by the binder arms or

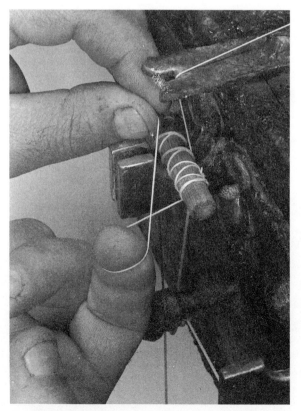

Forming the half hitch. Notice the path of the knot needed to follow the flow of the binding thread.

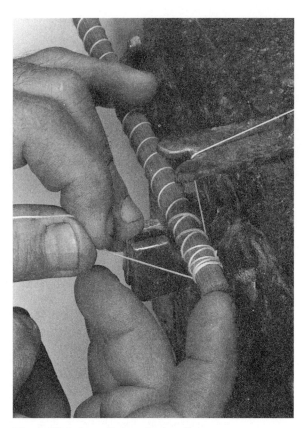

The half hitch applied to the bundle.

Moving the binding thread to allow the knot in the drive belt to pass by.

the feed guides? How's the thread — are there any cuts in it? Now is the time to correct any shortfalls in the system. Don't jump directly to binding strips of bamboo until you're satisfied that the binder is functioning correctly.

Progress on the reverse bind.

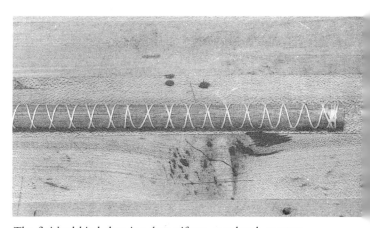

The finished bind showing the uniform crosshatch pattern.

Binding Strips

With the strips planed to untapered equilateral triangles, the next step is to bind them for heat treatment. The best way to hold the strips in place for the binder is with masking tape. First, arrange the strips in the proper order for your node-staggering method, then place a piece of masking tape 2 inches from the butt end. Skip to the midpoint of the strips and place a second piece there. And finally, place a piece at the tip of the section.

Use the 1½-pound weight for binding the strips before heat treatment. Place the bundled strips in the binder as you did the dowel, with ½ inch overhanging to the right of the center support arm. Double-wrap the drive belt on the strips, followed by the binding thread. Pull the slack back at the spool of thread.

Now, before you turn the wheel, remove the masking tape closest to the drive belt. This tape won't take the heat of the oven well, so it should be removed before it's buried beneath the binding thread. The best movement to remove the masking tape is when it's centered in the left support arms.

Run the bundle to the end and half-hitch the thread, then rerun the bundle but in the opposite direction and again tie off. To flatten any bends in the bundle, place it on your workbench and, with both hands, roll it back and forth, working your hands from the center of the bundle to the ends.

Heat-Treating Oven

To bake out the moisture and set a temper in the bamboo strips, they need to be heated to a temperature of 375 degrees F. Different rodmakers use different methods. Some prefer a piece of pipe and a torch. Others have special ovens built for this

The author's uniquely designed heat-treating oven.

job. One rodmaker I know from out West even uses a pizza oven for his heat treatments.

Not having any friends in the pizza business, and wanting an accurate heating device, I designed my own electric oven. It doesn't use liquid petroleum gas, which I'm not comfortable with. Rather than dispersing into the atmosphere like natural gas, this gas instead settles into low pockets waiting to be ignited. An accident waiting to happen!

I built my oven enclosure from two pieces of ductwork. Its inner dimensions are 4 inches by 8 inches by 59 inches long, while outside it's 6 by 10 by 60 inches long. To insulate the enclosure I used 1-inch fiberglass ductboard (compressed fiberglass with a foil backing placed on the outside).

To assemble the enclosure, cap one end of the 6-by-10-inch duct, then line the inside with

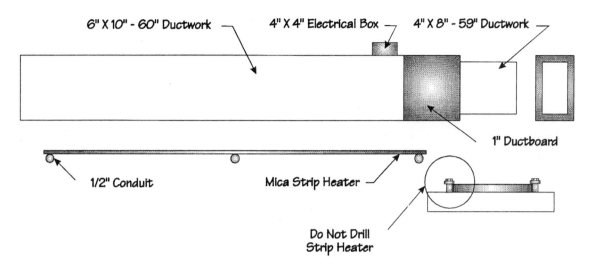

6" X 10" - 60" Ductwork

4" X 4" Electrical Box

4" X 8" - 59" Ductwork

1" Ductboard

1/2" Conduit

Mica Strip Heater

Do Not Drill
Strip Heater

An end view of the oven opening.

the ductboard. To do this, first cut two pieces of ductboard 10 inches by 60 inches, and slide a piece down each side of the 6-by-10 duct. Then cut two pieces 4 by 60 inches and slide them into the top and bottom of the enclosure. Cap the 4-by-8 piece on one end, and cut a 4-by-8-inch piece of ductboard. Place the ductboard in the opening and slide the inner ductwork piece in after it. Once the inner ductwork is in position, the two open ends of ductwork will be flush. To seal the unit, you can fabricate a reducing cap using the measurements noted above.

For a door, I merely cut a 4-by-8-inch piece of ductboard that would friction-fit in the opening. For a handle, use a carriage bolt ¼ inch by 2 inches with fender washers.

The heat requirement for this task is 963 BTUs (282 watts). But to get a faster warm-up, I chose to use a 650-watt heater. At first I tried a short 12-inch finned heater, but the box temperatures were uneven and it showed on the cane strips. I then went to a mica strip heater 54 inches long. To suspend the heater off the bottom of the cabinet I cut three pieces of ½-inch conduit and

attached them to the mica strip — one at each end and one in the middle.

For temperature control, I used a universal electric oven thermostat. To start the wiring, first mount a 4-by-4-inch electrical box that's 2½ inches deep on the top side of the enclosure near the front. Then drill a hole to the inside large enough to admit the thermostat probe and the two wires (⅜ inch).

At this point you need to add the inside rack. I built mine from ½-inch rat screen. Its dimensions are 4 inches by 4 inches, and 58 inches in length, so start with a piece of screen that's 12 by 58 and bend it into a U. The rack is now slid into the box. At about the halfway point, I wire the probe of the thermostat to the rack with bare copper wire, then slide the rack into place. Next the mica heater is installed. To attach the pieces of conduit, use sheet-metal screws placed alongside the strip heater. Note that *you must not drill the strip heater.* Just before the heater is fully in place, terminate the lead-ins to the heater. Remember, the wire used inside the enclosure has to be rated for higher temperatures.

Mount the thermostat control to a blank four-square box cover, add a plug-in cord, and terminate the wiring. Don't forget to case-ground the enclosure. That's the function of the green wire.

Anytime you work with temperatures in the range that this oven will create, safety is a priority. *Do not place flammable materials on the enclosure, and do not leave it unattended.*

I've built or supplied parts for about 20 ovens of this style and I'm convinced that it's a good workable design. Some rodmakers have told me that the rat-screen (hardware-cloth) shelf needs to be flat. During construction, the shelf can become buckled or have peaks and valleys in the supportive surface. If you leave these in place, there will be a tendency for tip sections to follow these irregularities during the postcuring of the glued sections.

Perhaps the best flattening technique is to use a flat board. Lay the board on the shelf, lift it until it contacts the upper oven housing, and then drop or guide it to fall against the shelf. A few taps should flatten the shelf. This will ensure that you aren't adding kinks to any rod sections, at either the heat-treating or the postcuring stage.

Heat Treatment

Bake for 7 minutes at 375 degrees F in a preheated oven, flipping end-for-end at 3½ minutes.

It may sound like a recipe off a cake box, but it's the heat-treating regimen for the bundled rod strips. Even if the culm was flamed, heat treatment is still required.

Heat treatment does several things to the bamboo strips. First, it's an effective way to relax the internodal sweeps and built-in tension. Second, it dries the moisture from the bamboo

and tempers it. Because the tip and butt strips are the same size at this point, I heat both for an equal amount of time.

After the bundle of strips is cooled, you need to remove the binding cord. I simply unleash the last half hitch that I tied, set the bundle on my workbench so that it will spin inward, and pull the string upward. I repeat this for the second string.

Nodes Again

After the rod section has cooled from its heat treatment and is unbound, an inspection of the strips may reveal a node that has risen to its pre-flattening hump. Occasionally the heat treatment will allow a node to resurface. This is an indication that when it was originally pressed, it wasn't softened enough. For the strips to lie flat in the final forms, all nodes must be flat. Any that resurface need to be reflattened.

Because you've now removed material to shape the strips into triangles, the amount of heat you'll need to soften the nodal area is reduced — as is the amount of pressure you'll need to flatten the enamel face of the strip against the jaw surface. However, the point opposite the enamel side may see some flattening from the pressure of the vise. This should not be a problem, because you'll remove more material in the final planing, which will once again bring this back to a sharp point.

Moisture Reentry

Each year I'm asked to make more and more rods, so I now do it on a year-round basis. During the winter months, when the outdoor temperatures are well below freezing, there's little chance that moisture will reenter my heat-treated strips. But as spring hits and the humidity inside the house starts rising, I begin storing unfinished rod sections in my heat-treating oven at 100 degrees F (interior cabinet temperature). At this heat range there is little or no humidity to affect the bamboo. If you live in a humid area, however — like rodmaker Frank Erlicher of New Orleans — you may have to store your work in progress in a heated atmosphere all through the year.

To know how local climatic conditions will affect you, there is a simple test that should become routine for every rod you make. Before you heat-treat a bundle of strips, cut a scrap piece and weigh it on a grain scale. (A grain scale is an extremely accurate beam scale that bullet reloaders use for measuring powder and bullets. There are 437.5 grains in 1 ounce.) Write the weight on the enamel side of this test strip. When you heat-treat the bundle of strips, put the test strip in the oven as well.

After heat treatment, weigh the test strip again and write this new weight on the enamel as well. Now you can keep this test strip with the other pieces that were heat-treated together; it will serve as an indicator of whether moisture is reentering the other strips. Simply weight the test strip and compare your result with the inscribed weight.

Interesting Facts

One of the rules of thumb you'll hear from heating contractors is that for every 4 degrees F that you raise the temperature of normal air, you lower the humidity by 10 percent. And by lowering the humidity, you increase its ability to absorb moisture. Using this as a general guideline, you can determine the approximate temperature that will produce dry air.

A good example of this principle can be seen in the mechanics of a clothes dryer. This appliance brings in room air and warms it, allowing it to absorb the moisture from the clothes. The higher-temperature moist air is then discharged. The temperature limit of most clothes dryers is usually around 135 degrees F. From a practical point of view, this is warm enough to completely remove moisture from clothes anywhere in this country, summer or winter.

Soft-Setting Rods

The phenomenon of extreme moisture reentry can be seen in what is best termed a *soft set rod* — a rod that, when bent to shape or direction, will stay in that shape or direction. Long-term storage in a damp basement is usually the culprit. The rods that I have seen fitting this description have been stored and forgotten about for years, and often retrieved by the next generation.

The moisture can be removed using the procedures I've already discussed. However, a normal side effect of drying out these rods is that the ferrules and other parts become loose, because they've been stretched by the added moisture in the bamboo. Sometimes these rods need to be completely rebuilt if they're to be usable again.

7
CREATING ANGLES

Forms

The biggest challenge in tooling up to make bamboo rods is creating or purchasing a good set of final planing forms. You may choose to follow the advice of Everett Garrison in his classic handbook. Or you may want to check out the options presented by George Barnes in his book *How to Make Bamboo Fly Rods*. He offers two suggestions: a wooden set of forms that can easily be made with a table saw, and a V-block system fashioned after the forms that the Herter Company used to sell.

intend to hand-plane bamboo to tolerances of 0.001 inch, shouldn't you be able to file and stone steel to the same precision? I thought I should build by own forms, even though I had no access to a mill. I did the job with the tools I had available in my basement.

Do stop to think about the length and weight of rods you intend to build before buying or building a set of forms. Otherwise, problems may arise. As prescribed by Garrison, the dimensional difference (the slope) between the adjusting stations of his form will only allow you to make

A Stanley 59 doweling jig is now a valuable collector's item.

For some rodmakers, spending up to $650 for a set of forms may be the best choice. But for others, this may seem like a lot of money merely to begin a hobby. I fell into the second category, although money was not my only concern. If you

rods of #4-weight and heavier. This reflects the fishing style of his day.

However, many rodmakers are now creating rods as light as #2-weight, which require a shallower slope in the planing forms. Garrison had his

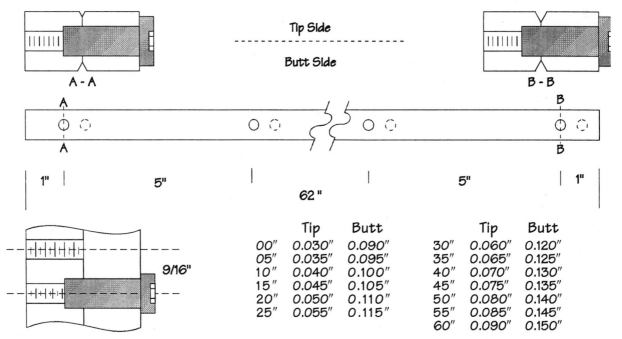

	Tip	Butt		Tip	Butt
00"	0.030"	0.090"	30"	0.060"	0.120"
05"	0.035"	0.095"	35"	0.065"	0.125"
10"	0.040"	0.100"	40"	0.070"	0.130"
15"	0.045"	0.105"	45"	0.075"	0.135"
20"	0.050"	0.110"	50"	0.080"	0.140"
25"	0.055"	0.115"	55"	0.085"	0.145"
			60"	0.090"	0.150"

A schematic for a set of final planing forms.

forms milled with a dimensional difference of 0.0075 inch between the 5-inch adjusting stations. This means that for lighter rods, the

would be a 0.005-inch dimensional difference between the 5-inch adjustment stations — or a 0.001"/1" slope.

With that thought in mind, here are my recommended dimensions for tip and butt sections.

	Tip	Butt
00"	0.030"	0.090"
05"	0.035"	0.095"
10"	0.040"	0.100"
15"	0.045"	0.105"
20"	0.050"	0.110"
25"	0.055"	0.115"
30"	0.060"	0.120"
35"	0.065"	0.125"
40"	0.070"	0.130"
45"	0.075"	0.135"
50"	0.080"	0.140"
55"	0.085"	0.145"
60"	0.090"	0.150"

Top of Form

b

a

30°

Tan 30°=.577350269

b=a x .577350269

An example of specific tip-form dimensions.

forms cannot be pinched together tight enough to be set correctly. Today the recommended slope

You'll also need a variety of tools for this stage. Again, this is my recommended list.

Hacksaw

Hand drill

Drill bits: $^3/_{16}''$, $^1/_4''$, $^3/_8''$

Tap wrench and $^5/_{16}$–18 tap

Stanley #59 doweling jig

Sharpening stone (India Combination)

Dial caliper

Depth gauge

Metal scribe

Mill file: 10"

Allen wrench set

Here's a list of the materials you'll need at this stage. Most are readily available at a building supply center.

Square stock: $^3/_4''$ x $^3/_4''$ x 12'

Layout die

12 dowel pins $^3/_{16}''$ x 1"

13 shoulder (stripper) bolts: $^3/_8''$ x 1"

13 set screws: $^5/_{16}''$–18 x $^3/_4''$

Your first step is to hacksaw the square stock into two 62-inch pieces. Then one side of each piece needs to be stoned flat. I use a standard India stone (6 inches by 2 inches by 1 inch). Pour some fuel oil in a Tupperware dish big enough for you to wash the stone. Working outdoors, place the steel strips on newspaper (a deck is a good work surface for this project). Space the strips about 1 inch apart so that you can stone them both at the same time. (This will help keep the stone flat to the surfaces.) Now simply wet the stone and polish the surfaces until all burrs and valleys are removed. Keep washing the stone in the fuel oil to clean it of all microscopic metal particles.

Once you have one side of each piece of square stock smooth, place the two pieces together with the smooth sides facing. Use a prick punch to mark the top side of each piece at the very end of the steel pieces. This identifies the forms for later indexing. The next step is the layout of the stock for drilling. Start by swabbing the layout die on the top and both sides at approximately the area that you'll be drilling.

Now it's time to round up your C-clamps and some flat stock. Before the actual laying out, clamp the square stock together and then clamp it again to the flat stock to keep the tops flush. I choose to clamp at 2 inches from each end and then at three other locations in between. Watch for the layout die, leaving about 1 inch of distance so the clamps won't interfere once the drilling starts. Laying the body of the C-clamps off to one side will also help with clearance.

The layout is straightforward. Starting 1 inch from one end of the forms, make a light mark every 5 inches with a metal scribe. Next, using a machinist's square, extend the original scribe marks across the top and down both sides. Finally, make a cross mark on both sides $^3/_8$ inch from the top. This gives you an entrance and exit point for drilling.

Before you start drilling on the forms themselves, it's best to check the accuracy of your doweling jig on pieces of scrap stock. Then you can shim the jig as required for proper alignment. Place the doweling jig carefully on a cross mark, taking time to align the center mark of the jig and scribe lines. I start with a $^3/_{16}$-inch hole. Then I use a drill blank driven through the hole for measuring accuracy.

I have a 6-inch dial caliper that I can use as a depth micrometer for measuring. Using the caliper, check first the dimension from the top surface of the forms to the top of the drill hole at both the entrance side and the exit side. If a dimensional difference exists, you need to shim the top foot of the doweling jig.

When I was first making forms, I decided to proceed with drilling when I could consistently be within 0.010 inch. I just started at one end of the forms and marched down the line until I reached the end. After I drilled a hole, I drove in a ³/₁₆-inch steel dowel pin to further hold the forms in alignment as I continued drilling.

At this point you have a decision to make: Do you want to use differential screws (the Garrison style), or do you want a push-pull system

The differential screw used on the author's original forms.

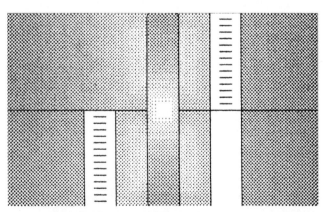

The commonly accepted push-pull adjustment method for final planing form.

of adjustment? The Garrison style is clearly illustrated in his book. By turning one bolt head, the forms are drawn together or spread apart. The push-pull method consists of a hex-head shoulder

(stripper) bolt that pulls the forms together, along with a set screw on the opposite side that pushes the forms apart. Both screws need to be turned simultaneously.

The push-pull system is the one I would adopt if I were starting again. It's certainly the easier method for the home hobbyist. The difficulty with the Garrison method is in making the differential screws. (I'll be describing the push-pull machining momentarily.)

For ³/₄-inch square stock forms, use a ³/₈-by-1-inch shoulder bolt. My suggestion would be to start at one end and work to the other, finishing each station before you skip to the next. First check your doweling jig again, but this time use a ¹/₃-inch drill. Then go to the forms. Drive out the ³/₁₆-inch dowel pin. Then mount the jig (now set up for ¹/₄ inch) and enlarge the original hole to ¹/₄ inch.

Leave the jig in place and switch to a ⁵/₁₆-inch guide. Use it to guide the ⁵/₁₆″–18 tap while tapping the entire hole. Once the entire hole is tapped, switch the guide again, this time to ³/₈ inch. The ³/₈-inch hole you're about to drill needs to be only 1 inch or so deep (just enough for the bolt to fully seat), so the drill bit needs a stop to indicate when you reach the correct depth. I simply measure the drill guide and add an inch. Then I wrap a piece of electrical tape on the bit at that location, drilling until the tape touches the drill guide. If the bolt doesn't seat all the way, I just tweak the hole again with the drill. I repeat this process until I've completed all stations.

One method of incorporating a push-pull system.

The set screws go on the opposite side of the shoulder bolts, but they need to penetrate only that side of the forms. So you can now take out all

Another variation on the push-pull system.

the bolts and separate the two halves. The holes are laid out ⁹/₁₆ inch to the left of the exit hole centerline and centered at ³/₈ inch from the top surface. Here I use a ¼-inch hole to start, then switch to the ⁵/₁₆-inch drill guide for tapping the hole to ⁵/₁₆″–18.

With all holes drilled and the form halves bolted together again, it's once again time to stone the forms. This time the top and bottom need to be stoned until the surfaces are flat. The method is similar to surfacing the sole of a plane, which I

described earlier (see chapter 3). You can watch the surfaces gradually grow together with a uniform sheen. Chances are that if one side is high (shine starting in the middle), then the other side will be low (shine starting on the outer edges).

This is, unfortunately, one of those "it-takes-forever" processes. However, it's good training for building cane rods that take 40-plus hours of precision handcrafting. Once both sides of the forms are stoned, wipe the forms dry. Then swab the layout die down the center of both sides and allow it to dry. Before separating the form halves, see if the index marks are still visible. If they aren't, redo them.

Now take a sheet of paper and create three columns. The first one represents the station locations (0 inches, 5 inches, 10 inches, and so on). In the second column are the depth dimensions of the forms at the appropriate station locations (0.030 inch at 0 inches, 0.035 inch at 5 inches, etc. — see the listing on page 72). The third column is the dimension of the guide mark on the top face of the forms to which you will file.

These numbers are calculated from the dimensions in the second column. To arrive at these numbers, multiply each dimension in the second column by 0.577350269. This is the tangent of 30 degrees. To better visualize this process, imagine that when the forms are separated you'll be removing a 30–60–90 triangle from the corner of the metal. After you've finished the calculations, the dimensions can be marked at the top face of the forms at the appropriate location. Then each of these "points" can be connected with a line.

The last thing required before the actual filing begins is a guide form. I make mine out of nine-ply Baltic birch plywood, which is ½ inch thick and very stable. First I glue two pieces of plywood together to form a 1-inch block that's 4 inches wide by 6 inches long. Then I set up my table saw to saw an exact 60-degree angle down the long side of the block. I use a precision angle gauge against the blade.

The ¾-inch square stock would fit in the miter gauge slot of my table saw. The slot is ⅜ inch deep, so I then undercut the 60-degree gauge block with a slot that's ⅜ by 1 inch. The gauge block can now ride over the square stock, and I can begin filing the stock until I've worked my way to the line. If you don't have a table saw that will accommodate the square stock, then make the gauge block 1½ inches thick and undercut ¾ inch instead of the ⅜ inch I suggest.

I try to file a small amount off the entire length of the form halves. This will give a smoother slope without creating any "bellies." Be careful to keep the file flat against the gauge block, and keep the gauge block flat against your work surface. When I file, I quit just before I hit the scribe line. I do this to both sides, and then I assemble the forms to measure my depth, and check against my chart to verify my progress. With a strong light also check the valley to see that the V is coming together without a ledge on one side. If a ledge appears, then you should file only the shallower form until the two are even for measuring.

This is where the work gets a little hectic, so make careful notes of your progress. Measure each station and record it, comparing that measurement with your target dimensions. Disassemble the forms and do additional dressing in needed areas; then reassemble and measure once again while recording your progress.

If the file starts to leave bad streaks in the metal, clean or replace it. Once you are within a few thousandths of an inch of your goal, you may also want to switch to a stone in order to get a more dressed finish. When one side of the forms is done, flip the forms and start working on the other (butt) side in the same manner.

This may seem like a time-consuming task, but don't despair. Try to be as accurate as possible and your efforts will pay dividends later when you produce a beautiful rod.

Push-Pull

As more and more become involved with the craft of bamboo rodmaking, better techniques begin to emerge. Such is the case with final planing forms. The current accepted standard is an improved push-pull adjustment method. This system breaks down to three elements located at each adjustment station: a set screw, dowel pin, and bolt.

To start, drill the form halves to accept the dowel pin. This holds the forms in alignment, both lengthwise and in terms of the surfaces being flush with each other. Then a form half is drilled to one side of the dowel pin and tapped to accept a threaded device. When tightened, this thread device acts to push the forms apart. On the opposite side of the dowel pin, drill a hole through the first form half, then drill the second half and tap it for a second thread device that, when tightened, will act to pull the forms together.

I've seen and used this adjustment system on a couple of different forms. One used a set screw and a socket-head cap screw; the second used two hex head bolts. My preference is the former, using a set screw and socket-head cap screw. My reasoning is simple: I touch my fingers to the edge of the forms when planing to stabilize the plane, and the first combination is softer on my fingertips. Now, there's nothing wrong with the form in the second illustration. It's simply the bolts that cause me problems. Bumping the sharper corners of the hex-head bolts with your fingertips can hurt. The simple way to fix the problem, of course, is to change the bolts.

In terms of dimensions, the adjustment system is open ended. The thread devices and dowel pins can be either ¼ or 5⁄16 inch, and the centerline spacing can be either ½ or 9⁄16 inch. And it doesn't matter which side of the dowel pin the push or pull is on — as long as this is consistent throughout the form.

Adjusting the push-pull forms isn't difficult. First, make a quick overall check with your depth gauge to see if the forms need to open or close. Then back off whichever thread device needs loosening in order to allow this movement. Do this along the entire length of the forms. If they need to close, back all the push devices out a few turns. If the forms need to open, back out all the pull devices.

Then, starting at one end, adjust the individual stations. Push or pull the forms to the desired dimension and lock in the adjustment with the other thread device by bringing it up snug but not tight. Continue to the next station, following up the last adjustment with a check of all stations. A final readjustment may also be needed.

Fine-Tuning

One of the keys to accurate dimensions is having each of your tools working at its peak. In the case of the planing forms, this means that the two surfaces are flat and the V is a correct 60-degree angle and free of any burrs.

The following technique works for new forms as well as used ones. With new forms it will ensure accuracy; on used forms the nicks and chatters (little ridges) from scraping can be removed. To prepare the forms, they should first be dismantled and cleaned thoroughly of any debris with a soft wire brush or stiff paintbrush. Then reassemble them with their inner faces seated, and set them on the workbench. To monitor your progress, coat the faces of the forms with either layout die or a colored marker.

Two files are used — a flat mill and triangle mill — and both will require some adapting beforehand. For surfacing, a flat mill file about 12

A view of the mill file used to flatten the forms. Note the screw attaching the handle.

to 14 inches long works best. To make filing easier, a handle is often added — but not in the way you might imagine.

To avoid rounding the form surface, you need to hold the file as parallel to the forms as possible. The conventional file handle prevents this from happening. Instead, you can mount a block of wood to one of the faces of the file just below the teeth, where the file is smooth. This smooth area isn't hardened and can be drilled and counterbored for a wood screw to hold the new handle. Counterbore until the screw head is recessed. Then you can bend up the normal handle slightly to get it out of the way.

A 6-inch mill triangle file is used on the V. For a handle, cut a piece of ¼-inch nylon or Plexiglas to the same width as the assembled

faces are squeezed together carefully and avoid excess glue, which might cant the file off angle with the handle. Again, bend the normal handle up slightly.

Besides the files, you'll need a file card or brush to clean the flat file. A toothbrush works well to clean the triangle file. And it would be best to have a paintbrush handy to whisk the filings from the forms. Finally, as much as I discourage the use of gloves while making rods, this is one of those times when a pair of jersey gloves will protect your hands and not get in the way.

A triangle file glued with epoxy to a piece of nylon.

forms and about 5 inches long. To attach the file to the handle, glue it with epoxy down the centerline of the handle's width. Be sure the two sur-

The surfacing of the forms is done first. Lay the file on the forms as parallel as possible, having the front of the file hang just over the edge of the forms and its rear just over the opposite edge. File forward with one hand on the handle and your other hand placing a light amount of downward pressure at the file's midpoint. Take a few passes in this file position, and then alternate the file so that it overhangs the opposite edges (forming an X pattern). Now take a few passes more.

Surfacing the forms. Notice the long angle used to ensure a flat surface.

You'll need to clean the file after just a few passes, but cleaning the surface of the forms will help make the filing go faster.

After a few passes, inspect your forms for progress. If they're new, you'll probably notice a few things right away. If the forms weren't surfaced after assembly, you might see removal at just the middle or just the edges. This is common due to the inaccuracies of steel manufacturing. Normally, if one surface contacts at the middle first, the opposite surface will contact the edges first. Also, check for flatness using a straightedge. Continue filing until the entire surface shows evidence of file wear. Both sides should be surfaced before you focus attention on the V.

Before the second phase begins, I recommend that you soften the sharp edges you've just created. With a flat mill file, chamfer the four corners of the forms. My reasoning is that in the next stage you'll pull the file down the forms with your thumb and first finger resting on these corners for a guide. If they're sharp or have burrs, your fingers are sure to suffer the consequences.

If you examine a triangle file closely, it'll be obvious that the corners don't come to a point but are instead flattened. To compensate, the forms need to be opened enough so the faces of the file contact the faces of the V. Perhaps the most accurate way to accomplish this goal is to set the gap using a pair of feeler gauges, adjusting from station to station. A feeler-gauge thickness of 0.060 to 0.070 inch is needed. The key to using feeler gauges is to have the same resistance to travel at each location.

Speaking generally, a triangle file is "pulled" the length of the forms starting at the deepest end. But there are a few fine points. After you place your file in the V, rest the middle finger of your right hand on it to hold the file in position. Then make a visual inspection of the distance between the form surface and the lower surface of the handle to ensure that the distance on each side is the same. If it isn't, this error needs to be corrected. Finally, with your left thumb and first finger pinch the side of the forms and the handle — and pull forward. After each pass, the file and the V should be whisked clean, and the V inspected for progress.

Remember that with each pass, the V is being filed deeper; too much filing (especially on the tip side) might not allow the forms to adjust to the required numbers. A compromise would be to bring the surface of the V to a 50 percent finish — that is, one in which 50 percent of the

The triangle file as it is pulled down the length of the forms.

V's surface shows evidence of filing. Needless to say, you should proceed with caution.

Depth Gauge

The correct instrument to set the final planing forms is a dial depth gauge. This instrument costs about $150, but there is a less expensive option. If you buy a dial indicator and fit it to a base, you'll have the same tool — but for only about $25. Part of the price difference is that the dial depth gauge

Using the depth gauge to adjust the final forms.

has accurate extension rods that allow you to measure to depths of 8 inches. A dial indicator will only measure up to 1 inch, which is all most rod-makers need.

The block I make is again built from Baltic birch plywood, 1 inch thick, 2¼ inches wide, and 1½ inches high. I use a doweling jig to drill a

¼-inch hole completely through the block, followed by a ⅜-inch hole drilled only halfway. The indicator is then slid into the ⅜-inch hole. If the hole is accurate, it will be a friction fit. If the gauge slips into place, put a little wood glue on the ⅜-inch metal collar to make the fit snug.

The gauge needs a 60-degree point. I had to order mine, but it only took a few days to arrive. The last time I checked a 60-degree point could be mail-ordered for about $4. You want to specify Starrett part 6632/6.

60 Degree Point

Correct

Incorrect

Measuring to ensure a true 60-degree point.

To set the dial to a zero point, loosen the lock screw, place the unit on a flat surface, hold it with light pressure, and then index the dial face to zero. Now tighten the dial's lock screw. It's also a good practice to recheck the zero setting before each use.

Metal Base

A helpful refinement to the depth gauge is the addition of a base made of either steel or aluminum. This will add enough weight to the base that it will sit firmly on the forms while you make the adjustments.

The base I made most recently was aluminum formed out of a 2-inch length of a 1-by-1½-inch rectangular bar stock. The ⅜-inch hole for the gauge collar is bored in the center of the 1-inch face. Once the gauge is in place, a drop of superglue will hold both together. Apply the glue to the collar of the gauge and allow it to flow down onto the metal base. This will form a buildup of glue in the corner where the two meet. One of the benefits of using aluminum is that the extrusion produces a finer finish than you'll find on steel.

Right Point

One common problem is that there are several depth gauge points that look right but aren't true 60-degree points. This is further complicated by the fact that the manufacturers don't always describe their products adequately. However, I've found the Starrett model that I recommended above to be consistently accurate.

A good test is to check your depth-gauge point with your 60-degree center gauge. It should fit the center gauge exactly; otherwise, you have the wrong point. Also, watch to make sure your depth-gauge point truly comes to a point. If it doesn't, it will throw off your measurements now and at later stages as well.

Index Fixture

One way to stop depending on the sharpness of the point to zero-set the depth gauge is through

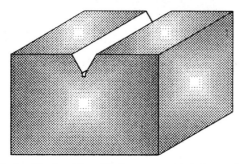

An index block with a 60-degree trough helps maintain accuracy of depth.

the use of an index block. This is a metal block with a 60-degree V cut across its top face. The base of the V is also squared out to ensure that all seating occurs between the faces of the point and of the block.

The exact depth of the V isn't necessarily important, but most of those I've seen are 0.100 to 0.125 inch deep. Knowing the exact depth of the V on the index block you use, however, *is* important. This depth is the standard for your block.

To use the index block, set the depth gauge on the block so the point seats to the V. Then adjust the dial until the indicator needle is pointing to the number equal to the standard of the block. Lock the dial face into place and the gauge is ready to be used to set the final forms.

Because I didn't have access to the equipment needed to make an index block, I bought mine. This is one of those items that's nice to own, but sometimes the cost can outweigh the benefits. Over the years I've fine-tuned my block with an abrasive stone, and it's still a few thousandths off in terms of precision. I describe an index block as an extra, not a necessity, when it comes to making rods.

Setting Forms

Before you start to adjust your forms to a new taper, take a minute and double check your math. Most taper listings give you the dimensions across two flats, which you must divide by 2 to in order to arrive at the dimensions of the individual strips.

You'll use these dimensions often when measuring the progress of the strips. A little trick I use is to place a strip of ¾-inch masking tape just to the back of the forms on my workbench, then write the dimensions on the tape in line with the 5-inch-spaced adjustment screws. This speeds up the process when I set the forms, and it's invaluable when I'm measuring the strips at the final stages.

Start at the tip end of the forms. First, use your dial indicator to measure the setting and then adjust the screw until you reach the desired dimension. Move to the next station and repeat the setting adjustment. Once you've adjusted all the stations for the section you're about to make, recheck the settings and readjust if needed.

A pitfall many novice rodmakers fall into is not planning for the amount of surface that will be removed later when the glue and binding thread are sanded away. I leave a slight haze of enamel on the finished strips to act as a release agent for the glue. Consequently, I *must account for this extra enamel* in the dimensions at setup time. On my rod-taper charts, then, I add 0.001 inch to the needed dimensions. When this extra layer is removed after gluing, the dimensions are again correct. Without such planning, though, you might find yourself making undersize rod sections.

Another Trick

The final planing forms are designed with the smaller dimension of both sides at one end. As a result, one side allows for setting the forms with the adjustment screws facing out and away from the workbench. But when you flip the forms to the opposite side, the adjustment screws face to the inside of the workbench. To make these screws accessible, you'll need to flip the forms lengthwise.

But before you do so, transfer the dimensions onto the forms. Writing with a felt marker, inscribe the dimension corresponding with each adjustment station onto the upper surface of the planing form. With the form flipped lengthwise, this will eliminate any confusion about the adjustment dimension for each station. Later, when the section is completed, you can remove the markings with a few passes of a block sander.

Final Planing

In the first stage of final planing you're removing more of the excess bamboo and developing the taper in the strips. In the last stages you're defining the final dimensions of the taper in the individual strips. I work all the strips through the two stages as a group, completing the first process before moving to the second. I believe it's easier to concentrate on one task at a time.

To begin, first set your planing forms on the workbench with the butt side up. To give the strips the greatest side support, intitially place the strips in the forms at the butt (larger) end,

Holding the bamboo as the plane is initiated at the end of the strip.

gradually working them toward the tip (smaller) end as you remove material.

After the cut is started, the hold position is shifted. Now the strip is being pulled, not pushed.

Starting with a freshly sharpened plane blade, adjust your hand plane to 0.004 inch. Readjust the forward foot as well. The throat opening (the distance from the blade to the forward foot) should be at most 0.010 inch. Plane as you did when you first formed the 60-degree angle. Start at the front of the strip and work your way back slowly with each pass of the plane. This time make three or four passes and then flip the strip, planing equally from each side.

If you're working on a butt section, plane until you're 0.030 inch above the forms. Then move the strips to their proper location in the adjusted forms. If you're planing tip strips, continue until they're flush with the forms, then flip the forms so that you can continue planing with the strips in their proper location. This completes the first stage of final planing.

The second stage obviously requires more precision. To start, lightly mark each strip with a pencil on the enamel side at each 5-inch set screw. The plane blade is now backed up to a 0.003-inch cut.

An overhead view of the plane at the start of a pass over the strip.

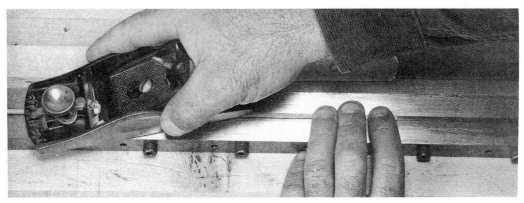

The proper way to hold a strip as the plane is moved through the cut.

At this point it's a good idea to check the dimensions of all three flats-to-points at each 5-inch station on all six strips. If your angles are correct, the measurements will be the same. If these dimensions aren't identical, then the angles are not a true 60 degrees. Use your center gauge to investigate the angles. Work on the flat that you find is out of angle with the enamel side. Small differences may occur if you press the points of the strips too hard with your dial caliper, so use caution.

Now place the strips in the forms at their intended position. Your planing strokes should run the entire length of the strips, and you should

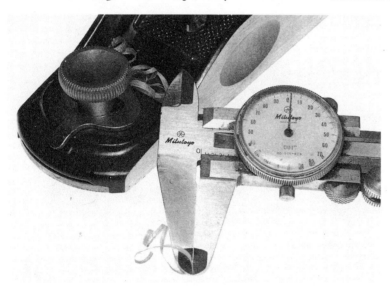

A shaving of 0.0025 inch created with the plane.

flip the strips on every second pass to balance the removal of bamboo. I normally plane until I'm 0.005 inch from touching the forms. I then remove the enamel surface and complete the finish dimensioning of the strips with a scraper.

If you're experiencing problems with chipped or lifted nodes, you can try to restraighten the node area. Then, instead of using a hand plane, try using a scraper to straighten the area before using the plane again.

Measuring Strips

You must measure the strips at two distinct stages during the final planing process. The first time is when the apex (corners) of the strips come to a point. This will clarify whether the angles are correct. And the second time is at the end of the planing, to make sure that your final work was accurate.

Measuring the strips is a straightforward process. With a dial caliper (or micrometer), take a measurement from the apex (corner) to the flat opposite it. Because the strips are triangle shaped, each location along the strip will have three measurement combinations. And because the triangles are equilateral, the measurements at each location should all be equal. If they aren't identical, the angles are incorrect.

When you're measuring the strips, you should take a couple of precautions. First, a dial caliper driven by a thumb can exert a tremendous

Decimal Equivalents

$3/64$	0.046875″
$4/64$	0.0625″
$4.5/64$	0.0703125″
$5/64$	0.078125″
$5.5/64$	0.0859375″
$6/64$	0.09375″
$7/64$	0.109375″
$8/64$	0.125″
$9/64$	0.140625″
$10/64$	0.15625″
$11/64$	0.171875″
$12/64$	0.1875″
$13/64$	0.203125″
$14/64$	0.21875″
$15/64$	0.234375″
$16/64$	0.25″
$17/64$	0.265625″
$18/64$	0.28125″

amount of pressure on the fragile apex (corner) of a strip. In fact, the bamboo can be crushed to a shape other than a point, which will yield an incorrect measurement. In practice, I hold the strips vertically, tip-end up, and apply only enough pressure to the dial-caliper slide that the strip is barely held by the dial-caliper jaws. If I suspect that I've damaged an apex, I remeasure 1/2 inch above or below the marked location.

The second precaution relates to the way you lift the strips, either from the forms or off the workbench. The lifting point should be to the butt side of the midpoint of the strip, *never from the tip ends*. This is, of course, common sense. The strips, especially those for tip sections, are fragile and can be damaged or broken by improper handling. Usually when you do lift the strips, it's to measure them. If you lift the strips midpoint, they'll pivot neatly to a vertical position.

Bad Angles

The discovery that your strips are not equilateral — with all corners at 60 degrees — can be very discouraging.

There are several factors, or combination of factors, that can lead to bad angles. And to add to the problem, the way that a hand plane characteristically functions can make these off angles hard to correct. The natural tendency of the hand plane is for the front foot to "jump" so it can seat with the already planed surface. To correct bad angles, you have to figure out what caused them in the first place — and then try to correct them, if you still have enough bamboo to work on.

The most likely cause of off angles is probably rocking the plane with your hand. You must work on the bamboo strips with the sole of the plane *parallel to the forms*, pass after pass. To visual-ize this technique, you might want to place a mirror at the end of your workbench so you can watch the alignment of the plane throughout each pass. This will help you learn the feel of the correct plane position.

A second tip in stabilizing the plane is to lightly touch the third finger of your plane hand to the corner of the forms. But first you want to soften the sharp corner of the form so you don't cut your flesh. A few passes with a mill file, followed by a block-sanding, will create an ever-so-slight radius at the corner that will be finger friendly.

Remember that excess downward pressure can aggravate a lack of plane stability. And it's human nature to push down harder when the plane doesn't appear to be cutting. The real cause, however, is usually a dull blade or a flipped burr. In either case, you need to stop and deal with the problem. The weight of the plane alone should provide all the downward pressure you need to make any cut. Besides losing control of the angles, you also burn up a lot of energy trying to force the plane to work.

The Blade

As you've seen, the leading edge of the plane blade needs to be parallel with the sole of the plane body. You can confirm this positioning with a visual inspection, making sure that these two parts "touch" one another. The Stanley 9 1/2 (or G12-020) has a lateral adjustment lever for just this purpose. Similarly, after sharpening the blade and making a few passes, it's wise to recheck the adjustment. It's always possible that the blade may settle against the exposure adjustment stop.

If you're using waterstones for sharpening, you may want to check the blade against a straightedge to ensure that the blade isn't crowned. If you do have a crowned blade and are planing off center, the blade will remove uneven amounts of bamboo and gradually lead to incorrect angles. A crowned blade can be prevented by flattening your waterstones on a regular basis, or by using diamond stones for the coarser metal removal.

Raised Node

The bamboo immediately in front and in back of all nodes should touch the face of the planing forms. If it doesn't, you'll soon run into problems. It's probably time to reflatten these areas and redress the problem with sanding as needed.

Clean Forms and Strips

It is essential that you keep your planing forms and strips free of debris, such as sanding dust and shavings. Even the smallest of particles can push the strips upward in the forms, creating undersize strips. A soft-bristled paintbrush works well to remove unwanted material. But be careful not to catch and leave bristles in the V of your forms.

The strips can also pick up debris, especially sanding dust, so they should be kept clean as well. However, use extreme caution when cleaning the strips. Here again you can use a soft paintbrush, but whisk only downward (large end to small). Whisking upward (small end to large) could destroy strips by driving the bristles into the end grain and lifting fibers.

Pink Pet (Pearl)

As the exposed surface of a strip grows closer and closer to the top surface of the planing forms, you may find that it becomes more difficult to hold the strip with just the contact of your fingers. I

noticed this particular problem in one of my classes. A student had suffered an accident with his hand earlier in life, and holding the strips became a challenge. The solution was a Pink Pet (Pearl) eraser. It was large enough for him to grip, and its rubbery texture held the strip in place in the planing forms.

Block-Sanding

To remove the remainder of the enamel and reveal the final surface, a block sander is essential. Now, I know that several makers use scrapers to take the enamel off, but I think this is a mistake. First, you don't want to cut into any power fibers. Block-sanding with 360-grit sandpaper may be a bit slower, but I feel it gives you better control of the enamel removal. Second, a scraper, especially a freehand (nonbodied) one, can leave minute chatter marks in the surface. On the surfaces that get glued together, these may go undetected — but later, as the finish is added, these chatter marks will be amplified. Looking down the length of a finished rod, you want to see a uniform sheen, not a surface broken with chatter ridges.

For block-sanding, it's best to use your planing forms as a holder. Once again, use your soft paintbrush to whisk the forms clean, and then insert the strip. One note of caution about block-sanding: Because of the grip that the sandpaper has on the strips, any reverse stroke can cause the strips to ride up and out of the forms. This could possibly buckle and damage the strips. Sand one way, from large end to small, lifting the sanding block at the end of each stroke. You will also find that you need to hold the strips in place by applying light pressure with your free hand. Here again, to prevent buckling, you should maintain the correct pressure so that you sand away from the butt.

Block-sand each strip until the power fibers can just be seen through the enamel. Do not completely remove the enamel at this time; leave a slight haze of it, which you'll remove later when the glue and string are sanded free. As I mentioned earlier, this haze amounts to about 0.001 inch.

Scrapers

At the final stages of dimensioning your strips, it may be a good idea to switch to a scraper. For those unfamiliar with this tool, there are basically two types. The freehand scraper is a blade or piece

bamboo can be lifted from the form, allowing too much bamboo to be removed. This is especially true of areas around the nodes. The result of using a Swiss scraper can often be seen as voids or chips in the glue joints of the finished strips.

There are several bodied scrapers on the market today; the two most often used by rodmakers are the Lie-Nielsen reproduction of the Stanley model 212, and the Conover Woodcraft scraper. The original model 212 has become a collector's item, highly sought after by rodmakers and other fine woodworkers. Current prices for an

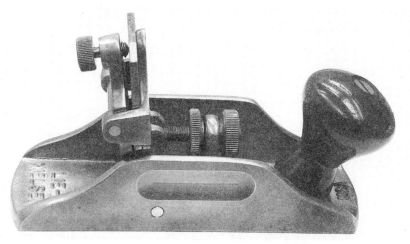

A side view of the Lie-Nielsen reproduction 212 scraper.

of steel held in your hand. The second type, known as a bodied scraper, has a blade of steel mounted in a body similar to that of a hand block plane.

The best-known handheld scrapers are the Swiss models. These come in a variety of shapes and are commonly used in finish woodworking. Most are fairly inexpensive and available at a variety of outlets. The drawback to using this type of scraper is that you have little or no control over the amount of material that they remove. In working with bamboo, there's a tendency to follow the grain. With no forward foot, the strip of

original can run into thousands of dollars (just like quality bamboo fly rods!). But in recent years the model 212 has been reproduced in bronze by Lie-Nielsen of Warren, Maine. The unit is not only functional but attractive as well. With this scraper it's easy to remove thin whisks of bamboo less than a one-thousandth of an inch.

The Conover Woodcraft scraper is also a reproduction. Ernie Conover, a rodmaker himself, saw the original in the American Museum of Fly Fishing. The entire unit is a mere $2\frac{1}{4}$ inches in length, and its wood and brass construction make it a very attractive piece.

There is no blade-adjusting mechanism on a bodied scraper. However, this is a simple process. The Conover scraper has a fixed blade angle, but the Lie-Nielsen 212 has an adjustable one. The best angle to use is 3 degrees forward. This makes the blade drag on the strips.

To set the depth of cut, place the scraper on a flat surface, then place a 0.0015-inch piece of shim stock under the very front edge of the scraper. Loosen the blade lock-down screw and, with pressure on the body and on the blade, retighten the lock screw. This should give you a removal thickness of about 0.001 inch. If you want a finer removal, then the shim stock used to set the scraper needs to be thinner. For amusement, I once sent Tom Lie-Nielsen a large plastic sandwich bag filled with shavings all less than a few thousandths of an inch thick.

Scraper Blades

Both the Conover and the Lie-Nielsen scrapers come with quality blades. Their metal composition and hardness will hold a lasting sharp edge. I sharpen both blades at a 30-degree angle (the same angle as used for plane blades). In fact, I use the same blade holder and exposure jig for both tools.

Because of the petite size of the Conover blade, however, sharpening can be a bit more difficult. To secure it in my regular blade holder, I had to fabricate extending arms. These arms represent two pieces of $1/8$-by-$3/4$-inch flat stock that's $2^{1/2}$ inches long. At one end of both pieces I filed a recess a little less than $1/32$ inch deep for the first $1/2$ inch. This recess accepts the blade and holds it in place when the arms are tightened in the blade holder. I set the exposure with the jig so that the blade angle remains constant from one sharpening to the next. And as with my other blades, I polish the back to remove the burr.

Handmade Scraper

Not long after I started making rods, I saw an all-wood scraper in the Garrett Wade tool catalog. It was made of tiger-striped maple and looked like it would work for scraping bamboo. At about the same time I was able to get an early version of Lie-Nielsen's 212 reproduction, so I abandoned the idea of the wood scraper — but it was a concept that never seemed to go away. My hope was not to buy one but rather to build one. It finally became a personal challenge.

I could have saved myself some grief and made it from straight-grained maple, but part of

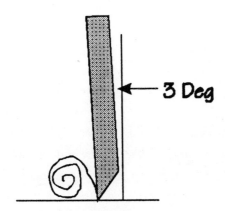

The correct angle for setting the scraper.

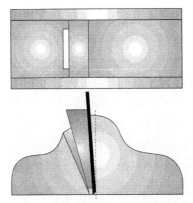

A rough plan for making a wooden scraper.

the attraction of the scraper in the catalog was the fact that it was made from figured wood. In fact, any good hardwood should work for the project — but because of the fineness of the work intended, a finer-grained type is perhaps best. Lignum vitae is the wood that my local wood supplier recommended, but it's quite expensive. The maple I used cost only a few dollars.

Originally I built my scraper around the dimension of the model 212 scraper blade (1³/₈ inches). Later I thought I should have used that of the Hock blade from my 9½ hand plane: 1⁵/₈ inches. Then I would've had to buy only one good blade.

The body of the scraper has four components: the front, back, and two sides. Because the front and back are 1⁵/₈ inches thick, I laminate them from two pieces of wood. To ensure an equal thickness from front to back, I first laminate pieces big enough for both parts, and then I cut them from the one laminated board. For the sides I plane one board to ⁵/₁₆ inch, then cut it in half.

With the four parts cut, I then glue and clamp them together using the bottom as my index. Once the parts are clamped securely, I clean any squeezed-out glue from inside the throat area. Any buildup on the blade or wedge faces will cause the blade to be insecure.

I finish the body by bandsawing the block to the required shape and then routing the edges. The sole is trued up by flat-sanding it. I use 220-grit sandpaper on the sole, and 150-grit on the rest of the body.

The wedge is then cut and the shaving relief is added. I trim the length of the wedge as needed. To do this, first slide the blade into place and seat the wedge. Initially the fingers of the wedge may stick out past the surface of the sole. I choose to cut them back until they are up into the throat about ³/₁₆ inch. You don't want to cut them back too far or you may get blade chatter. For a finish, I stain the maple to bring out the grain, and then I seal it with several coats of tung oil.

Set the blade depth just as you do on the other bodied scrapers: by placing a shim under the sole at its very front and securing the blade into place. The one difference is that instead of turning a set screw, you force the wedge into

The author's own wooden scraper.

the throat. I use only finger pressure to seat the wedge; I don't tap it into place.

Scraping

You're now down to removing the last few thousandths of an inch of bamboo. With a scraper, it's better to use a whisking action. If you were to stop the scraper with it still on the forms, chances are that you'd leave a cut ridge on the strip. Such a ridge — even one a few thousandths of an inch high — will cause a gap in the glue joint.

Once again, I make light pencil marks on the enamel side after I've sanded the enamel. This way I can make a pass with the scraper and quickly measure the strips to check my progress.

Keep It Clean

After each pass with the scraper (or even the plane), flip out or lightly blow out the shaving. This will keep you aware of the material you're removing with each pass and assure you of the pass's effectiveness. And when you're scraping to the final dimensions, it will also give you a sense of the delicate amount being removed.

How Close?

A reasonable amount of accuracy is important in making bamboo fly rods. Remember that the taper dimensions represent a specific line weight and casting character in a finished rod. If you make any radical departure, it might change these features. On your first few rods, I encourage you to aim for an accuracy of 0.002 inch on the individual strip dimensions. This equates to an assembled-section accuracy of 0.004 inch. To some makers with machinist backgrounds, this may not sound intimidating, but for most new rodmakers it will be a goal that requires intense attention to detail.

It's accurate to describe bamboo rodmaking as an acquired skill, similar to other life skills. In other words, it's something that you work toward. When it comes to accuracy, I recommend you set a level that is personally challenging and yet not self-defeating. Your skills will gradually increase, and so will your pleasure and success in this craft.

The Last Cuts

In an ideal world you could achieve proper dimensions by simply planing or scraping the

A shaving of 0.001 inch created with a scraper.

strips until no more material could be removed. This is a reasonable image of the process, but I recommend adopting a slower pace toward the end. Once the strip dimensions are within 0.005 inch of your target dimensions, it's safer to finish the work in segments, remeasuring after each pass with the scraper. This slower pace helps prevent unpleasant surprises — especially undersize dimensions.

The scraping and measuring process is best accomplished by starting at the tip end of the strips and continuing through the butt. The segments, both start and end point, lie midway between the adjusting stations. And to prevent leaving a cut ridge, you must lift your scraper at the end of the cut.

If you have several segments that need the same amount of material removed, they can be treated as one exercise. However, it's still wise to check dimensions at each station involved. After each pass, all the debris should be removed from the scraper body. This tells you how much material is removed with each pass of the scraper. Also, recheck dimensions with each pass.

Problems

Few rodmakers ever talk about them, but there are some nodes that chip and simply do not straighten. They can't be scraped out, and they definitely won't be planed out. These are the strips that normally get remade. But there is a way to salvage them if you recognize the problem early.

If a node area continues to chip as you're planing, stop chasing it just before the chip level gets below the finish surface of the forms. Once the chip level is into the forms it's no longer usable; a new one must be started. You can block-sand the chipped area until the chip has disap-

peared. To prevent the block sander from forming a belly, you need to dress a 5-inch section around the chip as well.

After the chip is sanded away, test the area by placing it next to another strip and comparing for any voids or misfit. This is the time to correct any flaws. Then you can go back to planing or scraping, although you must dress only the opposite side of the strip.

Ideally, planing and scraping is done evenly to both sides of the strips, alternating after a set number of passes. But I've learned that once the strips taper in on both sides, there's really no need to flip sides. The center fibers will still run the length of the strips, and no one will be able to tell which strips may have caused you problems.

Red X

After you've cleaned up a chipping node or some other problem area, I suggest using a Sharpee marker to place a red X on this area. This will act as a warning when you pick up the strip; the mark will remind you of a corrected problem area. As a rule, you can use only a scraper over a red X area. Trying to use a plane just aggravates the problem, and that could spell disaster.

Dimension Problems

If you're having problems getting your strips down to the needed dimensions, there are a few items to check.

First, you must determine whether a problem strip is flush with the top surface of the forms or above it. If the strip is flush, you might want to check whether your dial calipers are out of adjustment. This may be caused by debris on the measuring surface. Then check the depth gauge for zero adjustment. You might have debris on the foot surface. Finally, recheck the adjustment of your finish forms, which may have opened up.

We went through this sequence of checks once at a workshop I was conducting. A couple of the students had brought in some of their own equipment. No matter what they tried, they could not get their strips down to the final dimensions — nor could they find the problem. Finally, after a lot of rechecking and remeasuring, we discovered that the points on their depth gauges were not a true 60 degrees, and this was making their forms adjust incorrectly.

Another potential problem with the 60-degree point is that the very point can be "biffed" (flattened) easily. This can be caused by setting the point down on a metal surface too hard. The only solution is to change the point.

If the strips are above the surface of the forms, on the other hand, this suggests that you're not cutting the bamboo properly. Once again, there are three items to check. The edge of the scraper blade may have rolled back; resharpen it. Or some shavings of bamboo may have wrapped around the edge of the blade, not letting it make contact. Clearing the scraper of shavings will correct this problem. Finally, the scraper blade may be cocked sideways at an angle, not allowing the blade to touch the surface. A simple readjustment of the blade will solve this problem.

Another example of a rolled burr.

Cheat a Bit

The system I have described above works well — but only to a point. As you acquire more skills and try to achieve a higher degree of accuracy, it does break down slightly. Your technique will

certainly require some fine-tuning when you try to achieve that last thousandth of an inch. Even when your planing forms, depth gauge, plane, and blade sharpness are all operating at their best, the magic may still not be there. I'm thinking of those times when there's a 0.001 inch to be removed at a particular station — and try as you may, you just can't get the system to work.

One option is to pinch the planing forms inward slightly. However, if you're caught up in the moment and not receptive to taking the time to readjust, you might choose to cheat. Remember that if you slide the strip forward, you'll expose it above the top surface. The amount of forward movement needed to expose the required level of the strip can only be calculated by knowing the slope per inch. This is not a place or time for guesswork.

Tape and Test

With all six strips at their final dimensions, it's time to join them for gluing and binding. A single wrap of masking tape placed at 6- to 8-inch intervals works well, but I should add a word of caution. Masking tape becomes stickier as it ages, and your delicate strips can be damaged trying to rip off old masking tape. Keep a fresh supply, preferably of the auto-body variety. Also, when you buy masking tape, shop where there's a high turnover rate of supplies. Otherwise you may be purchasing something that has been on the shelf too long.

To start the strip assembly, place a piece of tape sticky-side up on your work area. Then place the larger end of one strip on the tape. Indexing from this strip, place the remaining five strips tight to one another in place on the tape, following the staggering method that you have chosen.

Once all six strips are in place, curl the tape up — bringing the strips into the familiar hexagonal section. Pinch the two free ends of tape together and tight to the hex shaft. Gently separate any intertangled strips, then place the next piece of tape and pinch it tight. Keep working down the section in 6- to 8-inch intervals, untangling the strips and mounting the masking tape until the entire hex shaft is bound. To finish the taping process, use a pair of scissors to trim the tag ends of tape to within ¼ inch.

This is the time to check for any flaws in your planed strips. It's better to find any chipped nodes or imperfect edges now than after the section is glued. At this point a flawed strip can be replaced.

Starting with the larger end, use the first two fingers and thumbs of both hands held about 1 inch apart to compress the shaft as if it were glued. Slowly roll the entire length of the section, looking for flaws. If you find any, mark them with a fine-point red marker for later evaluation.

If you find voids in the glue line, slice the tape with a razor blade or surgeon's scalpel and open the bundle flat. Check for any debris on the flats of bamboo, or for any end cuts left by the plane or scraper. These can be corrected with a light touch of 360-grit sandpaper. But if the void is caused by a chipped node or undersize bow in the strip, you'll have to make a new section.

If you find mistakes in your work, you must be willing to take the extra time to correct them. Strict attention to these important details shows that you are a rodmaker who will only accept the best in workmanship.

8
GLUING THE ROD

Glues

There are three glues that I have used successfully to assemble rods: Weldwood Resorcinol, American Cyanamid URAC 185, and Nyatex epoxy (10E007/10EH008). Each one has particular qualities that make it useful in different stages of rodmaking.

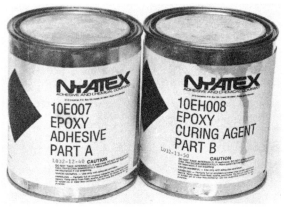

One of the author's three recommended epoxy glues.

Resorcinol was used on most rods in the 1930s and early 1940s. I had the opportunity to use the glue a few years ago when I reconstructed an entire butt section for a client. A rod glued with Resorcinol is easily detectable by its distinct wine-colored glue lines.

For the past 40 years most rods have been glued with URAC 185. This glue is water resistant, withstands heat well, and dries to a light tan color that matches the natural blond color of bamboo. Both Resorcinol and URAC 185 are two-part glues that use a liquid resin and a powder catalyst. When you work with either of these glues, it's always a good idea to sieve the powder through an old nylon stocking to remove any unwanted lumps.

One drawback to these glues is their quick setup time, although you can lengthen it by keeping the glues chilled as long as possible. The easiest way to chill the glue is to immerse the mixing container in ice water, and leave it there until cleanup. The glue can be prepared and spread from a chilled container, but make sure that the strips to be glued are at room temperature.

Mixing Instructions
Resorcinol

Mixing ratio by volume:

4 parts liquid resin
3 parts powder catalyst

Resorcinol can be thinned with up to 10 percent denatured alcohol.

URAC 185

Mixing ratio by volume:

4 parts liquid resin
1 part powder catalyst

Caution: URAC 185 cannot be thinned with any type of alcohol!

Nyatex Epoxy
(10E007/10EH008)

Mixing ratio by volume:

1 part resin
1 part hardener

Mix thoroughly, let set for 15 minutes, remix, and then apply.
Caution: Do not thin with anything!

With the exception of the rod mentioned above, I have had very little experience with either Resorcinol or URAC 185. In fact, I have used epoxy glue on practically all of my rod projects. I fell into this habit after watching a good friend use this epoxy to glue flocking (the fuzzy material that seals the crank-up windows on an automobile) to plastic parts. He was doing something unique with the epoxy glue: heat-curing it at 300 degrees F. At this temperature the glue cured in two minutes, yet it could sit in the application pot for four to six hours at room temperature.

Although there's a virtual cornucopia of epoxy glues out there for you to choose from, there are only a few that I recommend for gluing bamboo rods. And given the many varieties of resins and hardeners, the combinations may number in the thousands. But each combination or change of mix ratio produces a glue with different characteristics of strength, hardness, resistance to heat, and depth of penetration. Only some are obviously suitable for rodmaking.

I knew that the archery world had been using heat-set epoxies for years. Bows are laminated under pressure and then postcured with heat to add strength to the glue bond. The archery bow and the bamboo fly rod have several similarities. The glued material is tight grained, for instance, and the glue bond is stressed with the loading and unloading of energy.

I should warn you that unless an epoxy glue is specially formulated to be postcured, heat will only damage it. My suggestion is that if you can purchase an epoxy glue off the shelf in any store, don't use it to glue strips. It won't be the right type of epoxy for rodmaking.

Other Drawbacks

If you've ever used epoxy glue for repairs around the house, you know that it just doesn't wash off your hands the way other glues do. Nyatex epoxy is no different. If you get it on something it won't come off easily — if at all. For some rodmakers, this "use-it-and-throw-it-away" quality is a definite drawback. Your mixing equipment, spreading apparatus, and binder drive belt will all end up in the trash at the end of each session. Even your binder will accumulate a buildup that you'll probably have to tackle with a drill and a rotary wire brush after drying.

I certainly recommend that you wear an old shirt and jeans when you're working with this material. And to keep it off the hands, I suggest a pair of light latex, disposable custodial gloves. These are similar to the latex gloves that surgeons wear, but not sterile. If you do get some epoxy glue on your hands or other skin areas, white vinegar is usually the best cleanup material.

Shelf Life

If you chose to use Nyatex epoxy glue, the smallest available package contains a quart of each component. Remember that this company is an industrial supplier and 55-gallon drums are its normal sale. Because 1 ounce glues one rod section, a quart of each component will cover about 20 complete rods. For some craftsmen, this represents several years of rodmaking.

The Nyatex instructions suggest that this glue has a shelf life of only 90 days. However, in most cases it will last much longer. Nyatex is just being cautious. Many chemical compounds age at accelerated rates when stored at high temperatures. My experience is that in the cooler (65-degree) confines of my basement, the glue will stay fresh for upward of two years.

A few tips can help you extend this glue's shelf life even further. The first is to repackage the components into smaller units. Pint and ½-pint paint cans, available at a local automotive store, work particularly well. By repackaging, you'll reduce the air contact of the unused portions.

A more unusual storage method is refrigerating the glue. Placing it in your vegetable bin can add many years to its shelf life. Or you could tuck it into the freezer section, where it'll last even longer.

Gluing and Binding

For mixing glue, I purchase 1-ounce plastic cups; for spreading it, I buy soft-bristled toothbrushes. As with the binder drive belt, anything that comes in contact with epoxy glue should simply be thrown away. I get the mixing cups from my local rod component supplier. These are normally used for mixing epoxy wrap finish. They come 100 to each pack, and cost about $4. My wife, Brenda, is a nurse, and she uses the same type of cups for dispensing liquid medicines. I buy the soft-bristled toothbrushes at a local discount pharmacy. They cost 39 cents each, on sale.

I use two plastic picnic spoons for scooping the glue from their containers: one for the resin and one for the hardener. Even if you wipe the plastic spoons, you're risking cross-contamination if you try to use only one of them. For stirring I use round wooden toothpicks. I suggest purchasing a separate box for your shop. If you choose to use Resorcinol or URAC 185, all these items can be cleaned and reused.

Before mixing the glue, you want to have all your equipment ready: You're about to make a commitment, and knowing that everything's ready will reduce your anxiety. Load the proper-size binding thread on the binder. Pull some thread out to make sure that it isn't bound. Then make a new drive belt and mount it on the binder. Hang a ¾-pound weight on the pulley and test the belt by taking a few turns with the crank handle. Make sure the knife you'll use for cutting the binding thread is nearby. At your gluing area have the mixing cup, spoons, toothpicks, and glue ready. To protect the top of my workbench from glue, I spread out double-folded newspaper.

Next, the taped rod section needs to be opened. Using a sharp razor blade or surgeon's scalpel, cut off the tag ends of the tape tight to the section. Then you must slit the tape *at one seam* so

Trimming the excess tape prior to opening the rod section.

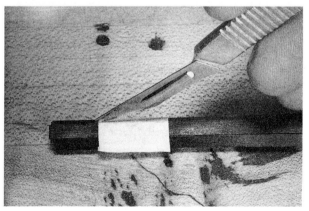

Splitting the tape at a seam.

the section will butterfly open. Starting at the butt end of the section, force the point of a toothpick into the seam just above the masking tape. This will cause the tape to stretch slightly and the seam to gap. Now slice the tape, using just the point of the blade. To move the toothpick to the next tape area, tilt the free end forward and drag it. Wooden toothpicks are made from white pine, which is softer than bamboo, so you shouldn't damage the planed strips. Continue this march until you've sliced all the tape wraps. Finally, lay the section on the newspaper to await the glue.

A toothpick is used to pry open a corner of the taped section.

Before I spread any glue on the strips, I always whisk them off with a clean toothbrush. This removes any debris that might cause a gap in the glue joint. And remember, you don't plane against the grain for fear of lifting bamboo so don't brush up grain either. Always brush from butt to tip.

After the glue is mixed, applying it is a simple matter. Dip the toothbrush in the glue and spread it onto the strips. The first coat may be a little uneven. However, by applying a second coat of glue, and then making a third pass with the toothbrush but no additional glue, you'll level the applications. I allow the glue to penetrate the strips for 15 minutes before I go any further.

Spreading the glue with a toothbrush.

To bind the strips, first gently lift them from the newspaper and lay them into the feed guide arms of the binder with the butt at the center supports. Then gently squeeze the strips back to a hex shape. This will cause glue to escape at the seams. Holding the section together with the left hand, wrap the drive belt around the butt with your right hand. Two wraps are required. It may not matter, but I always wrap the drive belt clockwise for the first pass. A bit of practice with a dowel rod will make this maneuver seem like second nature.

Now weave the binding thread into place and tie it off with several half hitches. Remember to leave enough of a tag end that you can make a hanging loop for suspending the rod during air-drying. Any slack should now be pulled back through the tensioners.

Start cranking the section through the binder at a slow speed. This allows the glue some time to squeeze out and lets you watch everything carefully. When a wrap of masking tape is centered between the supports of the binder, stop and remove it. Continue binding until the drive belt drops off the shaft.

To tie off the thread, first pinch it on the section to hold tension on it. Then slide the section in the guide arms until there's about 6 inches of free thread. Cut it and tie some half hitches while still holding pressure on the thread bound to the section. To finish binding, simply run the section

The glued rod section, bound and ready for drying.

through the binder again, but this time reverse the direction by wrapping the drive belt on the shaft in the opposite direction.

Straightening

A glued section may require one or two kinds of straightening. First, the section may be twisted or spiraled. Second, it may have some kinks or bends. If you look ahead a few pages, you'll find another section about straightening (see page 103). It's a simple choice: You either straighten now or you straighten later. And believe me, once the glue has dried it becomes a lot harder.

Before I check for any bends or twists, I roll the section against a flat surface with the palms of my hands. Place fresh newspaper on your workbench and lay the section on it. Starting with both hands at the center of the section, lightly roll it back and forth by shuttling your hands. As you roll the section, gradually slide your hands apart. Eventually one hand is at the butt of the section, and the other at the tip. Both hands are shuttled simultaneously. I usually make two passes over the section in this manner.

Again, practicing this maneuver beforehand with a $^3/_8$-inch wooden dowel is a good idea. It's an easy technique, but if you haven't done it before it can initially be awkward.

This palm-rolling achieves three goals. First, it blots excess glue onto the newspaper. Second, it

relieves stress on the binding thread, allowing the strips in the section to slide back to their natural position. Third, it rolls out most bends that might have developed in the section.

Because my workbench gets used for all kinds of projects, its surface is a little torn up. To compensate, I have a piece of $^1/_8$-inch tempered Masonite 6 inches wide by 4 feet long that I lay on the workbench whenever I want a smooth, flat surface. When the Masonite sheet becomes worn, I just replace it with another. (Whenever I mention a "flat surface," this is what I mean.)

The next stage of straightening is to check for and correct any twists that might remain in the section. Finding a twist is easy. Placing the section on a flat surface and starting at the butt, simply press down on one spot with one hand. With your other hand, skip ahead a few inches and press down at that location. If there's a twist in this part of the section, it will rock as you press on the second location. If the section rocks, you then have to determine the start and end points of the twist — which demands some careful testing and observation.

When you've located a point, place a light mark with a pencil on the problem section. To remove the twist, grasp the section at the pencil marks and twist it opposite the spiral. The amount of pressure needed depends on the severity of the twist. Several light applications of pressure are better than one massive effort, which might simply result in an overcorrection. When you can march down the section with your fingers and not detect a rocking of the shaft, you're finished.

Unlike a twist, which is common to all flats of a section, a bend can affect as few as two flats. You can detect any major bends by simply laying the section on a flat surface and observing if there are areas where the section doesn't touch the surface. But to find minute bends, you must roll the section on the flat surface using the corners of the hex shape as an indicator.

Any bends you find after you've palm-rolled the section are long bends, not kinks. However, don't try to straighten a bend by holding the section in both hands and pressing with your thumbs when the glue is wet: You'll end up with a section that has one kink followed by another.

You can straighten bends in two ways. With either technique, you first need to determine the start and end points of the bends. I don't mark these with a pencil; instead, I hold a finger on the section and visualize the approximate length of the bend.

The first method makes use of a wallpaper seam roller. Once I have the highest point of the bend up (whether it's a flat, corner, or combination), I apply the roller with light pressure until the bend is flat. The second method, which I prefer, is more tactile. With the high point up, I press on the section with the first finger of my left hand. At the same time I pull back on the section as if I'm drawing back a pool cue before the shot. I prefer this method because it causes the bonding thread to reposition itself, allowing the strips to shift. And for me, it's simply a faster process.

Drying

When I'm satisfied with the straightness of my freshly glued strips, I hang the section at room temperature to air-dry for 16 hours. This is one of the few times when you should bring the rod upstairs, where it's warmer and less humid during the summer.

To create a hanging loop, I tie a square knot in the free ends of the binding thread at the butt end. I then slip this onto a bolt in the beam connector

in our living room. (We own a beam-and-timber home that took several years to build.) If you have a more traditional house, then you need to find a warm place to hang your sections. Putting an eye-hook in a closet doorjamb, or using a clothespin on a hanging lamp, are other possible solutions.

I normally have the section glued and straightened by midnight. Then I let it hang and dry until I arrive home from work the next evening. This represents 16 to 18 hours of drying. The section is now ready for thermal-setting.

Thermal-Setting

Resorcinol and URAC 185, as well as postcure epoxies, all benefit from postcure heat treatment. However, Resorcinol and URAC 185 will not take the same temperatures as Nyatex epoxy.

Once the sections glued with Resorcinol and URAC 185 have dried at room temperature for 16 to 18 hours, you can place them in a heated environment at 100 to 105 degrees F. This will speed the final glue cure and also prevent moisture reentry. A minimum of 24 hours at this temperature is needed to ensure that the glue is completely dried. If you don't postcure the freshly glued sections with heat, it may take three to eight days for the glue to properly dry — depending on the room temperature and humidity.

Heat-set epoxies, such as the Nyatex glue I use, *will* air-dry, but there are several benefits to postcuring them. Because of their complex molecule structure, epoxy glues of this type cross-link when heat is applied. Cross-linking can be thought of as polarizing. I remember the science experiment I enjoyed as a child: I spread iron filings on a sheet of paper, then passed a magnet under the paper. The scattered filings all lined up end-to-end under the magnetic field. This is similar to what heat does to this type of epoxy glue. The cross-linking adds greatly to the structural strength of the glue.

Heat-set epoxies also temper under heat during postcuring. Heat deflection temperature, or HDT, is the temperature at which a glue fails under heat. By postcuring heat-set epoxies, you can raise their HDT significantly. The postcuring regimen I use for Nyatex glue is to air-dry at room temperature for 16 hours, then heat-treat at 235 degrees F for 3 hours. This raises the HDT from 121 to 193 degrees F. After the heat treatment, the sections are removed to cool.

Rebinding

Because of my preference for Nyatex epoxy glue, I spent years facing a hefty cleanup project after thermal-setting my rod sections. Once thermal-set, the glue-saturated binding thread and the bamboo had become one. To clean, I had to file or sand the glue-caked thread from the surfaces. This required extra time and caused some stressful moments when I couldn't determine the exact location of the flats.

The solution to this dilemma came from rodmaker Al Medved. He allows his rod sections to air-dry for 24 hours. Then before he thermal-sets them, he removes the binding thread.

Now, if you don't have the luxury of allowing your sections to air-dry for a full 24 hours, there's another option. Before thermal-setting the rod sections, remove the glue-saturated binding thread and rebind the sections with fresh thread. After thermal-setting, you'll be able to remove the binding thread with ease — allowing for a rapid cleanup.

Sanding

Because there are no nonvolatile solvents that will loosen excess glue from freshly bound sections, I end up sanding both the excess glue and the binding thread from the shaft after curing. This may sound like a lot of work, but in fact the glue sands off rapidly. Once again I use a block sander with 360-grit paper. As anxious as you may be to see the glued shaft, now is not the time to hurry. Be especially careful to sand parallel to the surface. Rocking the sanding block could round off the precise corners of the hexagon.

Start sanding at the butt end of the shaft and work forward. I prefer finishing one flat at a time. As the surface of the bamboo starts to show through, I focus my sanding efforts just ahead of that point. Instead of trying to get all the glue and thread off with a single pass, I make three: The first removes the bulk, the second leaves some area of bare surface, and the third cleans the surface of the final residue. Remember, I add 0.001 inch to each strip's dimension just for this sanding.

Once I have a clean shaft, I apply a coat of pure tung oil. This is compatible with most varnishes and some plastic finishes as well. However, to be certain that it'll work with the finishing product you plan to use, test the combination on some sample pieces.

Tung oil can be applied with a soft cloth or with your fingers. Begin by applying a liberal coat and letting it air-dry for 5 to 10 minutes. Before the oil becomes tacky, wipe off the excess. I slide the shaft back and forth through a soft clean cloth, indexing the flats so they're all wiped clean of oil. I then set the shaft aside and allow it to dry overnight.

Actually, that may not be entirely true. What usually happens is that I sit at my workbench and just look at the completed section. I slide it back and forth between my fingers. I feel the flats for smoothness. I look over each flat and corner to be sure there are no flaws. It is at this stage of making the rod that it first begins to take on a character of its own.

Just the Corner

Experience has taught me that as wasteful as it is, you should only use the corners of your sanding block. In fact, use only up to the first 1¼ inches in from the corner. By limiting yourself to this degree, you'll have a better visual sense of what's actually taking place on the rod sections. In other words, this is the safe way to sand.

Flaming

With the rod section assembled, your ability to retouch any light areas in a flamed section with a torch is long past. Any attempt to darken with a torch or bubble buster at this point would risk damaging the section. But darkening can still be accomplished with a butane lighter. As I explained earlier, you use the side of the flame in such a way that it leaves soot behind; the point of the flame would simply leave charring. Once the soot is in place on the rod section, wipe it around with a finger to achieve the required toning. If the area is still too light, simply add more soot from the lighter.

Close Your Eyes

One of my main objections to using a bodied or unbodied scraper to remove the last of the enamel is the quality of the surface it leaves behind. As I have suggested before, your eyes might miss the chattering — but your hands will certainly notice the difference.

If you lightly pinch a rod section between the thumb and first finger of one hand and then slowly pull the section between them, your sense of touch will indicate the true surface condition.

And to amplify your sense of touch, close your eyes as well. Besides chatter ridges, you'll also be able to detect any rises or washout areas. Have no doubt that troublesome areas *will* still be present after the finish is applied.

To give you an idea how acute your sense of touch can be, try this little experiement. Lay a sheet of typing or printer paper of a flat surface. (A small piece of Plexiglas will also do fine.) Then place another sheet of paper on top of the first, but with the edges offset. Now run a finger over the edge area where the pile goes from one sheet thickness to two. For me, the feeling is reminiscent of driving over a speed bump. In the same way, a scraped enamel flat will feel like a washboard gravel road.

First Look

Once you've sanded the glue and enamel haze from your shaft or shafts, you'll have a clearer vision of your finished rod. Of course, I hardly need to encourage you to inspect it. Your curiosity will already have taken over. If you find areas during your inspection that are less than satisfactory, there may still be time for adjustments.

Corner alignment may be one area that needs attention. For example, points of adjoining strips that don't meet to form a corner usually indicate that the angles of a strip weren't equilateral before gluing. One indication would be the point of one strip overshooting the point of an adjacent strip. But after you've sanded it more often, the area will appear as an odd long crescent. If the rod section is flamed, the crescent will stand out as being blondish.

If this is objectionable, sand the incorrect surface by tilting the block slightly to the incorrect corner. If the section is flamed and is lightened by the sanding, sooting with a butane lighter will mask this.

Some inconsistency in dimensions — usually up to about 0.005 inch — can be corrected by sanding. Any adjustment sanding should be done from midpoint of station to midpoint of station, or at the tip from midpoint of station to end. With each pass, stop your sanding stroke closer to the station (the measuring point). This will ensure a gradual transition. Remove an equal amount from both flats.

In essence, you're sanding into the power fibers, so you need to stop well before you sand through them. This shouldn't be difficult to observe. Carefully watch the fibers and you'll see how they gradually grow wider and then start to narrow again. This indicates that the sanding just passed the center depth of the fibers and should be stopped.

If the rod section that you're sanding was originally flamed, then you need to pause here for a moment. This is the time to retouch the tone of the sanded area to match the rest of the section.

Straightening

Now, without the binding thread or glue, you have a clear picture of your completed section. Hopefully you were successful in straightening the section before the glue dried, and you need only touch up a little now to complete the job.

At this point I am often asked: "Well, how straight does it have to be?" Only you, as the maker, can answer this question. To me, straight is straight. It seems pointless to settle for anything less after all the hard work you've expended to reach this stage.

To identify any twists or bends left in the section, use the same tests as before — but this time the flaws can only be removed by heating the section. The same rules apply as when you straightened the initial split strips. Use a wide application of heat for twists or long bends; use a narrow application for kinks. This time, however, you want to be less aggressive with the amount of heat. I suggest performing any corrections in stages, allowing the section to cool completely between each stage. And this time you can grab the shaft with both hands and use your thumbs to straighten out a bend instead of "pool-cuing" it.

In practice, I first roll the rod section on my workbench, holding the larger end of the section tight to the surface. As I roll the shaft, I look for light between the rod section and the workbench top. When I see light, or I see the rod section rise from the bench, I know there's a bend. I then roll the rod section back and forth until the gap is largest. This way I know that the direction for correcting the bend is toward the bench surface.

Then, as I hold the rod section tight to the bench with my right hand, I press downward on the raised area with my left. While doing so I carefully watch the rod section where it first lifts from the bench. I'm looking for the exact apex of the bend. That is the area on which I'll need to concentrate heat. Once I'm sure of the apex, I move my left index finger 2 inches to the left of the apex and place it on the uppermost part of the rod section. I follow this by placing my right index finger 2 inches to the right of the apex. Then I lift the rod section from the bench and place both thumbs on it opposite my index fingers.

As I lower my hands to their natural straight extension of the arm, the direction for the corrective bend is horizontal. I achieved this by twisting my hands so that the thumbs move outward. I now have a direction and an amplitude. After softening the apex, I pressure the rod section into an exact mirror of the initial bend. Any other position might cause me to chase a bend back and forth forever.

Bends and kinks come in all varieties, and each requires a different heat application. If the bend is confined to an exact location, I suggest applying heat with just the narrow width of the heat-gun diffuser. If the bend spreads to a broader area, then change the angle at which the rod section crosses over the diffuser of the heat gun to allow for a wider softening.

If you're trying to correct a lengthy sweep, the rod section will eventually be in line with the broad width of the heat-gun diffuser. At this point the rod section will need to be slowly shuttled the length of the sweep over the diffuser.

As you apply heat, it's important to rotate the rod section so that the girth of the area is warmed evenly. This should be done with a careful wrist action; otherwise, you'll lose the correct position of the rod section with respect to your index fingers and thumbs. And always remember to maintain a distance of ³/₄ to ⁷/₈ inch between the top of the heat-gun diffuser and the rod section.

I wish I had a magic formula for determining the exact amount of time needed to soften rod sections for straightening. Because of the many variations in rods and materials, though, there is no single, universal solution. Still, I have worked out a good commonsense guideline. If you start with a base time of three to four seconds at the tip and then add two seconds per foot as you move toward the butt, you'll be working with safe and reasonable start times.

Obviously these guidelines may not get the job done on a first attempt, but you should never overheat and delaminate anything. Make your first attempt following this time guideline, then add two seconds to each additional straightening attempt. However, after you've made two attempts at straightening an area, I recommend that you stop and let the rod cool to room temperature. Then take up the heating times where you left off. The corrective bending position is now maintained on the rod section for double the warming time. This ensures that the bonding material of the bamboo has hardened enough to hold the new position.

If the area that you're warming is larger than the heat-gun diffuser, the heating time needs to reflect this difference. Remember also that on long sweeps, the exposure time should not be even. Because of the difference in mass at the different locations along the rod section, you'll need more heat in the areas with larger dimensions.

9
WORKING WITH FERRULES

Making Connections

Because most fly rods are made with at least two sections, and many have three (or even more) sections, ferrules are critical in the rodmaking process. It makes sense to create the best possible connections between the parts of your rod by using quality ferrules and ensuring accurate and firm joints. You will need some special tools — especially a quality turning device — for working with these metals.

Inexpensive Lathe

The first metal lathe I used in rodmaking was a worn-out jeweler's model sold by Craftsman many years ago. Most of these lathes were made for Sears by Atlas, and parts are still obtainable today. But the model I had purchased was made by another manufacturer, and I was unable to get parts to rebuild it.

When I was in the market for a better lathe, I attended many machinery auctions and scoured the local paper's for-sale ads — all without much success. Prices for a used South Bend or Atlas lathe were running at $750 and higher. Finally I made a deal with a local importer on a 9-by-18-inch model he'd ordered for a customer who subsequently backed out of the sale. The price was $1,000. By this time I'd started earning a little money at making rods, so I felt I could justify buying the lathe. For some rodmakers, however, spending this much money for a few minutes of use per rod doesn't make much sense.

A wood lathe with a three-jaw, self-centering chuck is a good option for working ferrule stations, handles, and wood fillers. Grizzly Imports now offers a precise three-jaw chuck with the

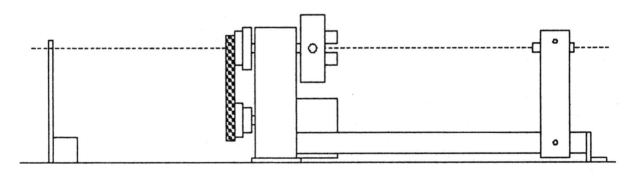

A simplified schematic of a lathe and support system.

¾″–16 thread that fits the spindle heads of most popular wood lathes. The company's chuck sells for $72. Wood lathes sell new for $225 and up, but I've seen good used Craftsman models go for $75 to $125. And, an occasional deal can still be found.

I now have both lathes: I reserve the metal one for machining reel-seat parts. Recently I developed a plan to mount a cross-and-index feed on the wood lathe using a milling vise. But for now I can turn ferrule stations simply by using a file and sandpaper.

Nickel Silver

Sometimes referred to as German silver, nickel silver contains no silver at all but is rather an alloy of nickel, zinc, and copper. There are two grades available, offering either an 18 or a 12 percent zinc content. You'll find that 18 percent nickel silver is the one most commonly used for rod components: ferrules, reel-seat parts, and grip checks. This metal can be machined well and polished to a jewel-like finish. Nickel silver is a tradition with bamboo rodmakers.

Ferrule Sources

Fortunately, there are still several sources of precision high-quality nickel-silver ferrules. In fact, both of the traditional ferrule styles are readily available.

Currently the most popular ferrule is the Super Z. Originally designed and patented by Louis Feierabend in the early 1950s, this ferrule was revolutionary for its time. Eventually it became universally accepted by well-known rodmakers as the only ferrule to use.

Feierabend, a mechanical engineer, designed his ferrule to maximize the strength of the connection between the rod sections by having both the male and female ends of the bamboo the same size. This broke with the tradition of undercutting the male section, which removed the valuable power fibers at the ferrule station.

The original Super Zs are instantly recognized by the trademark stamp on the barrel of the female: the encircled letter *Z* with the word *super* written over it. These ferrules found on classic rods made by Gillum, Garrison, Payne, and Young.

A second ferrule style, the Leonard, is also still available. It is, of course, the ferrule found on rods built by the H. L. Leonard Rod Company. For the restorer of quality rods or the Leonard aficionado, it's a real boon that this hardware can be easily sourced.

Standard Versus Truncated

In both ferrule lines — Super Swiss and stepdown — you can choose between a standard and a truncated length. (The truncated is just a short-

The different lengths of ferrules: truncated (left) and standard (right).

ened version of the standard.) Historically, the standard length was used for two-piece rods, and the truncated lengths on three-piece rods. In fact, the truncated version is being used to transfer more energy than the standard version. The bottom ferrule on a three-piece is lower on the rod and dimensionally must be larger than a two-piece to yield a similar action.

Prepping Ferrules

Whichever ferrule style you choose, the process of preparing them for mounting is the same: You need to slope or feather out their serration tabs.

The serration tabs of a ferrule as it is manufactured.

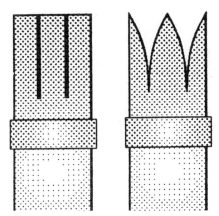

An illustration (before and after) of crowning the ferrule tabs.

The slope allows the ferrule wrap to make a gradual transition from the ferrule tubing to the rod shaft. Second, and more important, this reduction

of material diminishes energy that can build up in the ferrule and eventually cause the bamboo to fatigue at the joint.

To slope the ferrule, first mount a drill bit or drill-bit blank of the appropriate size in the three-jaw chuck of your lathe. If you're using a conventional drill bit, place the twist end in the jaws, leaving the butt to mount the ferrule on.

Next, slide the ferrule onto the butt end of the drill as if you were mounting it onto the rod shaft. The ferrule should slide on the shaft with light resistance. If it doesn't, then the drill bit should be sanded: Start the lathe and touch the drill-bit shaft with 400-grit sandpaper. Then try mounting the ferrule again.

Once the ferrule is in place on the drill bit, it's ready to be dressed. Take a ½-inch-wide by 4-inch-long piece of sandpaper and fold it in half to ¼ inch width. Start the lathe and wrap the sand-

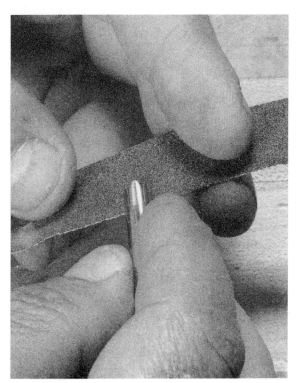

Sanding the crown into the serration tabs.

paper in a half circle around the ferrule. Hold each end of the sandpaper. Start with the sandpaper on the tip of the serration tabs and, as you rock the sandpaper back and forth by its ends, slowly slide it off the ends of the tabs.

Do not try to ride the sandpaper back on the ferrule tabs; you could catch a tab and lift it away from the drill bit. A few passes with 400-grit sandpaper should make the tips of the tabs paper thin. Make one last pass, but this time switch to 1,000-grit sandpaper to polish away any sand marks. The ferrule is now ready for mounting.

Over the years I have developed an extra touch that I like to add to ferrules. To give an even better transition to the shaft, I point off each serration tab before I slope it. This detail is only visible if the wraps are going to be transparent.

To point the tabs, stretch a ¹⁄₂-inch strip of sandpaper in your left hand. (The outward edge of the sandpaper must be cut, not torn.) Your first and middle fingers hold one end of the sandpaper, while your thumb and third finger hold the other end. This is a tricky maneuver at first, but it soon becomes familiar. An alternative to holding the sandpaper in your hand is to attach one end of it to your workbench with a pushpin, and then hold the free end.

When you slide the ferrule onto the sandpaper, make sure the sandpaper is in serrations that are 180 degrees apart. Slide the sandpaper about ¼ inch into these serrations, then sand the ferrule in a back-and-forth motion. At the same time, tilt the ferrule upward and draw it off the sandpaper. Because you're sanding two serrations at once, rocking the ferrule will put varying amounts of pressure on the front or back serration to even out the sanding pressure. The ferrule is indexed until all serrations are arched to a point.

I normally sand a little and then move to the next serration, forming the finished points after three or four revolutions of the ferrule. This is freehand work and best done slowly. Once the points are formed, slope the tabs as detailed above.

Do It by Hand

Because I crown my ferrule tabs by hand, I've learned to taper their thickness by hand as well. Obviously, crowning removes a good deal of material. But even if you choose not to crown the ferrule tabs, you can still taper them by hand.

As with the crowning, ¹⁄₂-inch-wide strips of sandpaper work well. It's better to slice the sandpaper strips with an X-Acto knife or surgeon's scalpel than to tear them. Slicing gives the sandpaper a smooth, straight edge.

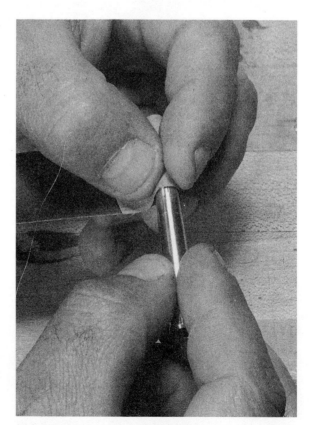

Tapering the serration-tab thickness.

Fold the sandpaper in the center to form a circle with the leading edges flush with each other. Then the tabbed end of the ferrule is inserted into the formed circle until the serrations are covered. To add pressure to the paper, squeeze the circled loop between your thumb and middle finger. You can obtain additional pressure by pressing your first finger to the top side of the sandpaper. This configuration forms a triangle of pressure points around the tabs.

The feathering is achieved by turning the ferrule with your free hand. As the ferrule turns, gradually pull it out of the circle of sandpaper. This puts the taper in the tabs by doing a light amount of sanding to the whole surface and a greater amount of sanding at the ends of the tabs.

A good way to practice is to spread out your tapering over several passes. One pass would involve moving the sandpaper the length of the tabs with three or four full turns of the ferrule. At the end of each pass, inspect your progress. A close look at the end of the tabs will reveal everything. The tabs need to flow to points at the tips, making a gradual transition from full thickness. If the tab ends are blunt (thick), they won't have enough flexibility. If you then wrap them with thread, it will fall off the leading edge and cause a gap in the wrap.

Casting Fractures

If you closely examine a rod that's been fished hard for several years, you'll often discover a fracture in the finish where the ferrule tabs extend onto the rod section. This fractured finish usually encircles the rod, forming a ring. Over time this initial fracture can spread, opening up the finish to expose the underlying thread wraps. Eventually this leads to deterioration of the wrap itself.

The serration tabs after the crowning process.

I've heard other makers wonder about this condition, questioning the glue or contaminate in the bond. But I'm convinced that the problem is caused by a lack of transition in the ferrule tabs. Those rods that I've seen with fractures had ferrule tabs that were never tapered.

Originally, I started crowning the tabs of my ferrules as a decorative feature. But I'm convinced that I am also creating a more flexible transition from a rigid ferrule to a flexing rod shaft — and thus reducing the likelihood of a casting fracture. Only time and many fishing trips will tell me for sure if my technique is successful.

Correct Lengths

Before you mount the ferrules, take a minute to figure out the exact lengths of your shafts. When the ferrules are mounted, you want all shafts to be of equal length — and of course you want your assembled rod to be the correct length.

If you're making a two-piece rod, then each shaft should be half the rod length plus half of the ferrule's seating dimension. If you have a 7-foot, 6-inch rod with a ferrule-seating dimension of 0.900 inch, for example, then each section would be 45.450 inches long with the ferrule parts mounted.

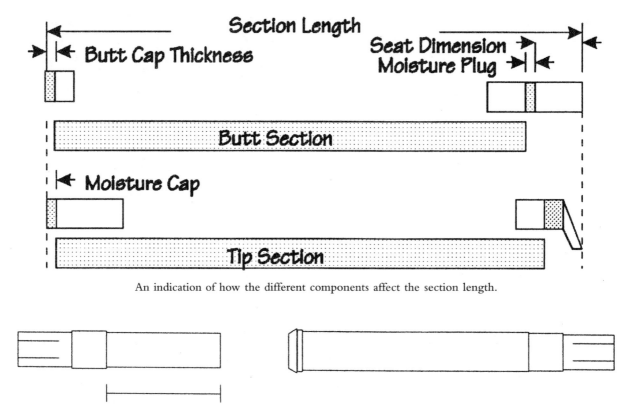

An indication of how the different components affect the section length.

Ferrule seating dimensions must be carefully calculated to ensure that the sections of the rod are equal in length.

On the tip section, the half that receives the male part of the ferrule needs only one correction to the section length: the thickness of the moisture cap sealing the male ferrule end. The shaft length would thus be 45.450 inches minus the moisture cap. On the butt section, the half that receives the female part of the ferrule needs a corresponding correction to the shaft length: Subtract the 0.900 inch seating dimension, and then substract the thickness of the moisture plug. The butt section would thus be 44.550 inches long (45.450 inches minus 0.900 inch) — minus the moisture plug.

Three- and four-piece rods are calculated a bit differently. Because each different ferrule size has its own seating dimensions, the total seating dimension is averaged among the shafts to make

them equal length. If a 3-piece, 7-foot, 6-inch rod had ferrules that seated 0.900 and 0.600 inch, then each section would be 30.500 inches in length. The butt-shaft length would be corrected to 29.600 inches minus the moisture plug. The mid-section shaft would be 29.900 inches, minus the moisture plug, minus the moisture cap. And the tip-shaft section would be 30.500 inches minus the moisture cap.

Practical Approach

What I've just reviewed is the mathematical explanation of how to calculate rod length. Let me now go through the practical approach.

To begin, you can add some insurance when measuring sections by butting them and the measuring tape against something steady. On the front left corner of my workbench, I've mounted a piece of ¹/₂-inch-thick plywood to act as a stop block for my planing forms. This stop block can now be used to butt against the section ends and the end of the measuring tape. As you proceed, you'll begin to see why this technique is useful.

Again, your goal is to find the point at which all sections are the same length unassembled and the rod length is correct when assembled. You can determine the seating dimension of the various ferrule sizes simply by measuring the length of the seating section of the male ferrule. The finished section length reflects the total length of the rod plus the total of the seating dimensions divided by the number of rod sections. The order of assembly is to mount the tiptops and the female ferrules, then measure and cut for mounting the male ferrules and the reel seat.

When you fine-tune the node alignment during final assembly and gluing, you may find that the ends of the sections have become somewhat staggered. To allow for full seating of the components, cut the small end of each section sharply. On the larger mid- and butt sections, a jeweler's or coping saw can be used. But because of their delicate dimensions, the tips should be dealt with differently.

First, place the tip section on your workbench or another flat surface where it can be rolled through a full revolution. Then, using an X-Acto knife or surgeon's scalpel, place the blade at the desired point. Continue until the waste piece is cut free. After cutting, radius the flats lightly with the block sander to remove the light ridge created by the shear.

One sign of a high-quality bamboo fly rod is that both tips are matched or butterflied — that is, when laid side by side the nodes fall in exactly the same spot on each tip. I mentioned this earlier when I described staggering and cutting the strips; now you'll do the fine-tuning.

If there are two tips for your rod, assign each a tiptop. The tiptops aren't glued on at this time but rather dry-fitted, to allow you to determine section length. I use the term *assign* here because of the inconsistencies inherent to tiptops in the way that they are constructed. Each may seat to a different depth.

After you've mounted both tiptops, lay the sections side by side on the workbench with the tiptop loops touching the stop block. Turn the sections until like nodes are visible, and measure any offset. Then index both strips to the next flats, and again measure any nodal offset. If you decide

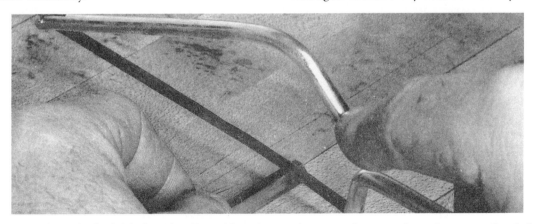

Trimming the end of a finished section. To avoid tear-out at the outer edge, cut only to the center of each flat.

that adjustment is needed, trim the longer tip section accordingly and retry.

When the tiptops are correctly fitted, cut the sections to length. With both tiptops and the measuring tape butted to the stop block, mark each section at ¹⁄₆₄ inch less than your target dimension. (This accounts for the thickness of the end cap of the male ferrule.) To prevent any material tear-out, cut at each flat — extending the cut halfway through the section — and then move on to the next flat.

After the sections are cut to length, proceed with mounting the ferrules. One note of caution

the section, indexing flat to flat as you make the cut. If the section is from the middle of the rod, then follow the same procedure as with the tip: Measure to ¹⁄₆₄ inch less than your target dimension. Once again, this accounts for the thickness of the male end cap. You can now proceed to mount the male ferrule.

If the section is a butt, then the cutoff point is determined by the thickness of the reel-seat cap or reel-seat filler plug — depending on which reel seat you've selected. In either case, the same method is used.

First, lay the measuring tape and section side

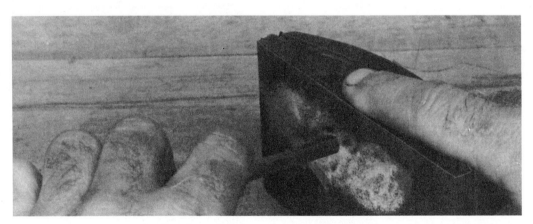

Sanding the end of the rod section after trimming.

should be added here: While you're turning the ferrule stations, take the tiptop off the section. The offset weight of the tiptop will cause the section to wobble when turned and may cause damage. Also, remember to do one section at a time, returning the tiptop when you're finished. This will keep the tiptops correctly assigned to the proper sections. (I'll deal with the mounting of ferrules momentarily.)

On the mid- (if present) and butt sections, the female ferrule is mounted once the small end is trimmed. Again, observe caution when cutting

by side, butted to the stop block. Next, with the reel-seat filler and cap or plug assembled, place it alongside the section, aligning the end of the cap or plug with the target dimension. Use a sharp pencil to make a mark on the rod section equal with the end of the reel-seat filler. Then inset a ¹⁄₄-inch dowel into the reel-seat filler bore hole until it bottoms. Mark the dowel flush with the upper end of the reel-seat filler.

Back at the rod section, lay the dowel alongside and index the two marks. The end of the dowel indicates where the rod section ends. Mark this location and cut to length. You'll also use the upper mark on the butt section as a starting point for the cork handle, so you can leave this mark for later use.

Mounting Ferrules

There are two methods of dressing the ferrule stations on your finished sections. The first makes use

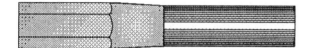

Dressing the ferrule station on a finished section.

of a metal turning lathe. The second is adapted to a wood lathe with a self-centering three-jaw chuck.

To prepare a section for turning, your first step is to measure the ferrule for the depth of seating of the bamboo. I normally use a depth micrometer, but a short piece of ⅛-inch dowel will work equally well. Simply determine the mea-surement from the tips of the serrations to the top side of the moisture plug. With a depth microme-ter, set the base on the serration tips and turn the spindle of the micrometer until the base is lifted from the serrations. With the dowel, slide it in the tubing until it bottoms and then scribe a line on

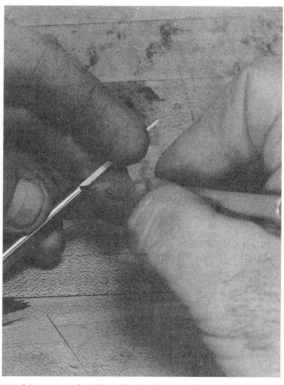

Marking a toothpick with the depth of the ferrule pocket.

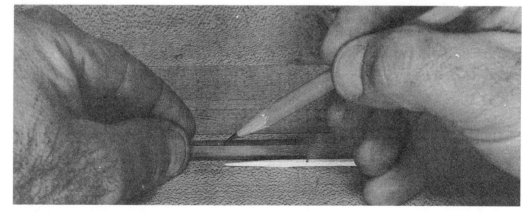

Transferring the depth from the toothpick to the rod section.

it at the tips of the serrations with a sharp pencil.

This measurement is then transferred to the ferrule station on the rod shaft. Lay the depth micrometer on the shaft with its base butted to the shaft's end. Then lightly mark the measure-ment on the shaft, using the depth rod as an index.

If you used a dowel, align its depth mark with the end of the rod shaft and mark at the end of the dowel to transfer the measurement. I scribe the measurement on all six flats. This mark is the total depth of seating.

Now you need to add a second mark, this one to indicate the length of the barrel of the fer-

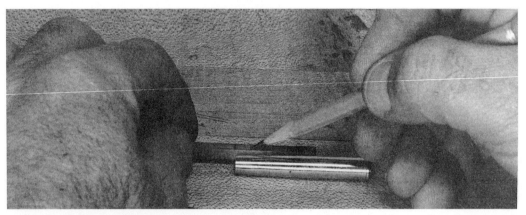

Using the ferrule to mark the end of the serrations.

The rod section prepared for the turning of the ferrule station.

rule (the total depth minus the length of the serrations). Using the actual ferrule as a guide, lay it on the rod so the serration tips align to the first mark. Add a second mark where the cuts of the serrations end. Again, I scribe this mark on all flats.

For turning, the section from the end of the shaft to the first mark will be cut to a uniform dimension. This is the area on which the barrel seats. From the first mark to the second, the bam-

boo is tapered to give a smooth transition from the smaller barrel diameter to the rest of the shaft.

Before mounting in the three-jaw chuck of the lathe, the shaft needs some protection so that it won't be marked or dented by the jaws. I use ³/₄-inch-wide masking tape rolled on at a 45-degree angle. This will create a tape cushion two layers thick. Use a little caution so that you don't overlap the base wrap and get three layers at the seam. I run the masking tape ¹/₂ inch from the last mark back up the shaft 2¹/₂ to 3 inches.

In my shop, which is cramped for space, the extension wing of my table saw is just off the end of the metal lathe. This is quite useful, because I've built a support — which rests on the wing — for the free end of the bamboo shaft. This part of the rod must be supported or you risk damaging it by having it snap off or crack. The same holds true when you're turning the cork handle: Some type of solid support must be provided.

With the shaft's tail end in the support, I slide its taped end through the three-jaw chuck until the last mark is ³/₄ inch out from the jaw tips. This leaves some room for the cutter holder to clear the rotating jaws. Check your setup before you start. You'll be using the cutter on the area from

Ferrule Puller

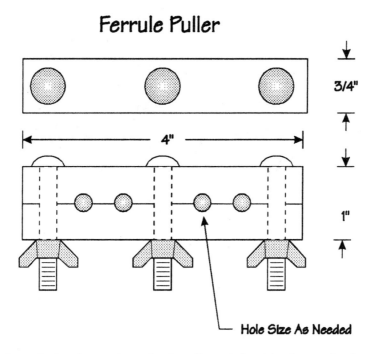

Hole Size As Needed

A rough plan for creating a ferrule puller to help with reluctant ferrules.

the end of the shaft to the first mark, so test for free swing with the tip of the cutter at the first mark. Roll the chuck by hand through a full turn, watching closely for any areas of contact.

Remember don't use a Live Center (a metal lathe tool) to hold the free end of the shaft. The pressure of the tapered point will simply act as a wedge and split the rod section.

Any wobble in the free end needs to be corrected before you start the cut. Wobble can be caused by an overlap of masking tape, or the shaft may need straightening. Move the cutter to the very end of the shaft. With a small gap between the cutter and the corners of the shaft, slowly turn the chuck and watch the gap. If it changes, something's wrong; examine the rod and fix the problem before you start any cutting.

For cutting the ferrule station, I use the slowest possible cross-feed and take a cut of only 0.005 inch. When cutting the shaft, I turn the

chuck by hand. This may sound a little odd, but on small ferrule stations I've seen the rod section pick up a vibration when the lathe is powered by the motor. Even at slow speeds the shaft sometimes bounces every time the cutter hits the corner of the section. Turning the chuck by hand takes a few minutes longer, but the finished shaft is cut much more accurately.

Always measure the shaft at the end of each cut to check your progress. When I'm within 0.005 inch of the target dimension, I advance the cut by only 0.002 inch. In fact, aim for a dimension 0.001 inch larger then the measurement of the barrel of the ferrule. This last 0.001 inch disappears when you sand the cut smooth.

Before sanding, I try to slide the ferrule onto the shaft. From this point onward you want to remove material only where the ferrule leaves a rub mark on the shaft. Using a narrow strip of 360-grit sandpaper, lightly sand off any marks. The technique is to sand at only three points as the shaft rotates once in the jaws. (This relates, of course, to the hexagonal shape.) This is a "sand-and-try" situation. Remove the rub marks until the ferrule slides onto the shaft completely.

Occasionally, the ferrule will lock on the shaft, and this is when a ferrule puller comes in handy. I've built these devices with a variety of

The rod section mounted in the three-jaw chuck of a lathe.

openings for the different sizes of male and female parts that might get stuck. A ferrule puller is a good tool for putting uniform pressure on a stuck ferrule without scratching it.

After you've fitted a ferrule to the shaft end, you need to taper the area between the first and second marks. Because I place the serrations on the flats of the rod, I file this portion into a hex shape with a small triangle file. Using the flat as a

guide, I lay the file between the marks and apply file pressure toward the rounded area. When one flat is feathered out, I move to the next flat.

If you're using a modified wood lathe to turn the ferrule station, the first few steps are the same. The rod shaft needs to be protected with masking tape, and the free end must be firmly supported. If the shaft tip wobbles when mounted in the three-jaw chuck, the shaft probably needs more straightening.

Most of the material you remove at this stage will likely be from the corners of the hex shape. To do this successfully, hold the file and sandpaper stationary, and don't let them wobble with the flat-to-corner spin of the rod section.

To start the fitting process, use a fine mill file. With the rod section spinning in a forward direction, place the front end of the file against a solid support on the back side of the lathe. Initiate contact with the rod section using the full width of the file while applying only very soft pressure. Starting at the tip of the section, slowly work your way back until the edge of the file hits the first scribed line. Concentrate on how straight you can move the file instead of how much material you're removing.

At this point you must continually check the corner-to-corner measurement at several locations along the ferrule station. If the results aren't good, you'll need to adjust future passes with the file accordingly. I strongly suggest removing just a slight amount of material on each pass and then remeasuring before you make the next pass.

At 0.005 inch over the final dimension, I switch to 360-grit sandpaper backed with a board. To hold the sandpaper in place, you might consider mounting a spring-loaded clothespin on the board, keeping it clear of the rod shaft. Again, remove as little as possible per pass, rechecking the measurements each time. As soon as the ferrule starts sliding onto the shaft, switch to sanding the rub marks left by the ferrule after you've tried to fit it on. When the ferrule slides home, you then taper the second section by filing the flats.

If the ferrule station is completely round (as some are when the ferrule is properly fit), then you should scratch a light cut on the bamboo from the tip to the first line. This gives any excess glue an escape route. Otherwise you may find yourself with air or glue trapped in the ferrule, which means that the bottom (if it's a male ferrule) or water plug (if it's female) may be pushed out if you use too much pressure trying to seat this section.

Additionally, sand off the second pencil mark on the rod section before you forget about it. If you make your wraps transparent, this pencil mark could show through as a last-minute and unwelcome surprise.

For glue, I recommend Devcon epoxy. This particular brand doesn't shrink as it dries. I mix only enough to mount each ferrule piece, spreading the glue out on a stiff piece of cardboard and mixing it with a toothpick. The toothpick also

The position of the sandpaper is critical in this detailed work.

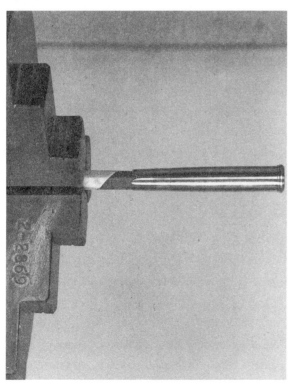

At this point the ferrule can be fitted to the rod section.

The author uses Devcon epoxy to glue the ferrule in place.

makes an excellent applicator for putting glue down inside the ferrule. A little dab into the bottom of the ferrule and a wipe or two around the sidewall should be sufficient. To ensure a complete bonding, I always roll the ferrule end of the rod section in the glue that remains on the cardboard.

Next, the glue-covered pieces are slid together. Because you're creating a tight fit with the wet glue, you'll want to apply only light pressure. It might take several gentle attempts before the excess glue and air escape. When applying pressure, be sure to press the ferrule against a solid surface. Also be certain that any pressure on the rod section is applied in an even manner.

Just before the rod section is fully seated, check the alignment of the ferrule tabs with the flats of the rod section and adjust them as needed. The ferrule tabs should always be centered on the flats of the rod section.

Complete the gluing by wrapping the fer-

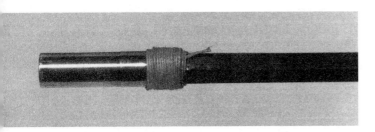

A completed ferrule with thread clamping the tabs to the rod section.

rule tabs with binding cord to draw them tight to the shaft. I make this wrap with the technique you'll use for the guide feet. Start by placing an overhand wrap on the barrel of the ferrule piece and then spin the shaft, laying down wraps of thread until the tabs are completely covered and the thread drops off the ferrule tabs onto the rod shaft. Tie off the thread with a couple of half hitches.

After the glue has dried (usually overnight), the binding thread is removed. By undoing the half hitches, you can pull the thread off the shaft just as you'd pull the rope-start on a lawn mower. The excess glue should then be removed with 0000 steel wool. Perhaps the easiest method is to roll the rod section on the tops of your thighs with a small cord of steel wool looped around the area that needs cleaning.

I get a little more serious about cleaning up this particular glued area. Recently I begged a few dental picks off my dentist. I use them to remove the darkened glue in the ferrule serrations and the last little bit of glue that remains around the serration tabs. I follow this cleaning by a light buffing with 0000 steel wool. Now the ferrule is ready to wrap.

Additional Thoughts

The fit between the rod section and the ferrule needs to be kept as tight as possible. And for sake of the overall length, the ferrule needs to be fully seated. Here is a good indicator: When you can slide the ferrule into position with light pressure and hear a soft tap as it bottoms out, you know the fit is correct. This will yield the tightest bond possible and prevent the ferrule from being mounted in a canted position.

However, if the design of the rod taper is such that the ferrule station is completely round, this degree of fit doesn't allow excess epoxy glue to escape easily. Seating the rod section with more pressure only increases the chance of pushing the moisture plug from the ferrule.

However, there is a solution. Start the rod section into the ferrule with light pressure. Then, using a vibrating sander without any sandpaper, press the ferrule against the felt pad of the sander.

As you apply light pressure to the rod section, flick the sander on and off. One short burst should allow the rod section to seat. If not, try a second short burst and perhaps a third. But don't overdo it. Once the rod section bottoms out in the ferrule, any further bursts of vibration will only act to throw needed glue from the bond.

It makes sense to set the rod section aside in an upright position while the glue cures. In my workshop I simply lean the rod sections against the back wall, with the newly mounted ferrule facing down. This ensures that if the glue were to move, it would simply sag into the ferrule and not create any voids. Laying the section flat, however, might allow the glue to drain outward — reducing the fill between the metal and bamboo, and possibly leading to eventual fatigue of the bond.

To track how quickly the bond is curing, place your toothpick into the pool of excess glue on the mixing palette. Then occasionally test the bond. Epoxy glue cures from exothermic heat and not exposure to air, so the glue on the mixing palette reflects the progress of the ferrule-to-bamboo bond as well. Once the sample has cured, you can discarded it, because you'll know that the ferrule bond has cured as well.

Seating Ferrules

The fit of the male-to-female ferrules when seated is said to be equal to the thickness of smoke. Today, most ferrules come with the males oversize by a few thousandths of an inch. This means that to get the parts seated properly, material on the male slide must be removed. However, the adjustment needs to be uniform over the length and circumference of the ferrule. Otherwise, there's a chance that the ferrule won't seat properly. One sure indication of an improper fit is a little click-

ing sound when you cast the rod.

To achieve a proper fit, sand the male slide to fit using strips of 1,000-grit sandpaper. But first, the female socket should be polished with a "noodle" of 0000 steel wool. This will remove any debris that might hamper the seating. From a roll

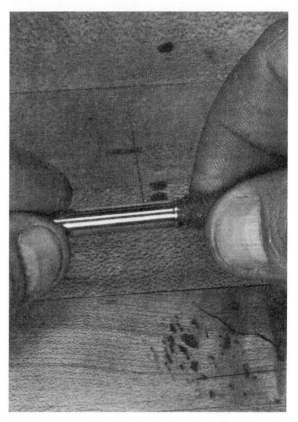

Polishing the inside of a female ferrule with 0000 steel wool.

of steel wool, tear a 5- to 6-inch length of fibers that, uncompacted, represent a ³/₄-inch-diameter bundle. Once in hand, compress the loose bundle to a smaller diameter by spinning it. (I always twist the bundle in the same direction as if tightening a nut, using a clockwise rotation.)

Next pack the steel wool bundle into the female socket. It'll help you feed the steel wool into the opening if you turn the rod shaft as well. You can simply use your hand, or you might try this alternative: Lay the rod shaft across your legs at midthigh and then roll it toward your knees by palming it with a flat hand. After three or four passes, inspect both the steel wool and the female socket. If the steel wool shows any signs of residue, repeat the polishing using fresh material.

At this point the female socket should be mirror reflective on both the sidewall and bottom plug surfaces. Finally, hold the rod section upright with the female opening pointed downward and snap your finger against the outer sidewall as if you were shooting a marble. This will allow any loosened debris to fall out.

The difficulty when fitting the male-to-female joint is in not forcing the ferrule to seat when you test the fit. You may be able to force the two together, but you'll have a tug-of-war on your hands trying to get them apart again. For lack of a better example, the ferrule should seat with the same effort as replacing the cap on a stick deodorant.

Strips of 1,000-grit sandpaper are used to sand the male seating surface. These strips should be cut to the approximate width of the surface. A cut edge will allow sanding up tight to the seating shoulder for a full fit. Two to three strips cut from the narrow side of a sheet of sandpaper should be sufficient. Again, I find it quite convenient to roll the rod section on my legs, palming it with a flat hand. Now, however, you can palm the shaft up and down your legs in a back-and-forth motion.

To use the sandpaper efficiently, form a teardrop by connecting the free ends, with the cut edge of each end aligned. Grip the ends with your thumb and first finger at a point midway across the width of the sandpaper. Then, with the rod section placed across your legs, slide the loop of sandpaper over the male seat until it butts to the step-up, and apply light downward pressure.

It's important that the pressure of the sandpaper against the seating surface be uniform so that material is evenly removed. Uneven pressure between the sandpaper and the seating surface can result in a tapered seat — which could then result in a loose fit. To stabilize the sanding, move the rod section in or out as needed until the hand holding the sandpaper rests against the leg.

With the sandpaper in place and light pressure applied, palm the rod section back and forth on the legs. Be sure to roll the rod section through at least a full revolution. This ensures that material is removed uniformly from the circumference

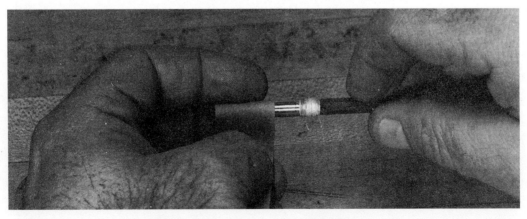

Sanding the male slide area to fit the female.

of the seat. Two to three passes up and down your legs is all the sanding you want to do at a time. Then switch from sandpaper to a bundle of 0000 steel wool. Polish the freshly sanded surface to a mirror finish with several passes as well, rolling the rod section up and down your legs.

Test the fit of the seat after each cycle of sanding and polishing. Here again, don't force the fit. Start the male into the female, if possible, and with light pressure attempt the seating. When correct, the male will seat into the female until the step-up of the male contacts the front face of the female. And when pulled apart with light pressure, you'll hear the familiar pop of air pressure — once again signaling a good fit.

Once the male begins to seat, then the width of the sandpaper can be reduced so that you're sanding only the portion that doesn't seat yet. The

between the seating surface and the sandpaper. When you look at the sandpaper, you should see a uniform spread of material — then a bit more removed material toward the capped end of the male. If the sandpaper shows more material being removed toward the step-up shoulder, you need to adjust the direction of pressure in future sandings. To get a fresh sanding surface, simply offset the ends of the sandpaper strips. But always remember to keep the cut edges aligned.

As slow as this process appears, it's still a good idea to sand only three or four rolls of the rod section between seating attempts. Even when the male does fully seat, the fit may still be too tight. You should need to apply only light pressure to seat and unseat the ferrule. If you find that you're tugging at the rod sections, lightly sand the entire seating surface to loosen the fit.

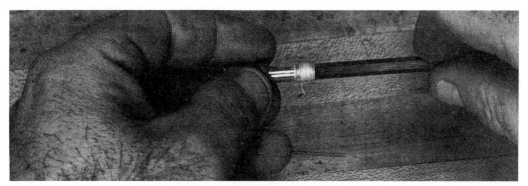

Polishing the male slide area with 0000 steel wool.

light scratch marks left on the male will give you an indication of the seating depth. Regardless of how narrow a strip of sandpaper you use, always do the follow-up polishing with the 0000 steel wool over the entire length of the seating surface.

A visual inspection of the sandpaper will show you the evenness of the contact pressure

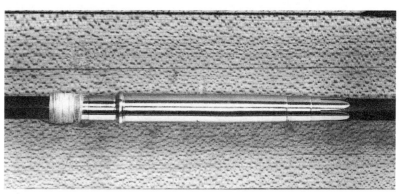

The seated ferrule.

10
HANDLES AND GUIDES

Cork

Most of the cork for the rings used to build rod handles is grown in Portugal. This soft wood is actually the outer bark of the cork oak, an evergreen tree. It's harvested at 10-year intervals, with the best-quality cork occurring at the fifth stripping of the tree. At this point the tree is usually about 70 years old. Cork oaks can be productive, however, throughout several centuries.

Once the raw bark is harvested, these 2- to 2½-inch slabs are steamed and flattened. Then they're machined into a variety of common products, such as bulletin boards, coasters, and dart boards.

Cork rings are referred to as "specie" cork in the trade because their size and shape resemble old coinage. Today 1⅛- and 1¼-inch-diameter rings are available. Each ring is ½ inch thick and the standard bore is ¼ inch, although other sizes are obtainable.

Cork, the outer bark of cork oak, is sold in rings for making rod handles and reel seats.

Because of the increased interest in fly fishing these days, and the high rate of graphite-rod production, top-grade cork has become difficult to obtain. Prices have also increased accordingly. I find that even when I purchase the best available cork, I only use about 60 percent of it. Fortunately, I have a friend who wraps graphite rods and is quite happy to take what I don't use.

Cork Press

I built this simple little tool to make the cork rings compact when I glue them to form the handle. There are two things to watch when you build

Cork Press

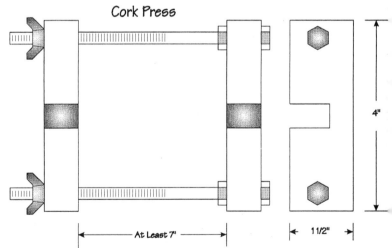

A schematic for a press used to make cork handles.

your own press. First, keep the slots through which the rod passes as small as possible. Second, the holes in the mobile arms must not bind on the threaded rods.

Handle

Before you start gluing any cork onto your rod, sit down and make a full-scale drawing of the handle. Consider not only the shape of the cork grip you want, but its length as well. Visiting a local fly shop might be the best way to see and feel the different grips.

Handle Design

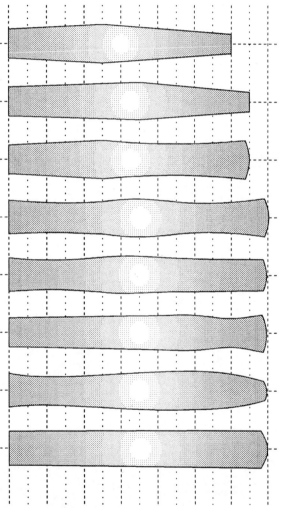

Eight common designs for fly-rod handles (grips).

Also, you need to locate a starting point for the grip. This is dictated by the length of the reel seat you intend to use. Most trout-rod reel seats are 3½ inches long. But keep in mind that the

thickness of a reel-seat cap can add about ¹⁄₁₆ inch to the length of the section. This may require cutting off an equal amount of shaft to keep the butt and tip sections equal in length.

Fashioning a flawless grip is a difficult task. Here's a trick that I learned from one of the graphite pros: Sort through your supply of cork, and reserve the best rings for the first and last cork of your grip. These locations are the only ones that actually show both the face and the flat of the cork.

Another hint for building a good grip is to pick your cork so the best part will be exposed when it's sanded to the shape on your plan. Simply use the diagram to find the diameter of the cork grip at the different locations. Visualize that diameter on the cork rings, choosing the ring with the pits located in a way that will minimize their exposure. Then stack them so the rings get placed on the rod in the location you've determined.

Because the ¼-inch bore in the cork rings is usually too small to mount them on the butt section of a rod, you'll need a cork file to increase the diameter of these holes. My local tool supplier actually makes cork files from pieces of rejected graphite rods. He coats the graphite with an adhesive and then sprinkles on an abrasive powder. This produces a cork file with a gradual taper. And if you need a different size, he merely cuts it from a different location on the rejected blank. (I've often thought about buying the adhesive and abrasives from him so I could make my own hex-shaped files from a scrap section of bamboo rod.)

I begin by sliding all the cork rings onto the butt section, leaving about an inch between each ring. I then dab a light coat of glue on the shaft ½ inch in front of the grip starting line. The first cork is now moved down the shaft until it's butted up to the starting line. I apply glue to the next ½ inch of shaft, and to the flat of the cork that's in place.

Now slide the second cork down and into place, being careful not to move the first cork. Glue should ooze out from around the joined cork. I wipe this ooze off and reapply it onto

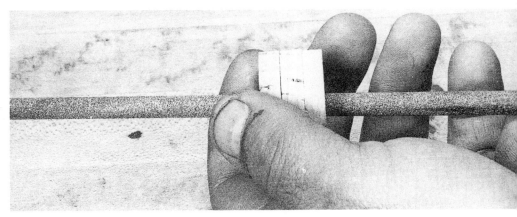

Reaming the inside diameter of the cork rings so they will fit the rod section.

the flat of the next cork ring, along with additional glue applied to the shaft. I then slide the third cork into place. I follow this pattern until all the cork rings are glued into place.

After I open a piece of newspaper on my workbench, I set the cork press on it carefully. The rod is placed in the cork press, using caution not to get any glue onto the pressing surfaces. I place the butt end of the rod at the stationary end of the press. This keeps the cork that is indexed to the starting line from being moved. I then put pressure onto the cork by turning the wing nuts, compressing the cork to ⅛ inch shorter than the normal length of the handle. If I used 13 cork rings, that translates to 6½ inches in length, so I compress the rings to 6⅜ inches. After I've measured the gap at each side of the press and have the correct dimensions, I set it aside to dry for the night.

Before you can shape the handle, the rod section again needs to be protected from any marring by the jaws of the lathe. Spiral-wrap ¾-inch masking tape on the part of the shaft to be chucked into the lathe. To keep the free end of the rod from flopping, remove any tooling that might be mounted in the tailstock. The reel-seat section can slide into the taper portion of the free arm, but first it should be built up with masking tape.

Apply the tape in the same direction that the shaft will spin. I find it easiest to start the masking tape on the rod section and then simply turn the chuck in the appropriate direction, allowing the tape to build up. Don't use too much; I normally leave a ⅛-inch clearance between the tape and the surface of the taper. This will prevent the tape from binding in the taper and causing damage to the rod section.

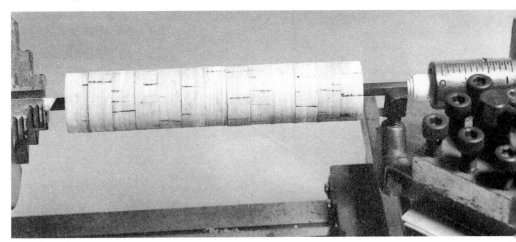

Ready to shape the cork handle. Notice the buildup of masking tape inside the tailstock.

Shaping with 100-grit sandpaper.

being cautious to keep the sandpaper moving at all times so that I don't create unwanted flat spots. As I get closer to the desired shape, I start using finer and finer sandpaper, until I eventually end up with 600-grit for final polishing. If you haven't worked with cork before, you'll be surprised how fast you can remove material with such fine sandpaper.

Because the corks can be out of alignment with each other, your first task in forming the handle is to make sure it's true. Otherwise, you'll turn an egg-shaped handle. Using a block of wood with 100-grit sandpaper wrapped around it, gradually lay the block against the entire length of the glued handle. You'll notice that the high spots are the first to rub the sandpaper. After you've knocked off these high spots, switch to a full-width piece of sandpaper cradled around the handle. Sand the handle until you have a smooth, even, round surface. Then, using your drawing as a guide, measure the diameter of the handle. I sand with this

When I'm finished, I brush the handle off with a soft-bristled paintbrush to remove the sanding powder. And to keep the finish looking new, I wrap the majority of the handle with plastic food wrap. I leave only the ends exposed,

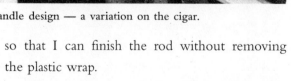

The author's favorite cork handle design — a variation on the cigar.

technique until I'm ¹/₃₂ inch from the largest diameter that I want in my finished handle.

Next, I start shaping the desired form of the handle with 150-grit sandpaper. I use wide pieces for convex shapes and narrow strips for concave,

so that I can finish the rod without removing the plastic wrap.

You can use several glues for assembling the cork handle, although most waterproof brands will be satisfactory. The characteristics to look for when you consider glues are the working time and the cure time. Choose a glue that will give you enough time to get the handle into the press before the glue starts to set. However, you also want a glue that will dry completely in a reasonable amount of time.

A Correct Fit

Among my pet peeves are some of my fellow fly fishers' exotic notions of grip size and how a grip should fit the hand. To prevent fatigue from a long day of fishing — and perhaps physical damage to your wrist — the grip on your fly rod needs to fit your hand in a natural manner. But getting such a fit doesn't have to be complicated.

ratio of 7:5 for a 6-inch grip and proportioned accordingly for longer grips. Starting at the front of the handle the grip rises in diameter, crests at the seventh $^1/_2$-inch cork ring, and then diminishes again over the last five corks. The front dimension is usually $^5/_8$ to $^{11}/_{16}$ inch, and the back is $^{13}/_{16}$ to $^7/_8$ inch, which allows for a slight radius at the corner where the length of the cork meets the face of the cork. This makes a nice transition into the grip check of the reel seat. The slopes from the cresting down can be slightly arched or held straight.

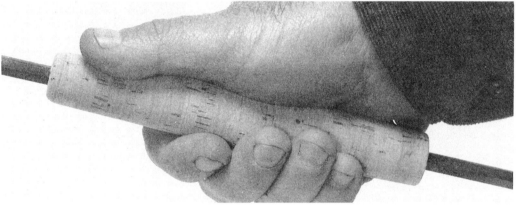

Fitting the grip to the hand. Notice the gap between the third finger and the pad below the thumb.

Here's my practical advice on the subject. When your hand grasps the rod, there should be a $^1/_8$ inch gap between the palm of your hand just below the thumb and the third finger. Without this gap, your fingers are pressured into your palm and bent back. Therefore, you must apply more wrist pressure simply to hold the rod. A common dimension for this cresting area of the grip would be $1^1/_{16}$ inches. Now, many people will argue that the grip of a petite midge rod should be smaller to reflect the character of the rod. But my contention is that the grip should always fit properly — regardless of the rod size or its use.

One shape that I've used successfully many times is the cigar or modified cigar grip, with a

Another interesting discovery is that even though most male fingers are longer than their female counterparts, they're also fatter. And this padding on the inside of the centerline of the finger actually reduces the diameter gained by the lengthier fingers.

Prepping Guides

Before you mount the snake and stripper guides, their ends (known as "feet") should be given special attention. First, the length of the forward and rear foot should be equal. Second, the end of each foot should gently slope down to meet the rodshaft surface. This will make the wraps look even in length with no thread separations — those

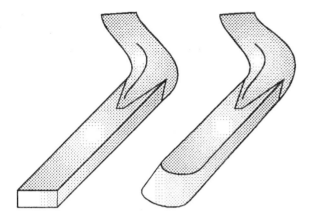

Prepping the feet of the snake guides.

spaces between the lines that seem to shout, especially between dark-colored threads. And finally, the surface of the guides and stripper should be smooth and free of any grinding cuts or burrs.

The length of the snake guides and stripper feet is a personal preference. But remember that the rod flexes when you cast it; the longer the feet, the more susceptible they are to skidding on the surface of the rod as it loads into a cast and then recovers. If the foot skids forward in a cast, it takes part of the thread wrap with it. When the rod recovers, the thread wrap stays forward and will soon unravel. My personal length preference is $^5/_{32}$ inch for all sizes of snake guides, $^7/_{32}$ inch for stripper sizes 8 and 10, and $^9/_{32}$ inch for size 12 strippers.

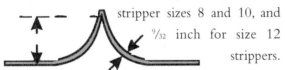

Snake Guide Dimensions			
Guide Size	X/64	Decimal	Wire Diameter
4/0	3	0.046875	0.022
3/0	3½	0.0546875	0.022
2/0	4	0.0625	0.022
1/0	4½	0.0703125	0.028
1	5	0.078125	0.028
2	5½	0.0859375	0.034
3	6	0.09375	0.034
4	7	0.109375	0.034

The snake-guide and stripper feet not only need to be ground to length, but also need their ends tapered so the wrapping thread can wind down neatly from the guide foot to the bamboo. The angle of this slope should be in the 15- to 20-degree range. If it's much steeper it'll be hard to keep the thread from sliding downhill when you wrap the foot to the rod shaft.

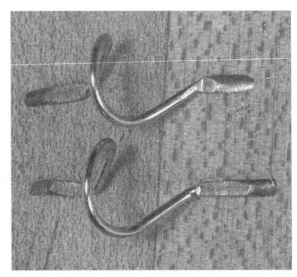

Snake guides before (bottom) and after (above) prepping.

Once the feet are ground, they should be polished with 400-grit sandpaper. This is done mostly for cosmetic reasons. Without color preserver as a base coat for the finish, size 00 thread wraps become very transparent, almost to the point that the feet appear to be held to the rod shaft by some magical transparent paint. The appearance of the guide feet below is another of those details that's so important to a good craftsman. A rodmaking friend once suggested that I just use color preserver and not attempt such painstaking detailwork; "It's like showing off your underwear," he said. But I do the detailwork for practical reasons as well. Leaving nicks or rough edges on guide feet can lead to cut or frayed thread and eventually cause premature thread wrap failure.

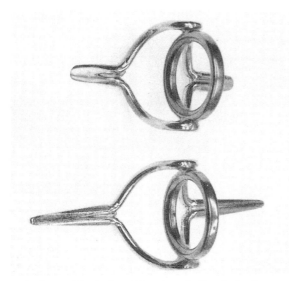

Stripping guides before (above) and after (below) prepping.

For grinding guide feet, I use the standard Craftsman bench grinder with a fine 6-inch stone on one side and a 6-inch brass wire brush on the other. Grinding guide feet may be my worst area with regard to safety. Here I want you to do as I say, not as I do. I know that I should hold the guides with a pair of hemostats and keep my fingers at a safe distance from the grinding wheel. But when I'm grinding guide feet,

A Dremel grinder mounted in a vise, ready for the grinding stage.

even those of a 1/0 snake guide, I often end up with the ends of my fingers within a mere fraction of an inch of the grinding stone.

Using a Dr. Slick to hold the snake guide during grinding.

Grinding the feet is a very delicate job. It doesn't take much time or effort to remove a large part of the foot. First, you grind the feet for length. With a machinist's scale in my left hand and the guide in my right, I lightly touch the foot of the guide to the side of the grinding stone. I measure the length of the foot, repeating the cycle until I reach the desired dimension. Then I flip the guide end-for-end and do the second foot. I prefer to grind all guides to length first, then follow up by grinding the slope. As I've mentioned, I prefer to concentrate on one task at a time.

When I grind the slope on the guides, I want it to be just a single-plane slope. Later, I'll round the slope slightly with 400-grit sandpaper. Once again I use the side of the grinding wheel, which isn't normally a practice I recommend. But because it's such delicate work with minimal pressure, there's little or no risk to the grinding wheel. Holding the guide by the opposite foot, I gently touch the foot to the wheel.

For support and for a constant anchor point, I encircle the wrist of my right arm with my left hand and lean both forearms against the edge of the workbench on which the grinder is mounted. Holding the guide with thumb and first finger, I gently ease it to the wheel and then retreat. I pivot my wrist to inspect the thickness of the guide end and then return to the previous position for further grinding if needed.

The grinding action is a slow and delicate process.

This movement should keep you at a constant angle to the grinding wheel and will yield a true angle on the guide foot. As you inspect the end of the guide, you can watch its blunt end slowly diminish. When the blunt end becomes a knife edge, it's time to stop.

Finally, with a narrow swatch of sandpaper (1/2 inch by 4 inches), polish off the ground slope. As you drag the foot back and forth on the sandpaper, gently rock the guide. This will round off the square-cut edges for a smooth, rounded finish. Complete both feet, then lay the sandpaper on a flat surface with the guide on top of it. One or two back-and-forth strokes will remove any burr that may have formed on the bottom of the foot.

Finding the Spline

No matter how careful you are in planing the strips for your sections, there is always a weakest flat. This is the one on which you want to mount the guides. The better your planing technique, the harder this flat is to find.

Perhaps the easiest way to find the weak flat is to roll the rod with some pressure applied to it and feel for the kick or jump. First, set the ferruled end of the section on your workbench and hold the other end in your left hand. Then with your right hand placed in the center of the rod section, roll the rod slowly. As the rod rolls over each corner, you'll feel some resistance and then a jump as the corner rolls over the center. What you want to find is the flat that makes the strongest jump or kick. This is the side to which the rod is most easily bent. The side opposite your hand will be the weak flat.

If the rod has been straightened correctly, a second test is to set the ferruled end on your workbench with the shaft perpendicular to it. Then apply enough pressure on the other end of the rod to cause it to spring into a bow. The weak flat will be on the concave side of the bow.

Number of Guides

Most fly fishers agree that the more guides that are on a rod, the easier it is to shoot line. One rule of thumb that I've heard and used is that a rod should have at least one guide for every foot of length, plus one. On rods from 6 feet through 7 feet, 6 inches long, I mount seven snake guides and one stripper. On 7-foot, 9-inch rods I mount eight snake guides and one stripper.

On 8-foot models I mount nine snake guides and one stripper.

The sizes of the snake guides are standard for the seven guides I mount: one 0, two 1s, three 2s, and one 3. As I add snake guides for the 7-foot, 9-inch and 8-foot models, I merely mount additional size 3 snake guides. For strippers I use Mildrum model SRMC. This is a lightweight Carboloy casting guide that bamboo rodmakers have used for many years. For #2- or #3-weight rods I use size 8. For #4- or #5-weight rods I use size 10. For #6-weight models I use size 12.

Guide Spacing

In the past I have experimented with several guide-spacing methods. Eventually I found that the model I preferred was one where the space increased by $^9/_{16}$ inch per guide. Having chosen this spacing increase, I was able to write a basic formula for different-length rods. I simply measure the dimensions for the ferrule guide and then calculate the locations of the remainder of the guides.

On two-piece rods I always place a guide immediately below the ferrule. This is what I call the ferrule guide. The space between the end of the ferrule serration and the end of the guide foot is 0.075 inch. This is just enough space for 15 wraps of size 00 thread — 5 wraps to finish the snake-guide foot, 5 wraps to finish the ferrule wrap, and 5 wraps as a decorative tipping.

The exact distance from the tiptop can vary from rod to rod depending on the size of the ferrule that the rod shaft requires. This explains why I decided to use a formula rather than a spacing chart. If you decide to leave the feet longer, or to use a different ferrule style, my formula can easily accommodate these changes.

Wrap Tensioner

I'm amazed when I watch my friend Bob Hoekstra wrap guides on a rod without the aid of any accessories. He simply holds a spool of thread in one hand and twirls the rod with the other. He makes it look so simple, and he achieves professional results. I tried his method once with only fair success. The worst problem I had was that the oil on my fingers would stain the thread, even if I had just washed my hands.

There are several ways of tensioning the wrapping thread, and most of them are inexpensive. They range from running the thread through a Sears catalog to building a dual thread rack, as I did. With a dual tensioner you don't have to change spools of thread to switch to a tipping color.

Thread

Thread size and type are, and have always been, areas of polite disagreement among rodmakers — and it appears that the arguments will continue. It essentially boils down to tradition versus practicality.

Thread Dimensions

Size	Diameter
00	0.0045
Elephant silk	0.006
A	0.007
24/4	0.012
16/4	0.016
10/4	0.021
75#	0.036

Silk is the traditional wrapping thread. It lies flatter because it's a softer thread, creating more of an oval shape than nylon. Its drawbacks are that it frays more easily and has a lower breaking strength than nylon. But it *is* traditional.

Perhaps it's best for all rodmakers to reach their own decisions on thread material and color. I can remember ordering one of each of the colors that Gudebrod and Elephant made, then wrapping and finishing test sections on a piece of scrap shaft. This helped me decide which colors I wanted to use on my rods.

Some of the author's thread-wrapping equipment. Note the tension mechanisms on the spools of thread.

And I do make the choice of color. Some rodmakers let their customers choose the color thread that they want. This, at times, can be a mistake. Unless the thread is color-preserved, it will often change shades when a finishing material is applied. Thus the right shade may well become the wrong shade. I spent several nights, for example, trying to get the correct purple wrap on our daughter's rod.

Magnifying Glasses

While I'm wrapping a rod, I wear a pair of 2½-power magnifying lenses mounted to my regular glasses. When I'm burnishing and packing, I flip the magnifying lenses down. When I'm done, I flip them up and out of the way. In these instances the lenses amplify the work, allowing me to be more critical. I feel this advantage improves the end quality of my rods.

Wrapping

There are four types of wraps that are commonly used on bamboo fly rods. The first is the wrap at the transition from the ferrule to the rod shaft. The second is the wrap that's on the shaft only. The third is the wrap that holds the guides to the rod shaft. And the fourth is the tipping wrap.

Each has its unique details, but the basic wrapping, burnishing, and packing methods are the same. (Note that the instructions I'll be giving are for making the wraps from left to right with the rod in front of you.)

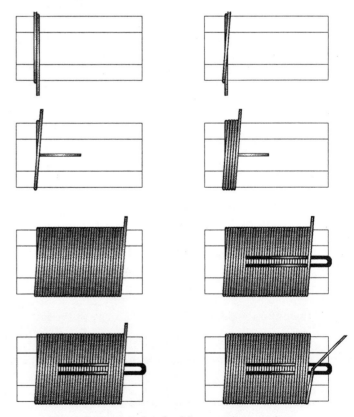

The delicate steps involved in wrapping a rod.

Before I begin doing any wraps, I always make up a pull loop, which is used to pull the end of the thread back under the wrap. I make the loop ahead of time so I don't have to fiddle to create one midway through a wrap. I start with an 8-inch piece of wrapping thread. Then I fold it double and tie it in an overhand knot near the free ends.

The ferrule wrap is the hardest wrap to begin, because it's started on the polished barrel of the ferrule. The wrap starts with a loop around the ferrule. The thread comes from the tensioner, over the top of the ferrule, and wraps around to the right of the initial thread. Hold the free end of the thread with your left hand and the rod with your right. If the thread isn't where you want it, you can slide it to its proper place by shuttling the rod back and forth and dragging the thread by the tag end.

The wrap begins by crossing the thread from the tensioner over and to the right of the thread that's around the ferrule. However, one wrap won't hold the thread from sliding on the polished metal. To add more wraps successfully, you must pass the free end of the thread around the rod section. The thread is passed from the thumb and first finger of your left hand to the thumb and first finger of your right hand and back again as you spin the rod shaft in order to add further wraps. The thread usually requires five passes around to gain enough grip on the ferrule to stay in place. As you add wraps, the thread from the tensioner must lie down tight against the existing wraps.

Once the wrap stays in place on the ferrule, you may have to readjust its position. For pushing the thread around, I use a plastic burnishing tool. These tools are available from most rodmaking suppliers for a few dollars. An alternative to a burnishing tool is the plastic cap of a ballpoint pen.

To move the wrap of threads on the ferrule, use the blunt edge of the burnishing tool. As you spin the rod to add more wraps, gently nudge the wrap in the direction that you want it to move, pushing on the wrap at 8 to 10 places per turn.

When I have about 10 wraps or so on the ferrule, I cut the free end with a surgeon's scalpel or single-edged razor blade. Then continue wrapping until you're 3/16 inch from where you want the wrap to end. At that time the pull loop of thread needs to be wrapped under so the finish end of the thread can be pulled back under the wrap.

When I'm at the end of the wrap, I cut the thread so I have a working piece about 6 inches long. To keep the wrap from unraveling, I press on the threads with the thumb of my left hand. Using my right hand I slide 3 inches of the free end of thread through the pull loop. I then pull on the knot of the loop, pulling the free end under the wrap. When the free end is under the wrap, I pull it snug but not tight.

This completes the thread part of the wrap. To finish, I now burnish the wrap by gently rubbing the rounded surface of the burnishing tool over it. This flattens and spaces the threads of the wrap evenly. As a last touch I pack the wrap inward slightly at each end, using the blunt edge of the tool.

By burnishing and packing the wrap, you eliminate any voids that may have been present until this point. If you choose to finish the wraps as I do, without color preserver, these voids would become quite visible when the finish is applied.

The wraps that are turned on the hexagonal section are much easier to start. I always start these wraps so that the initial crossover is on the flat opposite the guides. The thread will usually hold in place on the first wrap. Carry out the wrapping as described, including the burnishing and packing.

The trim wraps are a little more difficult. Mine are limited to five turns. This means that I must start the wrap with the pulling loop already in place. And both free ends are trimmed after the wrap is completed.

Twenty-Three Turns

To maintain uniformity from wrap to wrap and from rod to rod, I count the number of full turns to create each wrap. The most common count is 23 turns. This is the length of the wraps at all snake guides and at the tiptop trim using 00 thread. Remember, I dress all snake-guide feet to ⁵/₃₂ inch.

Here's the sequence I use. I make the crossover for the first turn, doing it on the flat opposite (three flats each way) the guide. I then make four more turns for a total of five. I cut off the tag end at this point. I continue the wrap until the 15th turn, which is where I place the pulling loop under the thread. Here again I put the pulling loop in when I'm at the flat opposite (three flats each way) the guide. I make seven more turns for a total of 23 and finish the wrap by pulling the tag end through with the loop and trimming it off.

I place the pulling loop in with seven turns left because the thread is still two turns from the end of the guide foot. By doing this I keep the thread from forming a gap at the very end of the guide foot, which would be hard to burnish out. The other important numbers are 40 turns for the cork wrap and 16 turns each for the signature and client wraps.

The ferrule wraps are treated individually because of their varying lengths (depending on the ferrules' size and whether they're standard or truncated). Because the distance from the last ridge on a ferrule to the end of the serrations is equal on male and female ferrules, I make sure I use the same number of turns on the male ends as I do on the female. Starting with the female I make five turns, keeping them packed tight against the ridge. The tag end is trimmed off. And then I continue, counting each turn, until the tip of the serration is two turns from being completely covered. I place the pulling loop in place and finish off the wrap with seven more turns. I now wrap the male counterparts with the same number of turns. To maintain uniformity of length, I burnish and pack each of the wraps with equal effort.

Rod Turner

A rod turner is used to keep the freshly applied finish on the thread wraps from sagging to the bottom side and drying into an unwanted glob. Most rodmakers use one of these devices, although the rod could be cradled on two support arms and moved from flat to flat until the wrap

The author's 1 rpm rod turner.

finish tacks. There are several models of rod turners available. A good source is a supplier that specializes in rodmaking components. Prices start around $20.

When you're considering a rod turner, look at its rpm rating. Most rodmakers who purchase power turners use them when applying the finish to the wraps. Look for a unit that turns at 1 to 8 rpms, which is a nice speed for controlling the flow of the finish application.

Notice how the rod is firmly supported to the left of the working area.

Sealing

Whatever material you choose to finish your rod (I'll describe your options in the next chapter), you should use the same or a compatible material to seal the wraps. If you intend to use varnish for a final finish coat, use it to seal the wraps as well. The only exception comes if you intend to use tung-oil finish on the rod. Then you should finish the wraps with a tung base varnish before applying the finish coat of the tung oil. If you don't know the components of your chosen finish, check the label or contact the manufacturer.

Be aware that if you want to emulate a famous rodmaker of the past by using a particular product,

you may not be getting the same stuff today. Back in the early 1970s most paints and varnishes had to be reformulated to meet new EPA standards. If you want to find some of the same varnishes that were used on fly rods built during the 1940s and 1950s, you'll have to go to estate sales and hope to come across a can that's still usable.

I add the finish to the wraps as the rod is being turned. Using a toothpick, I apply finish first to both ends of the wraps, and then to the middle. A single drop of finish at the end of a toothpick is a manageable amount. As the rod is turning, I use the toothpick to draw the drop of finish to the very edge of the wrap. Because of the slow

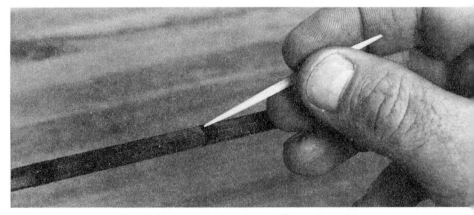

The finish on the wraps is carefully applied with a toothpick.

turn rate, the finish has time to soak into the thread as it's being applied.

I try not to overload the wrap with finish. This can cause the finish to push out onto the rod surface, or it may collect at the bottom center of the wrap as an unsightly glob. If I do get a glob I simply touch it with a dry toothpick; the excess finish flows off the rod. Avoid wiping with a paper towel or cloth, however, as this will leave lint or smear the finish.

Even after I've applied the finish to the wraps, I often let the rod turner run for another hour or so. This ensures that the finish is smooth and even. Once it has dried, usually overnight, I trim off any fuzzes that may show in the wraps. I do my trimming with a surgeon's

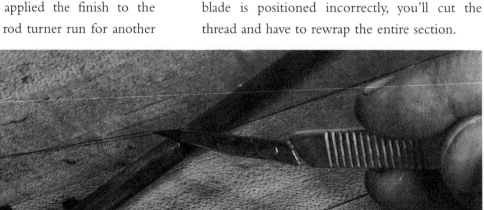

Any excess finish that has flowed onto the rod is trimmed tight to the wrap.

scalpel, but an X-Acto knife or a single-edged razor blade would work as well. After trimming, I add more coats of finish until the thread in the wraps is entirely embedded in finish.

Dress Wraps

No matter how careful you apply the finish material to the wraps, you often end up with some finish that runs off or spreads onto the rod shaft. This is especially true of the area under the guide roll-up. If you leave this excess finish in place, it will show through in the final finish of your rod.

This may sound like a nitpicky thing, but I remove this excess finish so there is a distinct drop-off at both ends of the wrap. Using a straight-bladed surgeon's scalpel, I slice the finish tight to the wrap just as you would slice a pad of butter. And yes, this is flirting with danger. If the blade is positioned incorrectly, you'll cut the thread and have to rewrap the entire section.

If you do this slicing before the finish is fully cured, it won't require as much blade pressure. Keeping the blade square to the shaft, and you won't damage the surface of the bamboo under light pressure. I don't know how much pressure it takes to damage the bamboo. However, I do know that you don't want to use a sawing action, which will score the bamboo. Once again, care and patience will produce a quality rod with obvious attention to the fine details.

11
THE FINISHING PROCESS

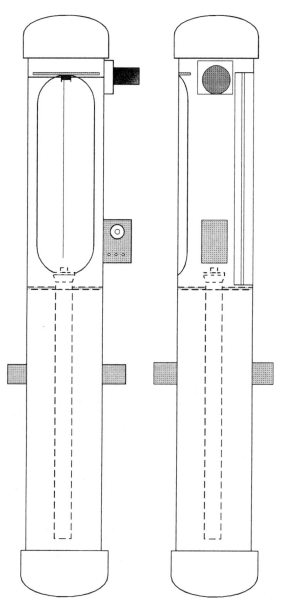

The author's dip finishing tube, constructed of PVC pipe, is waterproof and dustproof.

Finishing Tubes

My wife, Brenda, is fairly understanding about my rodmaking as long as it doesn't spread throughout the house. When I wanted to build a finishing cabinet alongside our spiral stairway, however, she drew the line. So I had to devise an alternative plan.

First I made a mental checklist of the features I wanted in a finishing tube. It had to be self-contained with no setup required, and it had to be located where I could use it anytime without disrupting other normal household activities (such as my family sleeping at 2 A.M.). That only left my shop area in the basement. The total height from floor to ceiling is only 8 feet, 8 inches, which meant that I would have to place part of the tube below the concrete floor to get the 10-foot height I'd set as a minimum. This raised the next hurdle: The finishing tube now had to be waterproof.

The solution was simple: Sch-40 PVC pipe. By capping both ends, the enclosure becomes both waterproof and dustproof. The size I chose was a 12-inch-diameter pipe that would accommodate the lights and other items I wanted inside. Unfortunately, plastic pipe holds static, which attracts lint, dust, and other undesirable air-borne items.

For a test, I first helped rodmaker Wes Cooper put a similar tube in his shop. From the start we could both see that this design was going to be successful. Instead of trying to deal with an entire roomful of potential contaminants, we were working with only what was in the cylinder.

The tube is divided at the 5-foot level. This is where the liquid tube support was going to be mounted, so my layout plans evolved from this feature. Once the tube was in place, I cut a door opening 48 by 10 inches. For the actual door, I cut 2-inch strips of clear vinyl, which I purchased at a local store. It came in a 54-inch width on a bulk roll and is normally used to protect fancy table-cloths. I overlapped the strips 1 inch, creating a reach-through curtain. (You may have seen these at a local grocery store in the frozen food coolers.) The strips were attached to the tube using a 1-inch sheet-metal strap at the center points of each vinyl strip.

With the access opening cut, I then began mounting the attachments. The first item was the liquid tube support, a 6-inch-wide piece of ½-inch plywood. It's held up by three ¾-inch pieces of ½-by-½-by-⅛-inch angle iron. I placed two in the back and one in the front. On top of this I mounted a ⅛-inch Plexiglas circle that I'd cut to fit snugly inside the tube. I added this feature because Wes kept talking about items that had to be retrieved from the bottom of his tube. The Plexiglas would stop anything from falling down the tube.

Mounting the pulling unit was the next task. A friend gave me a 0 – 90 DCV gearmotor and the SCR control to run it. The gearmotor was linked to a ⅜-inch shaft using a Lovejoy coupling. I built a spool 1 inch in diameter and 1½ inches wide, with 2½-inch-diameter endplates that mounted on the shaft.

For those of you who haven't worked with large pipe before, there's an old pipe fitter's trick for getting a straight line around a pipe: Use a wide, straight-edged belt pulled tight around the pipe with the ends overlapped. This will give you a line that's square to the pipe.

To mount the shaft, I first marked a straight line around the pipe, then used a flexible rule to measure the circumference. I divided this measurement by 2 and marked the end and exit points. Using a ¹³/₃₂-inch-drill, I drilled the two holes. Then I worked the shaft in place from the inside of the pipe, mounting the Lovejoy as the last item.

The gearmotor was made for a flat mounting, so I had to make an adapter to mount it to the round pipe. Once again I raided our son's supply of 75-pound-test braided kite string, this time for a winch cable. (I knew that the braided string wouldn't spin when loaded with weight.) With the string in place, I attached a plumb bob. Lowering it to the liquid tube support, I now had a location for the hole.

The liquid tubes I use are copper tubing, because this metal doesn't hold static to attract particles. A 48-inch-length of 1¼-inch L hard

Some of the hardware components used to create a finishing tube.

copper holds exactly 1 quart of liquid. The copper tubing is capped at the bottom. For a top fitting I wanted something that I could seal, but I also wanted it larger than 1¼ inches so that I could watch the rods as they were lowered. I didn't want to submarine the cork handles. I used a 2-by-1¼-inch extended reducer coupling and a 2-inch female X-fitting adapter. I then sealed the tube with a 2-inch PVC Sch-40 plug.

The copper fittings were soldered together using 50:50 solder. Then I washed the tubes with acetone to remove any debris, such as flux or shavings. By drilling a 1⅝-inch hole in the tube support, I allowed the liquid tube to slide neatly into place; it's stopped by the reducing coupler. If you try to copy the finishing tube, just show this description to someone knowledgeable at your local plumbing warehouse.

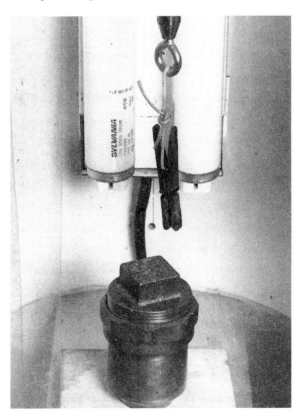

An inside view of the top of the finishing tube.

For cabinet lighting I added a two-bulb, 48-inch fluorescent light mounted to the back side of the pipe. Later, I found that this added just enough heat (75 degrees F) to compensate for my cooler basement (62 degrees).

One last feature I added (although I'm now rethinking its usefulness) was a blower with a Hepa 100 filter mounted in the entrance duct-work. The purpose of the blower is to pressurize the finishing tube with clean air, forcing out any contaminating particles. Even though I now question its practicality, I do know that it works. And with a friend who works in the clean-air business, the price of the filter was right.

I should point out that these are not your ordinary furnace filters. Hepa filters are rated by the number of 3-micron particles they pass per cubic foot of filtered air. A 100 filter falls into the microchip assembly category. This filter is preceded by other coarser filters to add longevity to the Hepa unit. At any rate, when running, the blower moves 75 cfm of air through the upper 5 feet of pipe. The reach-through curtain acts like a relief damper, allowing air to escape through the bottommost part, carrying any particles of dust with it.

I've been involved in installing three different finishing tubes, each one reflecting its maker's own ideas. For example, one craftsman wanted to add 200 watts of light at the very bottom of the tube to warm the finish and chamber. The lights are switched on and off thermostatically by a warm-air control placed higher in the tube.

In addition to its value in finishing rod sections, the tube can also be used to finish reel-seat fillers. I fabricated a small stand that sits on the liquid tube support. It's just large enough to support a quart can of finish. I then follow the same regimen that I use for rod sections. I suppose I could use the liquid tube for both, but I don't want to contaminate the finish with any stain residue. (I stain the tiger-striped maple to match my flamed rods.)

Making a finishing tube doesn't have to be an expensive project. Here are some other ways to save money:

• Make a tube out of 4-mil clear plastic, stapling it to the ceiling of your basement.
• Hang a pulley from the ceiling and reel the string by hand or with a fly reel.
• Use a barbecue rotator with a drum on it.

Personally, I've stopped keeping track of how much it has cost me to make cane rods. You might say it's similar to fly tying. Do you really want to know how much money you've spent to fill your tying chest? But if I'd bought everything that went into my finishing tube, it would have come to about $750. With the help of some friends, I figure I spent about $35 for the entire rig.

Finishes

The three types of finishing materials that I've worked with are tung oil, spar varnish, and polyurethane. All of the finishes I have used are tung based and work well over the initial tung-oil seal that I use on all rod sections.

A tung-oil finish is a low-gloss finish that is preferred by a few purists who feel fish can be spooked by the flashy finishes of spar varnish and polyurethane. As time passes, a tung-oil finish can be buffed out, or new layers of oil can be added at will. I don't use pure tung oil for a finish, but rather a low-gloss tung-oil varnish. You apply these finishes with a soft cloth or your fingers. Let the finish dry until it's tacky, then buff off the residue with a soft cloth.

Three of the finishes recommended by the author.

Tung-oil finishes do very little to fill in sanding gouges, so caution is needed when you're doing node or surface sanding. A good tung-oil finish requires a minimum of four coats; I've applied as many as seven. Tung oil can be slow drying and may require several days between coats. If you want a glossier finish at a later date, you can sand the tung-oil finish and use it as a base for a spar varnish or polyurethane. I caution you to use only a tung-based spar varnish or polyurethane finish.

Tung-oil is a highly air-reactive substance. For long-term storage, all air must be removed from the container. When resealing the container, first squeeze it until the liquid level comes up to the cap. Then cap the container. If you don't eliminate the air from the container, tung oil will gel very quickly.

Spar varnishes are the traditional finish for bamboo fly rods. These varnishes are water resistant and will produce a high-gloss finish. A plus for spar varnish is that it can also be buffed or polished if it becomes scratched. Many classic rodmakers used a combination of beeswax and rottenstone (a natural abrasive) to polish spar-varnish finishes. Modern car polishes also work well as a polish for spar varnishes.

Unfortunately, the drawback to spar varnishes is that they can break down under heat. You may have heard of rods that have gone into varnish meltdown. This is the ultimate disaster, and requires the rod to be completely stripped down and refinished — an additional challenge on an old or antique rod. As I mentioned earlier, the formulations of most varnishes were changed in the early 1970s to meet new environmental laws. This means that the varnishes used on many of the popular rods of the past don't have the same formulation as those you can buy today. Trying to re-create an old finish can be a real challenge.

The newest entries in the category of finishing materials are the polyurethane finishes. They dry to a tough high-gloss surface that resists water and heat. This is the material that I use for my standard finish. The worst drawback is that if a polyurethane finish is marred, it cannot be buffed or polished out. In all cases you should follow the label directions for each finish. Most finishes work best, for example, if they're recoated within a 24-hour period.

I prefer a finish that tack-dries quickly. This not only reduces the chances of lint attraction, but it also keeps the applied finish from drooping. When a finish droops, its natural tendency is to pull away from the corners and well up in the center of the flats. This poses a dual problem. First, it leaves the corners bare of finish — which can add to the number of coats you need to get a good buildup. Second, it creates a crown in the middle of the flats, which requires more sanding to bring the surface level again.

Linseed Finish

I usually avoid any finishing products that contain high levels of linseed oil. Before latex paints, linseed-based paints were the favored finish for exterior use on houses. Other types of paints would blister up and peel relatively quickly. But the explanation was simple. Most older homes were constructed without vapor barriers. These hold in the humidity generated in a house during the winter from cooking, showers, and the like. Linseed-based house paint didn't blister or peel because it allowed the internal moisture to pass through it. Other paints blocked the moisture in the wood, causing it to freeze and thereby separating the paint from the wood.

The purpose of the finish on a rod is to block out moisture. If you use a finish that contains a high level of linseed oil, you're flirting with the chance of moisture reentering the rod.

Straining Finishes

Before you put a finish into your finish tubes, it should be strained to remove any debris and clots. Standard paint strainers will work, but a better alternative is to use a pair of old pantyhose. It acts as an excellent sieve and is obviously disposable as well.

The finish tubes I built have a 2-inch pipe adapter at the top that narrows down to the 1¼-inch tubing size. This makes a natural funnel. But if you're using anything smaller in diameter, I suggest that you incorporate a funnel to guide the finish into the tube.

For straining, I place a double layer of pantyhose in the 2-inch neck area. I pour the finish gradually into the tube. If the pantyhose clogs, I stop pouring and slide the hose to expose a fresh area to the tube opening.

Finish Storage

As I mentioned, the finishes that I use are all air reactive. And because I finish rods on a regular basis, I leave the finish material in my tubes all the time. This accomplishes two things. First, it saves time cleaning the finish tubes if I were to return the finish to its original container. Second, it slows down the clotting of the finish, because the surface area exposed to air is reduced. (The tube is 1¼ inches in diameter; a quart container is 4 inches.)

However, regular maintenance is needed if you're going to maintain the viscosity and cleanliness of the finish. Every six months I dump the finish back into its container, adjust its viscosity, wash the tube out with paint thinner, and then strain the finish as I return it to the tube.

Aged Finishes

Eventually, a finish will start to clot badly. This is when it should be replaced. The usable life of a finish will vary depending on its storage tempature and exposure to air. From my experience, two years is not an unrealistic period of time for a finish to remain usable.

Finish Viscosity

Unfortunately, there is no standard viscosity for varnishes or polyurethanes. Each finish manufacturer packages its product at the viscosity it deems best for the blending of its finishing materials. And it holds true that each brand of finish works best at a different viscosity. Since the viscosity of a finishing material changes as it sits due to evaporation of the carrier material (paint thinner or turpentine), you need a good way to measure viscosity.

There are several monitoring methods available, but it's easy to devise your own. I measure the time it takes for a given amount of finish to flow through a restriction device. This may sound complex, but in practice it amounts to recording the time it takes to pour a quart of finish through a funnel. There are special funnels marketed for this very purpose, but I use a standard kitchen funnel that I have modified by inserting a rubber stopper, with a ⅛-inch hole, at the neck.

Here's a helpful tip for those of us with short memories: I write the target times of the different finishes I use on the side of my finishing tube for later reference.

Determining Viscosity

There are many factors that determine the ideal viscosity for a finishing material. However, its temperature is the one that most affects its flow. You may have read about rodmakers who apply their finishes at a temperature of 90 to 105 degrees F. My experience is that the finishes I use have less gloss and tend to sag easier at these temperatures. I've never heard a good explanation of the need for high-temperature applications. I assume that these makers were trying to get the finishing material to tack off (dry to the touch) quicker, to reduce the exposure time for dust attraction. Because the finishes I use tack off quickly, I apply them at normal room temperatures, which vary from 64 to 75 degrees in my basement.

To test a finish viscosity, I practice with a ¼-inch hard maple dowel rod. The finish characteristics of this wood are similar to those of Tonkin bamboo. To mimic a rod section, I even mount a few guides on the dowel rod. The withdrawal speed I use is 4½ inches per minute, but anywhere from 4 to 6 inches also works well. I prefer a film thickness of from 0.00075 to 0.001 inch. At this thickness the finishing material will stay in place and not run, yet it fills the micropores enough so that I can obtain a final finish in three coats.

In sampling the many finishes on the market today, I did find one that was too thin from the can. All the others had to be reduced. The thickness of the finish I use would be comparable to Mrs. Butterworth's pancake syrup. (If that brand is not available in your locale, you'll have to do some experimenting to find a similar comparison!)

Personal Marks

Once the glue is dry and the hardware mounted, it's time to mark your rod. Like most makers, I sign my rods. After five years of drafting classes I print almost everything, so naturally I just print my name and other pertinent information on my rods.

Marking rods is quite simple. In fact, I've found that the best tool for the job is probably a

A marking pen used by the author to personalize his fly rods.

technical inking pen. These are commonly used by draftsmen and artists to produce inked drawings. Technical pens are readily available from drafting and art suppliers, and most large office supply stores also carry them. The width of line they produce is determined by the point size of the pen. I have an inking set that contains the pen or holder and five of the more commonly used point sizes. My preference is a 00 or 0.3-millimeter width, which leaves a nice readable line.

Before you mark a rod, you should seal the surface of its shaft. Otherwise the ink will be sucked into the pores of the bamboo and cause blotchy, undefined lines. It's the same as trying to write on an absorbent paper, such as a napkin or paper towel.

Because the finishes I use are tung-oil based, I prefer to use a single coat of tung oil for a sealer. I use pure tung oil (Hopes) instead of tung oil with varnish added. And I apply it to the shaft just after I sand off the glue and string. I think it also helps seal the rod and guard against the chance of regaining moisture.

I then mark my rods with India black ink, but there's a wide variety of colors available. I once tried a red ink that matched the color of the wrapping on a rod, but being conservative I have stayed with the black.

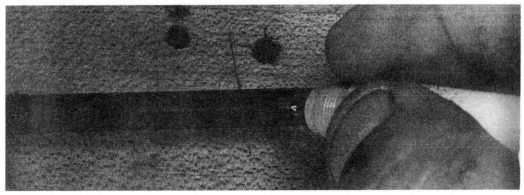

The actual lettering in progress.

Another personal touch is to stamp the butt cap with your name. I just recently started adding this signature; it's fairly simple to do and not very expensive. I spent about $100 for the die and jig.

When I first looked into getting a die built, I thought I'd want a roller die that would fit a knurling tool I could use on my lathe. After calling several local die engravers, I found out that this type of work used a specialized pantograph (a reduction duplicating device), and I couldn't locate one in my area. A New York firm that specialized in roller dies could make the die for my knurling tool, but at $250 this would be a little expensive.

Finally I talked with a fellow who had been doing die engraving for some 40 years. He said I could save money by using a flat die and making a jig where the cap was mounted on a pedestal.

The design I chose is like that of most rod-makers: I have my name on one line and the word *maker* on a second line. This is enclosed by a rec-

tangle with rounded corners. The outline helps ensure that the die does not skip on the cap and blur the imprint.

The jig you'll need for working with a flat die is quite simple. It involves a pedestal that the butt cap fits over, and a shafted bearing that the die rolls against. Both are mounted to a piece of ½-inch flat stock. I made my jig on a 4-by-6-inch base, which is larger than necessary but mounts nicely to my workbench.

To accommodate the different styles of butt caps I use, I designed the jig to work with all types. The difference in the butt caps is the outer wall angle, which ranges from 0 to 3 degrees. Instead of trying to drill accurately for the pedestal and bearing, I centered them at 1¾ inches and merely added shims as needed for the different cap styles.

For proper loading, first determine the correct shimming for no loading and then add 0.020 inch. The marking itself goes quickly: Just slip the cap on the pedestal, drop the die and shims in place, and then gently tap the die through the jig. If you're marking formed butt caps with reel-foot relief, you'll have to develop the proper starting point to get the marking centered.

The mounted bearing I used was a McGill Camrol #CF3/4S, which I bought at the Detroit Ball Bearing Company. I'm sure these are available nationally through local suppliers. The die can be made by most die engravers. Check your yellow pages to find a nearby shop.

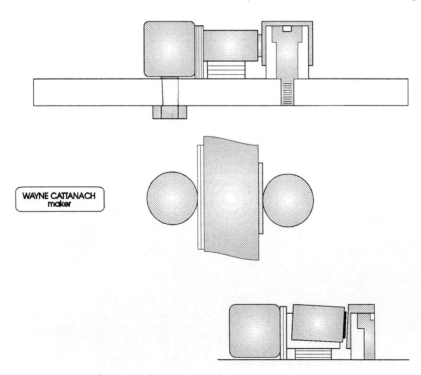

An illustration of a jig used to stamp reel-seat caps.

Finishing

Once I have a rod wrapped and its windings sealed, it's time to start the finishing coats. I begin by running the blower for approximately five minutes. Then with the blower off, I mist down the inside surfaces of the finish tube with a spray bottle of water. I turn on the lights and loosen the plug in the finish tube. As I've mentioned, I check the viscosity if the liquid has been sitting for a long period, such as over the summer.

At this stage I take special precautions. Because I have oily skin, I could leave fingerprints on a rod section, which would get buried under the finish. For this reason I wear a pair of lint-free, cotton inspection gloves whenever I handle rod sections.

Prepping the rod section is the first task. I start by wiping it down with a cotton diaper dipped in turpentine. I recommend that you not use paper towels, which leave lint. I follow up with an inspection for lint, removing any particles with a camera lens air bulb and a whisk brush.

Now I gently pass the shaft through the curtain and suspend it in place. I give it one last inspection, then uncap the finish and run down the shaft with the gearmotor drive. As the shaft approaches the correct immersion level, I gradually reduce the speed until I reach an inch:minute rate of approximately 1 inch:3 minutes. At the correct level I shut off the gearmotor and allow the shaft to stay submerged for two to three minutes. I reverse polarity, set the resistance dial for 6 inches per minute, then turn on the gearmotor, raising the shaft from the finish.

Here's a handy trick that another rodmaker taught me. After a guide has cleared the liquid, I stop the shaft midway on the lower wrap and wait for 2½ to 3 minutes before proceeding. This

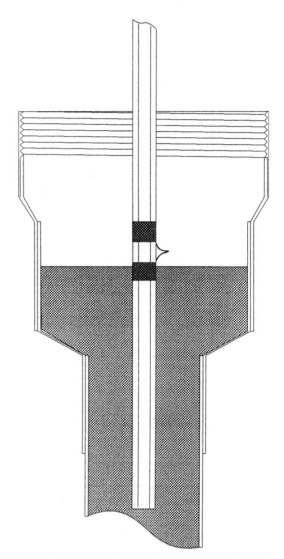

Remember to stop the withdrawal at the middle of the bottom wrap at each guide.

allows the finish that has bridged the circle of the guide enough time to run down; otherwise, a run can show up just below the guide in the same flat that the foot is on. This means that a tip section can take as long as 30 minutes to pull from the finish.

When the last of the shaft is clear, I reach in carefully and screw the plug into the finishing tube. I allow the newly coated section to set until the finish has become dust-free. If I'm finishing more than one section, I keep extra clothespins mounted directly to the pipe to hold shafts that are drying. If you use them, make sure that the guides are facing the pipe so you don't accidently brush fresh finish against the wall of the pipe. I leave the finished sections in the tube with the light on until they're ready for a second coat, or until I feel the finish has hardened enough to go into service.

I've been out in public showing my rods enough to observe that the general fly-fishing population doesn't look past the shine and smoothness of a bamboo rod's finish. If this finish isn't so smooth that a mosquito could slip and bust its butt, then they look no farther. This is unfortunate but true.

Sanding

To obtain a mirrorlike finish, I use 1,000-grit or finer sandpaper on my rod sections at the finishing stage. The 3M Company now produces an Imperial grade of wet or dry sandpaper in 1,000-, 1,200-, and 1,500-grit. Body shop supply stores are also a good source.

The first two coats of finish are filler coats. You apply them to fill the microfissures in the surface of the Tonkin bamboo. When I sand the first two coats I'm sanding away virtually the entire finish coat, leaving only the finish that's filling these valleys. This is the point where careful use of fine sandpapers for node and other surfacing work will be rewarded. If there are deep sanding gouges in the surface, you must fill them or they'll show through the finish as well. Deep sanding gouges may require you to apply more than two filler coats, which means that any time you saved earlier will now be negated by the extra time you'll need to sand additional coats of finish.

The key is to flat-sand the surface, watching the abrasion marks as an indicator of progress. I use a single folded piece of sandpaper and slowly work over the rod section until I've sanded the entire shaft. I put special emphasis on avoiding buildup in the center areas of the flats, which might give the finished rod a rounded appearance.

I spend as much as an hour sanding each section between coats, which equates to nine hours of sanding for the standard two-piece rod with a spare tip. Even with a 0.001-inch depth of finish per coat, the total depth of my finish after all three coats is only 0.0015 inch.

Avoid the temptation to merely degloss the finish with steel wool between coats. Steel wool will only follow the contour that the previous coat of finish has made. Without flat-sanding between coats of finish, the hex shape will become more rounded in appearance, losing the distinct sharpness of its corners and flatness of its surfaces.

Final Fitting

With the basic rod finished, you're ready to dress the ferrules so that you can join your various sections. As I noted earlier, the clearance of the ferrule fit is only "the thickness of smoke." To be more exact, the male ferrule is actually smaller than the female by only 0.0002 inch — "two-tenths" as machinists call it.

At this point I use narrow slices of 1,000-grit sandpaper to fit the ferrules. I start at the very end of the male slide and work inward. This way I don't overdress the male and create a loose fit.

Sitting in my rocker, I first lay the section with the male end across my legs in a position that allows me to roll it. The male end is to my left. Folding a strip of sandpaper, I hold it with the thumb and first finger of my left hand. I then loop the sandpaper over the male end and slowly roll the rod section a few times with my right hand. Then I polish the male end with 0000 steel wool to remove any debris, and I try to fit it into the female.

I continue this process, gradually working up the male surface until it seats completely. A correctly seated ferrule makes a moderate popping sound when the two sections are pulled apart.

12
REEL SEATS AND ROD CASES

Reel-Seat Filler

Part of the "jewelry" that rodmakers like to add to their rods is a reel-seat filler fashioned out of exotic grained wood. Several reel-seat manufacturers offer highly figured or special-grained fillers for their hardware. But these are priced at a premium, and for good reason. One special filler represents a lot of time spent culling through wood, looking for good samples. Burled wood can also fracture easily when machined. If you have an assortment of wood or just wish to build your own wood fillers, it's a relatively simple process. A metal lathe, however, is essential for this task.

Start by creating turning squares $3\frac{1}{2}$ inches long. Then use a doweling jig to bore a hole ($\frac{1}{4}$ inch by $\frac{5}{16}$ inch by $\frac{3}{8}$ inch) so that you can mount the square on a mandrel. (A 6-inch bolt will suffice.) The mandrel is chucked up in the jaws of the lathe. Then slide a spacer onto the bolt to give some clearance from the chuck to the barrel — so you don't hit the chuck with the cutter or holder. Slide the turning square onto the bolt, followed by a flat washer and nut.

Three sizes of reel-seat fillers are commonly used by hardware manufacturers: 0.650-, 0.685-, and 0.730-inch outside diameters. To determine which size you need, just measure the inside of the butt cap. The uplock and downlock styles are the simplest to make. Once the barrel is turned,

they're finished and then undercut to properly fit the threaded locking section.

Slide bands, on the other hand, are a little harder; they require mortising for the reel foot. The biggest drawback is knowing where to purchase the correct router bit. It's called a "fingernail bit" and comes in a $\frac{5}{8}$-inch diameter.

There are some reasonably inexpensive router attachments that do this job, or you may choose to create your own. I simply mounted a

The fixture that holds the reel-seat filler barrels when you're milling the reel recess.

router to a piece of plywood and C-clamped it to the extension wing of my table saw. For a guide fence I use another C-clamp to mount a straight-edged board to the plywood.

To complete the necessary setup, you'll need to fabricate a pair of guide blocks. First, drill a hole lengthwise in a 1-by-1-by-3-inch wood block. The hole is centered at $1/2$ inch by $1/2$ inch. Once you've drilled the hole, cut the block in half to create two $1\frac{1}{2}$-inch-long pieces. Using a bolt again, mount the reel-seat barrel between the guide blocks.

Adjust the height of the bit so that both tips of the cutter touch the wood barrel. The guide fence is adjusted to obtain the proper depth of the mortise cut. It should take a few passes to get the correct depth. Make a shallow cut, then try the slide band with a reel foot. Continue this

A view of the author's router conversion, which he uses to mill the reel recess into the reel-seat fillers.

cycle until the fit is correct. Eventually, you'll develop a set of standards so you can merely measure the distance across the wood barrel to ensure the proper depth.

A view of the router bit as it is adjusted to cut the wood correctly.

I should add that the choice of woods or rather the shade of reel-seat fillers can be important. Many rodmakers feel that the tone of the filler should be balanced with that of the rod shaft itself. If the rod shaft is flamed, then the filler should be of an equal brown tone, obtained either through choice of wood or from staining. This same group of rodmakers feels that there should be a consistent flow of tone through the length of the rod. A mismatch between the shaft tone and the reel-seat filler, they argue, interrupts the flow. One extreme example they find offensive would be a blond-shafted rod with a dark walnut reel seat.

Reel Seat

The final task in completing your rod is to mount a reel seat. Because I make my own reel-seat fillers, I can bore the barrels undersize and then ream them to the correct size for mounting. If you're purchasing your own hardware, however, you may need to shim the rod shaft to get a proper fit to the reel-seat bore.

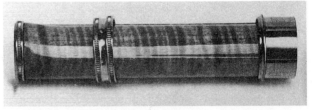

The finished reel seat.

The method I used before I started making my own fillers was to shim the rod section with wraps of masking tape. Starting from near the handle I made three buildup areas. The first was spaced to create a ¼-inch gap from the tape and the cork handle, the second was centered, and the third was positioned to create a ¼-inch gap between the tape and the end of the rod section.

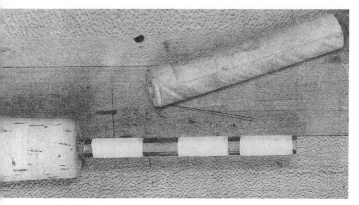

On petite rods, masking tape may be needed to build up the diameter for the reel seat and make it fit correctly.

To make the buildup, wrap masking tape on a rod section over itself again and again until it's built up enough to keep the reel seat from sliding over it. Then start removing short pieces of the masking tape until eventually, the reel seat will slide over it. Move on to the next buildup, until all three areas are sufficiently raised and the reel seat will slide over all of them.

To mount the reel seat, use a standard two-part epoxy that has a curing time of 45 minutes.

The rod is set on the workbench with the handle over-hanging the edge, and the reel seat is mounted and aligned.

With the masking tape in place, mix up a small amount of the epoxy glue. Using a toothpick, spread a light film of glue on the surface of the masking tape. Then, with the cork check in place on the reel seat, slide the seat into place over the masking-tape buildups, pausing to make sure the alignment is correct. (The cork check is the petite metal trim piece that creates the transition from the cork handle to the wood filler of the reel seat.)

With the reel seat in place, and with the rod section in a vertical position with the reel seat facing up, you need to mix more epoxy glue. This will serve as a filler to seal the void between the hex shaft and the inside bore of the reel seat. Fill this void until the surface of the glue is level with the surface of the end of the reel-seat barrel.

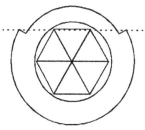

Epoxy filler will seal the spaces between the hex shape of the rod and the reel-seat barrel.

Then take the reel-seat cap and spread a light film of glue around the inside of it, where it'll make contact with the wood filler. Just before you place the cap over the filler, add a dab more to the glue-filled end of the filler to create a crown of glue. Then slide the cap onto the filler, making sure that the alignment is correct.

An impressive attached reel seat marks the end of the rodmaking exercise.

Rod Bag

My mother was a home economics teacher. Her attitude was that even men should know how to cook and sew; that way they had a bit of independence. By the age of 10 I could therefore run a sewing machine. Fortunately, as far as sewing projects are concerned, rod bags are a relatively simple exercise.

I fabricate my rod bags from basic tan poplin cotton, but I've seen some very attractive bags created with satins and silks. There's even a fly-patterned material available. Just be sure that your material "breathes" and won't scratch any of the sensitive surfaces of your fly rod.

The pattern I prefer for rod bags incorporates a rollover flap, which keeps the sections in place. Otherwise your rod sections may slip out of the bag and get unnecessarily damaged.

Cut the material to fit your pattern, then place the good sides of the cloth facing each other. Sew the outer seams, leaving the allotted seam allowance, and turn the bag right-side out. Ironing with a hot steam setting will flatten the edges, take out the wrinkles, and give the rod bag its proper form. At this point you can finally sew in the section partitions so that the rod parts will stay straight and separated.

Rod Cases

I'm the world's worst offender when it comes to keeping a rod in the case where it belongs. In fact, I've been known to go a whole summer with my fly rod sitting on the dashboard of my vehicle. If someone happens to comment on my carelessness, I tell him I'm conducting a rod test that involves total cruelty — including direct exposure to sun and intense heat. The truth is that I should protect the investment of time I put into the rod. It ought to be returned to its case at the end of every fishing session.

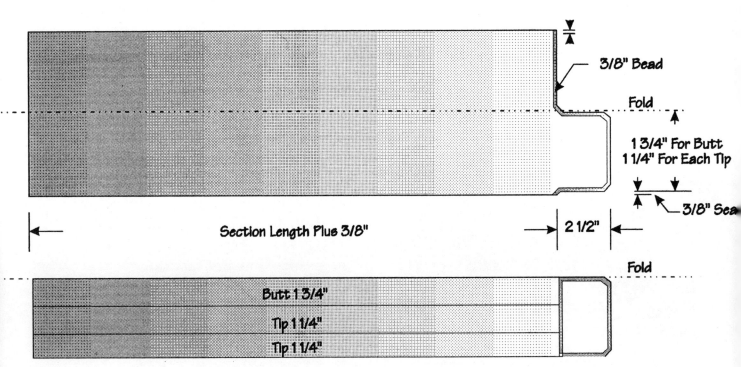

A pattern designed by the author for custom rod bags.

All the cases for the rods I make are handcrafted by Ron Barch of Hastings, Michigan. Ron is the inventor of the distinctive hexagonal wood rod cases that you may have seen in fly-fishing magazines or at fishing shows. Those he builds

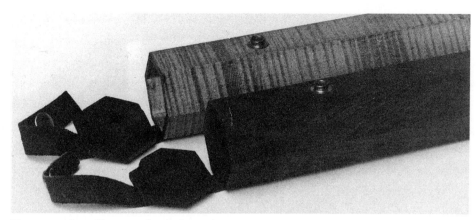

Two examples of hexagonal wooden rod cases.

for me are either tiger-striped maple or walnut. Both feature a leather strap closure. Our business arrangement is based on a close friendship that started with my first rod and continues today.

Many types of cases will protect your fly rod from damage, but I go by the philosophy that a special rod deserves a special case.

Wood Selection

There is nothing more appealing than a burled walnut rod case. But hidden in the beauty of the wood can be potential disaster. Due to the disconnected nature of the fibers or grain of this type of wood, it can have relatively little structural strength. Adding further weakness is the practice of matching the burl from flat to flat. Given the wrong set of circumstances a case could actually break into two pieces — usually taking with it the fly rod stored inside.

Between the simple, straight-grained woods and the weak, highly figured burls, you'll find a vast selection of safe types and patterns from which to choose. Personally, I prefer tiger-striped maple, which is native to Michigan and readily available. It also has eye appeal while offering excellent strength. Tiger-striped maple can be stained, which is how I match the reel-seat filler

to the tone of my flamed rods. This adds balance and the aesthetic "flow of tone" I mentioned above.

Rod-Case Fit

I should add another caution concerning rod cases, whether they're made of wood or any other material: They need to be properly fitted to the rod they store. The inside storage length of a rod case should be only $\frac{3}{4}$ to $\frac{7}{8}$ inch more than the length of the disassembled rod. Anything longer and you may go to assemble your rod someday only to find a broken tip.

Given enough room, a rod will slide back and forth in the case, picking up momentum. The first part to strike the end of the case will absorb all the impact. If the tiptop is the first part to hit the end and it has enough momentum, chances are the section will end up fractured just below the tiptop.

Wood Case Construction

As a practical matter, a rod case with a $1\frac{5}{8}$-inch inside diameter will hold two or three pieces housed in a rod bag. With a traditional bamboo fly rod — which of course has two tip sections — this diameter is adequate for what is termed a two-piece rod (three actual pieces). But a $1\frac{5}{8}$-inch diameter becomes a little tight for a three-piece (four actual pieces) rod. Even with the added volume of the hexagonal shape, a rod case with an inscribed diameter of 1⁵⁄₈ inches is a little crowded for a three-piece rod. But merely adding ⅛ inch to this diameter, bringing it to 1¾ inches, certainly makes it adequate. (Note that these figures are the inside flat-to-flat dimension.)

Now let's work outward. From trial and error I found that using ¼-inch-thick wood pieces gives a good balance between the strength of the glue joint and the appearance. So in going

An end view of the prepared wood slats for a hexagonal case.

from an inside dimension of 1¾ inches, the outside flat-to-flat dimension becomes 2¼ inches.

Apply a little geometry to this figure and you'll find that each flat of the hexagon should be 1.3 inches in width.

To calculate a target length, start with the total disassembled length of your rod and add ½ to ⅝ inch. This is

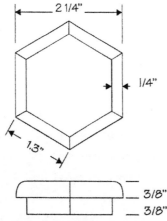

Cutting dimensions for the rod and cap case.

the total length of storage you'll need. To this figure add the thickness of the wood you'll use to make the end caps. Each end cap will be undercut half of its thickness to insert into the case. You now have the total length of the tube. However, it might be wise to add a bit to this dimension and trim later as needed.

Normally, wood isn't available in a ¼-inch thickness; you have to cut it in some fashion from thicker stock. If you're using a table or other saw that leaves blade marks, the initial cut will need to be thicker than ¼ inch. Later, you can remove the excess by further face dressing (sanding or jointing). A ⁵⁄₁₆-inch cut should work well.

There are a few ways to get ⁵⁄₁₆-by-1¼-inch slats, depending on the thickness of the wood you have available. If you're limited to a ¾-inch thickness, then cut 1¼-inch strips and resaw each into two ⁵⁄₁₆-by-1¼-inch pieces. A second option may be to obtain ⁶⁄₄ material and resurface it to 1¼ inches. When lumber is first cut at a sawmill, it's milled to a multiple of ¼ inch. Thus ⁶⁄₄ rough-sawn lumber is 1½ inches thick. After you plane both broad sides smooth, the wood is usually 1⅜ inches thick. Additional surfacing will allow you to achieve the suggested 1¼-inch thickness.

The ⁵⁄₁₆-inch slats are then cut from this slab. Remember that you should use a push stick when the cutting gets near the end in order to keep your fingers safely away from the blade.

You might also be able to leave one saw-cut side undressed and place it to face inside. But then you run the risk of catching the rod bag on the roughness inside the tube.

After cutting and dressing the slats, readjust the table saw to cut a 60-degree at 1¼ inches from the rip fence. Instead of trusting the indicator of the saw, use a 30–60–90 triangle against the blade for adjustment. Widthwise, check to see that the saw is cutting the slats to a full sharp corner. Again, use your push stick at the end of the cut to keep all fingers away from the blade area.

Before cutting, always choose which face of the slat you want on the outside and saw accordingly. And inspect the cut angles for any defects. If necessary, you can make a second cut by creeping the rip fence inward a bit. But if you retrim one slat, I suggest you retrim all six pieces to ensure a proper fit.

In preparation for gluing, place the slats side-by-side with the V facing up. The slats can be held in this position by attaching masking tape to what will be the outside face. Three pieces should be sufficient: one placed 4 inches from each end and one centered. Then *sparingly* apply wood glue. There should be enough glue to wet the surfaces, but any excess can form beads inside and out. Inside, these beads are hard to remove and can catch on the rod bag.

To reduce beading, after the glue is applied you should roll the slats into shape. Then secure the shape by sticking the tag ends of the masking tape together. Lightly squeeze down the length of the tube with your hands, forcing the slats together as if clamped. Afterward, slit the tape open on one corner with a sharp knife and lay the tube open on a flat surface. Using a damp cloth, remove any visible beads of glue.

To clamp the pieces in shape for drying, use electrical tape. With the slats rolled back together forming the hex shape, apply at one end a "stress cone" of electrical tape (electrical stretch wrapped over itself three or four times). Then spiral-wrap four to five turns down the tube, leaving a 1½-inch gap between each turn. Make another stress cone and continue this cycle until you reach the end of the tube — where you finish with a final stress cone.

Electrical tape makes an excellent gluing clamp.

The reason you need the stress cone is that electrical tape will not adhere to the wood properly — but it will stick to itself, creating an anchor point. Once the glue is dry, you can pull the electrical tape from the tube.

If you notice beads of glue inside at the corners, remove them. You can slide a small board down inside the rod case for this purpose. The corner of the board should obviously fit to the inside corners of the rod case. But waiting an hour or more might also be a good idea. Then the bead will be filmed over, and you can remove it without it spreading.

It's likely that some glue will also spread to the surfaces of the outside of the tube. Block-sanding with 100- or 150-grit sandpaper is perhaps the best removal method. If you choose a pad sander, use caution not to round the corners of the tube or leave swirls.

After referring to the dimensions again, clean up one end and trim it to length. Use a shallow cut, saw through one flat at a time, and always encircle the tube with masking tape at the cut. These three tips will reduce the likelihood of tear-outs.

The end caps are made from 2¼-inch strips of wood, but there are a few jigs you can build that will make cutting these parts easier and safer. Both make use of the rip fence as a guide. The first jig is used to cut the caps hexagonally. To set it up, first measure corner-to-corner on the tube. Now make an X on the 2¼-inch strip.

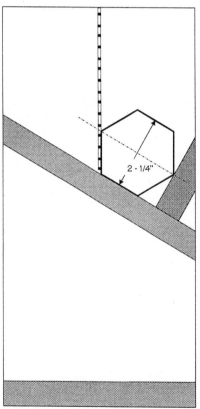

A jig used to cut the square wood into a hexagonal shape for the cap.

First, one end of the 2¼-inch strip needs to be cut square. Measuring from the square end, the first leg of the X is the corner-to-corner dimension; the second leg is the center point of the strip.

Place the 2¼-inch strip into the jig with the square end against the stop. Using a straightedge to extend the inside cut of the blade, adjust the rip fence until the extended cut line and the X cross. Once this is adjusted, slide the jig forward and cut the first 60-degree angle. Then flip the strip side-for-side and cut the second 60-degree angle. Now you can flip the strip end-for-end and cut the third and fourth 60-degree angles, creating a hexagonal piece.

Use the second jig to make the ¼-inch-wide undercut in each of the six sides. It can be set up by making a mark on the cap piece at ¼ inch in from the edge. Again, extend the inside cut line of the blade and adjust the rip fence until the two meet. Remember that the blade height also needs to be adjusted.

Perhaps the easiest method is

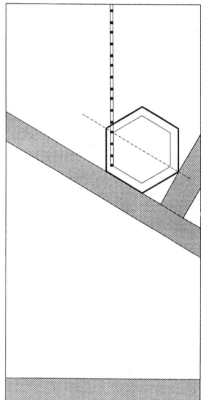

A jig used to undercut the caps so they will fit snugly into the case.

to set the jig against the blade and measure from the jig to the crown of the blade. Move the blade up or down as needed until ⅜ inch is measured. Set the cap piece in the jig and you can cut the six sides in rotation. After the first pass, back the rip fence away from the blade so that with a second pass on each side you'll remove the remainder of the wood at the outer edge.

WOOD CASE CONSTRUCTION **157**

If your work has gone according to plan, the end caps should slide into the tube with the sides flush. If not, you can try rotating to different flat combinations — or you may need to recut or do some trimming. Looking ahead, one end cap will be glued into place, but the other needs to be a bit loose fitting so that it can swing out on the leather strap. Knowing this may help you decide which cap to use for each end.

At this point you need to work with the end caps separately. Start by fitting what will be the fixed cap. When it slips in and the sides are positioned so they can be sanded flush, mark both the tube and cap with an X on one flat for an index. Apply glue to the cap at the cutout and to the lower inside edge of the tube. Slide the two together. Now set the tube vertically until the glue is dry. The vertical positioning prevents the glue from flowing into the tube. When the glue is dry, sand the corners of the cap to a ³/₈-inch radius, flush with the sides of the tube.

As I noted, the upper cap needs to be able to swing free of the tube. This suggests that it will fit a bit loosely in the tube. To allow you to sand flush with the sides, wrap masking tape around the recess to reduce this gap to a snug fit. Then sand the corners to a ³/₈-inch radius, blending them flush with the sides. When you remove the cap, use a nail to make a light dent in both the end of the tube and in the lip of the cap — for later indexing.

Next, mark the cap's center point on the bottom. To plot this point, draw a line from each pair of corners. Using a Bradpoint drill, make a hole at this point to a depth of ⁷/₁₆ inch. Follow this by drilling a ¹³/₆₄-inch hole through the remainder of the cap.

Inspect all the surfaces of the tube and address any areas that need extra sanding. It's a good idea to apply a soft repairable finish to all the surfaces, both inside and out; I recommend Antique Oil Finish by Minwax or Watco Oil. These applications should bring your finish to the desired level.

You can find all the leather parts and bindings you'll need for a tube at a Tandy Leather store. My local outlet cut and punched the necessary holes and even mounted the snap. However, the screw that mounts the snap stub to the tube needs to have the head lathed down a bit, and the store couldn't help me with this task.

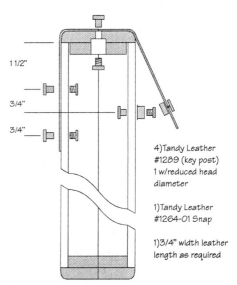

1 1/2"

3/4"

3/4"

4)Tandy Leather #1289 (key post) 1 w/reduced head diameter

1)Tandy Leather #1264-01 Snap

1)3/4" width leather length as required

The rod-case assembly with leather fittings and hardware.

First, mount the leather strap on the cap. When you place the strap on the tube, you can make marks for the drilling of the other needed holes. A small ratchet screwdriver can be useful for tightening the two screws inside the tube. Also, for safety's sake, use a thread-lock liquid on all the threaded fittings.

To add individualism to my cases, I had an imprint die made with my logo. The flared-out area on the strap that's next to the snap is perfect for this logo.

Recommended Care

A bamboo fly rod actually isn't as fragile as some people suggest. But like any fly rod, it should be treated with respect — both in the stream and during storage. Here are some guidelines:

• A fly rod should always be kept clean and dry. If you're caught in the rain with a rod, always dry it and the rod bag and tube before you store them.

• Before assembling the ferrule, always wipe the male end to remove any grit.

• If you're hooked on a snag or in a tree, always point the rod directly at it to pull loose.

• When playing a large fish in close, always hold the rod out at arm's length and at an angle.

• Never lean a rod upright for long periods of time. This may cause it to take on a set.

• Never leave a rod assembled for long periods of time. The ferrule parts may oxidize together, making it difficult to disassemble them.

I give my rods an occasional waxing. This makes it easier to polish them up after a show or gathering. Quite often they get handled rather a lot at these occasions, and a quick polish before and after refreshes the gloss of the finish. The product I use is a beeswax and lemon oil mixture that not only yields a nice shine but also adds a pleasant lemon aroma to the rod. Here's my recipe for a reliable rod wax:

Wayne's Microwave Rod Wax

⅛ ounce beeswax
¾ ounce lemon oil
1 plastic 35-millimeter film canister
1 round wood toothpick

Place the beeswax and lemon oil in the film canister and microwave on high for five minutes (or until the beeswax is dissolved), stirring after two to three minutes. After the beeswax is fully dissolved, stir the mixture for one minute to ensure that the components are blended. Then let it cool.

Because the film canister is used to store the wax, I prefer the screw-cap design. I keep a canister in my tackle duffel bag, along with a piece of cotton flannel. This keeps the wax handy so I can properly store my rod — rather than trying to do it after I return home.

The formula makes a wax with a consistency equal to soft fly flotant. If you prefer a more liquid polish, add more lemon oil. Reheating the wax doesn't seem to hurt it. I use this wax not only on rods but on woodwork around the house as well.

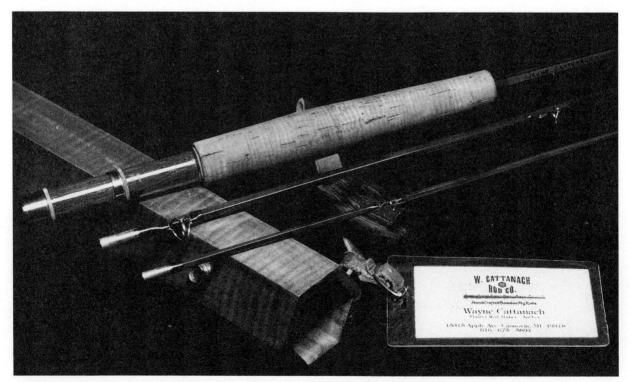

The final product — a custom fly rod with accessories.

13
FLY-ROD REPAIRS

Accidents

Once you start to make fly rods for others, it won't be long before you get "the phone call": A past client has suffered an unfortunate mishap and a custom fly rod is now broken and awaiting repairs.

There are a few simple truths in the life of a fly rod. The first is that most broken fly rods get that way within 10 feet of a door. In fact car doors, cottage doors, and garage doors all seem to attract bamboo rods like magnets. The delicate tips, of course, are particularly susceptible to these disasters.

The second truth is that even if several hundred dollars changed hands when you sold the fly rod originally, it's still yours by virtue of the fact that you are the maker. Along with the fly rod, you sold part of your soul. It would be impossible to ignore it in an hour of need.

Also, once a rod is repaired and back in it's owner's hands, it has gained stature. As in the landing of a memorable fish, the rod has become the victor. And as a rodmaker, you'll find it rewarding to be part of this process.

Previously Owned Rods

Brenda and I occasionally go to estate sales, where I can sometimes pick up a rare bamboo fly rod for $5. When I get it home I evaluate what it would take to make the rod serviceable again. Unfortunately, in most cases I can make and finish a complete rod in the same amount of time that it would take to properly restore these bargains.

But if you like a challenge and have time on your hands, the previously owned rod can be a way of learning new skills and ending up with a fishable bamboo fly rod. I have a friend to whom I send my "finds." If a rod is less than 8 feet long, he attempts to restore it to that length. If it's an 8½- or 9-foot three-piece rod, he sometimes makes a 5-foot, 8-inch or 6-foot rod from parts of

Fly Line Conversion

Line Size	Weight /30'	Old DT	Old WF		
#1	60				
#2	80			A	0.060
#3	100	IFI	IFG	B	0.055
#4	120	HFH	HFG	C	0.050
#5	140	HEH	HEG	D	0.045
#6	160	HDH	HDG	E	0.040
#7	185	HCH	HCF	F	0.035
#8	210	GBG	GBF	G	0.030
#9	240	GAG	GAF	H	0.025
#10	280	G2A	G2AF	I	0.022
#11	330	G3A	G3AF		
#12	380	G4A	G4AF		

Older rods often have cryptic fly-line designations. This graph will help you determine the appropriate line weight for an old rod.

it. He enjoys these restorations as much as I enjoy making new rods.

Original Parts

The actual time you need to restore a previously owned rod is often less than what you'll spend in hunting for any missing parts. Many of the guides and ferrules that were used on rods of the past are no longer available. Whenever I travel the countryside, I try to stop at sports shops and hardware stores looking for only these parts.

Over the years I have narrowed my most-wanted list down to a select few items. Fortunately, you can discover some surprising things in the least likely of spots. When you walk into a retail business, don't just see what it's like today — try to imagine what it might have looked like years ago. Some of the basements of these stores hide true treasures for dedicated rodmakers.

Cleaning Cork

As a fly rod gets fished over the years, the cork handle is the first part to show its use — yet a quick scrubbing with soap and water will refresh its natural look. I mix up a cup of dish soap and water and use a toothbrush to whisk the dirt off, followed with a freshwater rinse. My only precaution is that you should let the cork dry well before storing it away in your rod bag and case.

Steaming Cork

Small dents and impressions in the cork can be swelled back into shape by the use of steam. A vaporizer can be used, but it needs to be a hot vapor unit. A better choice is to use a damp washcloth with a steam-and-dry iron. Adjust it to its hottest setting and put it on steam, allowing it to preheat before use.

The technique is very simple. Lay the washcloth over the dents and press the iron to it. If the dents are going to rise, you should see some movement with the first application of steam.

Rehandle

If the dents in your cork handle are really just rounded nicks, your only alternative is to replace the unit. If you're refinishing the rod, you can slide new cork onto the shaft from the ferrule end; otherwise, it must go on from the reel-seat end. This means you must remove the reel seat.

To free the reel seat from most rods, the glue must be deteriorated. However, some reel seats are pinned in place with nickel-silver wire. On these rods you'll have to remove the wire before you can take off the reel seat.

To loosen the bond of the glue that holds the reel seat, you must apply heat. I use a heat gun with the rectangular diffuser I described earlier (see chapter 4). You must apply the hot air in short bursts or you'll damage the finish on the filler. After applying heat, wiggle the reel seat to help free the grip of the glue. Once the seat starts to move, just keep wiggling and it should slowly come off.

A protective wrap of masking tape on the rod shaft will keep the warm glue from spreading on it. You'll also need this tape when you chuck the rod section in a lathe to shape the new handle. (Mounting and shaping the cork, of course, were discussed in chapter 10.)

Polish Varnish

A simple step in the restoration process is polishing the varnish to bring back the rod's luster. The traditional polishing material is rottenstone, the fine brown abrasive powder that I also mentioned earlier (see chapter 11). Rottenstone is used with either an oil-soaked rag or a piece of beeswax. A more modern product worth considering is automotive polish.

Before you start in on an entire rod, first polish a small test area. One spot that's quite hidden is the area between the wraps under the guides. It can be a little difficult to reach, but using a Q-tip swab will make the access easier. If this yields the results that you want, then attempt a larger area.

If the varnish does not respond to polishing, perhaps the finish is too thin. In these cases you'll need to lightly sand the finish and add a new final coat.

Overvarnish

The preparation for adding a new final coat is just as I described in chapter 11. However, there are a few precautions to take when you're adding a new final coat.

Before purchasing a finishing material, read the label for recommended recoating instructions. Be forewarned that many of the polyurethanes on the market today do not adhere well to varnish. Check the ingredients list: If tung oil isn't listed, the material is highly unlikely to be compatible with the rod's existing varnish. Again, try a sample area under a guide.

Second, you should thoroughly inspect the existing finish. If it has separated in any spots, they must be sanded away and feather-edged into a solid finish.

Finally, the rod may have been waxed during its lifetime. A good washing with turpentine or paint thinner on a soft cotton cloth is the key to removing lingering wax.

Strip and Redo

There comes a point when the finish on a fly rod is no longer salvageable. At this point stripping and refinishing is your only option. But before you start ripping off all the guides, decide what thread you are going to use to remount them and what finishing material you plan to use.

I raise these concerns so that you'll think through the project before you begin. If you're working to restore the proverbial "hardware" rod, it may not matter if the thread color is only *close* to the original. But if the rod is a more valuable piece, anything less than an exact match will detract from the rod's final value.

Don't forget to measure and record the locations of everything, especially guides and intermediate wraps. If all the wraps are intact, you may choose to recover and reuse the wrapping thread. But you need to keep track of the guide and location for each thread. One method is to use a 2-inch width of poster board with notches cut every ½ inch on both sides. As you remove the thread, wind it in the appropriate notches in the poster board. Before reusing the threads, clean them up with paint thinner on a soft cotton cloth.

The old finish can be taken off with paint remover on a cloth. (I usually avoid painting the remover onto the rod shaft.) If you intend to leave the inscription or decals intact, work around these areas with paint remover. Make the break points occur at the corners of the rod section. Later, you can blend in these areas by lightly sanding over them.

Once you've removed the bulk of the old finish, a good washing of the shaft will neutralize the paint remover film. Any last traces of finish can be cleaned up by sanding with 360-grit sandpaper. If the rod has been flamed, use caution when sanding. Working the sandpaper too much in one area may remove the delicate flame-toning. Any finish that was left intentionally needs to be deglossed for adhesion and feather-edged to blend in with the new finish.

Rewrapping the guides with the old thread can be a little challenging. You don't want to trim off any more thread than necessary, but you'll probably lose some in order to accomplish the task.

Whether you decide to use color preserver on the wraps depends on the look you want to achieve. One way to reduce the transparency of the wrap without color preserver is to rub the wrap between your thumb and first finger when its finish is still a bit tacky.

Once the wraps are sealed, apply the finish as I described in chapter 11. The sanding between coats also follows the same technique.

Breaks

Many light fly-rod breaks can be repaired, but only if all the parts of the break have been saved. The secret is to unravel the layers of the break and separate them with pins. Then each layer is laid back in place in wet glue. Wrap the repair to tighten the glued layers.

This sounds fairly simple, but in reality it can be quite complex. The problem is getting the layers to compress as they did when the rod was first made. The breaks that I've tried to repair have all ended up with bends at their centers. As a result, I'm not very enthusiastic about repairing breaks. Another challenge is that there's usually a piece missing, which makes the repair even more obvious.

Growing Parts

A better way to repair a broken section is to "grow" it. The parts are not actually grown, of course, but a new piece is "scarfed" onto the existing section.

Instead of using a consistent *angle* for the scarf joint, I make them a consistent *length*: 2½ inches for butts and 1¼ for tips. This means that I build a new scarf block for each joint I repair. Although this may seem like a lot of work, after a few joints you'll have a collection of blocks to cover most repair situations.

In a scarf joint you're actually combining new parts with old, so you need to know the dimensions of the rod on which you're growing the parts. For me this has been one of the more enlightening aspects of rodmaking. Of the few rods that I've grown parts on, none was accurately made in the first attempt. I ended up averaging the across-the-flats dimensions.

The replacement part is made at least one scarf-joint length longer than the original. Then the two halves of the joint are planed to fit as a continuous rod section. I also prefer making the scarf joint to start at the top flat and finish at the bottom flat.

Once the parts are dry-fitted together, place a pencil mark midway across the joint. This will be your alignment mark when you glue the two pieces. As I suggested earlier, I use Nyatex epoxy to glue the joint, because I feel that it gives the strongest bond.

I've seen some scarf joints done by other makers. The joint is usually spotted by reinforcing wraps at the ends of the scarf. I prefer not to reinforce-wrap my scarf joints, however; I'm confident of the strength of the glue, and I try to blend the joint to be invisible.

If a rod's finish is in good condition, I refinish the rod only from the guide wrap closest to

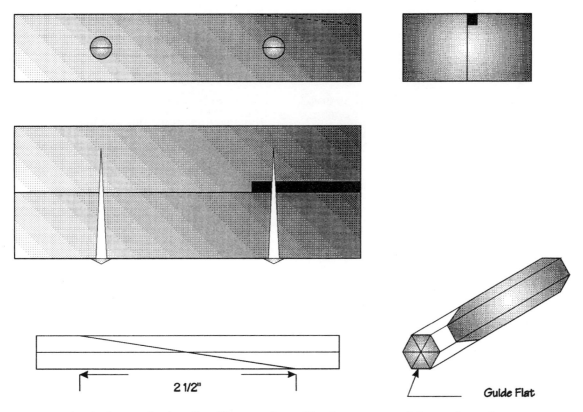

One way to repair a broken section is to "scarf" a new piece of bamboo onto an existing section rod.

the joint through to the end of the section. However, this means that I have to match the quality of the finish. A finish that changes from something acceptable 20 years ago to mirror quality is a sure giveaway of a repair.

Making Parts

There comes a time when it is easier to make a new section than to try to repair an existing one. And sometimes when a rod part is missing, your only option is to make a new one. Once again, you need to determine the dimensions of the parts that you intend to make. If the old parts are still available, this won't be a problem, but without the parts it becomes more of a challenge.

If you know who made the rod and have the model details, chances are that someone has the taper dimensions. Without this information you must rely on your knowledge of how tapers graph, and on determining how the client wants the rod to cast.

The next challenge is to match the new section with the other ones. The toning, node staggering, guides, guide wraps, and quality of the finish all must match. If duplicating the finish becomes a problem, you can do an overvarnish on the other parts to give every section a uniform look. This is easier than stripping all the sections and redoing them.

Polishing Metal

The metal parts of a rod can be polished to bring back their brilliance as long as they're solid metal and not plated. Nickel silver and aluminum, for example, can be polished with fine steel wool or polishing rouge. If you use steel wool, use either 4/0 or 6/0 grade. If you decide to use rouge, buy one especially designed for that metal.

If the parts have become blackened, it may be that the protective finish has deteriorated. Now you have a tough choice. Sometimes it's easier to remove the blackening and start over.

With plated parts, the best technique is probably to buff them with a chrome polish. Steel wool or rouge will eat away the plating quickly, so if you use them be careful.

When you're polishing, be particularly careful in the male ferrule area. It's better to have a corroded part than a loose-fitting ferrule.

Loose Tiptop

When you encounter a loose or missing tiptop, usually the trimming wrap will be intact. If this is the case, you can often reset the tiptop without redoing the wrap. To protect it from glue, place a few turns of masking tape around it. Then with 360-grit sandpaper, lightly degloss the gluing surface.

If you're reusing a tiptop, it certainly needs to be cleaned. I prefer denatured alcohol as a solvent. Clean the socket with a toothpick dipped in alcohol, then use Devcon epoxy to secure both tiptops and ferrules. Here again a toothpick is an efficient way to get the glue into the socket of the tiptop. When it's set, don't forget to align the tiptop with the other guides.

If you spot a buildup of glue squeezed from the tiptop, wipe it off quickly before it has a chance to dry. If you wait to trim the excess glue later with a sharp blade, you risk cutting the trimming wrap.

Finally, apply a finishing material to the wrap and tiptop to make the connection watertight.

Loose Wrap or Missing Guide

On many of the rods of the past, guides either are missing or have wraps in need of attention. This is probably a result of the use of color preserver or a failure to shorten the guide feet. Remember that the repair needs to run only from the front wrap to the back wrap.

If a guide is missing, prepare a replacement that's the same type as the rod's other guides. The feet of the guide should also be filed (proportionally) in the same manner as the others, and the end should be similarly trimmed. If the guide and wraps are in place but in need of repair, decide whether you need to save the thread and deal with it accordingly.

With the guide removed, it's time to address the finish between the far ends of the wraps. First, a light sanding is needed — enough to create a good base for the final finish. Follow this by wiping well with a rag soaked in paint thinner.

Now you can mount the guide and wrap it in place. Before you apply any finish, though, wrap each end of the thread wrap with masking tape. This will stop the wrap finish from creeping down the rod shaft.

Loose Ferrules: *Metal to Metal*

When the fit between the male and female ferrules loosens enough so you no longer hear a distinct *pop* when the two are separated, the female socket should be pinched in a lathe chuck to tighten the fit. But before you attempt any alteration to the female, protect it from the jaws of the lathe chuck with a wrap of masking tape. Always apply the masking tape to the ferrule at an angle so the tape overlaps itself midway.

I prefer a self-centering, three-jaw lathe chuck to tighten ferrules: You turn the handle only once to tighten all three jaws at the same time. The difference between a loose fit and a tight fit is a matter of thousandths of an inch. So take it easy with the pressure you apply to the handle of the lathe chuck.

I start by tightening the handle to pressure the ferrule at three jaw locations. After the pressure is released, I move the ferrule 60 degrees to place the jaws between the first contact positions. Then I repeat the process and apply more pressure. This will tighten the ferrule at six evenly located points. If you tighten the female too much, the male will need to be re-dressed (see Final Fitting on page 146).

Loose Ferrules: *Metal to Bamboo*

The best clue that you have a loose ferrule-to-bamboo connection is the clicking sound you'll hear when casting the rod. To correct the problem, you must first determine which connection is loose. Once you've found the faulty part, the rest is straightforward: The ferrule and ferrule wrap are removed, and the ferrule is reset and rewrapped. Here again, if you'll need to reuse the thread, you should carefully remove and save it.

A good break point in the finish is at the end of the wrap. To protect the finish beyond this point, place a wrap of masking tape at this juncture.

Meanwhile, you can fatigue the glue that's holding the ferrule part with short bursts of heat and the wiggling technique I mentioned on page 160. Many short applications of heat are better than one continuous one. The shorter applications protect the surrounding areas as well as the rod section from heat damage.

When the ferrule part is off, this is the time to polish its finish. If it's a male part, however, be careful not to polish away its fit to the female.

The ferrule should be reglued with epoxy. To get a good bond, lightly sand the existing glue and scribe a light V to allow excess glue and air to escape. Also, clean the ferrule socket with denatured alcohol and allow it to dry.

Once again, I use Devcon epoxy because it doesn't shrink when curing. I mix a small amount of glue using a round toothpick, which I also use to drip the glue into the ferrule socket.

Set the rod section into the ferrule socket with several applications of light pressure instead of one massive one. This allows the excess glue and air to escape without popping out the welt plug of the female or the end of the male ferrule.

With the section seated and the serration tabs in place, wrap some binding thread around the ferrule serration tabs and allow the glue to set. On the flat areas exposed, dried glue can be cleaned away with 4/0 steel wool; use a surgeon's scalpel or dental pick in the serrations and around the edges. Now you can wrap and finish the ferrule.

Filler

A good filler that you can use to repair hook digs, chip-outs, and missing parts at breaks is Acraglas. This is an epoxy bedding kit manufactured by Brownells, Inc. Many stockmakers use it to tighten the fit between a wood gun stock and the barrel and action.

The Acraglas kit includes resin and hardener as well as floc and a brown dye. This epoxy can be toned from a light blond to a dark brown to match most repairs. However, it will often still be detectable. The trade-off for a rodmaker is to reduce the obvious flaws without resorting to making new parts.

14
FINISHING TOUCHES

Blackening

Many makers prefer to blacken a rod's trim parts, including the line guides, ferrules, and reel seat. In the past there were several concoctions that would oxidize nickel-silver parts and turn them black. However, they often contained toxic chemicals that should be handled only by a registered chemist. I remember once trying to purchase the ingredients to brew a blackening agent; I got a distressed look, as if I were a terrorist trying to build a bomb.

Fortunately, I got some good advice from rodmaker Bob Hoekstra, who suggested that I try Birchwood Casey's Brass Black. This company produces a variety of gun repair and refinishing products that can usually be found in larger gun shops.

Blackening is done after the components are prepped for final use. After sanding and buffing, you'll need to clean the nickel silver to remove any oil residue or contaminants. Denatured alcohol followed by a water rinse makes a good cleaning combination. Remember that you have oil on the surface of your fingers, so touching the parts with bare fingers will leave fingerprints that may show in the blackening process.

The instructions that come with Brass Black suggest that you apply the agent with a saturated swab. Instead, I prefer immersing the parts in a small cupful of the liquid. A 1-ounce measuring cup filled enough to cover the parts completely works well. The reaction then takes about one minute. After immersion, wash the parts with water and dry them thoroughly. A light buffing with a soft cloth brings out the shine. If you want a darker look, just reimmerse the parts.

Once you're satisfied with their color, the parts can be coated with a clear enamel spray to protect their beauty. This last step is optional, but without a protective surface the blackening will eventually rub thin and need recoating.

Staining Maple

My first choice for making wood fillers is fiddleback hard maple. It can be a little hard to machine because of the tightly swirling grain pattern. Still, this grain is what gives the wood its character — if you know how to enhance it.

I've heard of several homemade concoctions that can be used to highlight the stripes in this wood. The most exotic brew involved dissolving a plug of chewing tobacco in a pint of turpentine. Fortunately, I've had enough success with several other recipes that I've never had to try this one.

To understand how to highlight the stripe, you need to know what the grain of the wood is actually doing. If you've ever stained wood, you already know that the end grain of a board absorbs stain at a faster rate than the side grain. In this type of maple the grain doesn't really know which way it's going. When you see the finish surface of one of these filler barrels, you're actually seeing both the side and end grains all tightly intermixed. The secret of good highlighting is to use a solution that reacts better to one facet of the grain than the other.

Oil stain is the simplest way to accent the grain. I formulate a special mixture that matches the flame-toning of my rods — adding just a hint of red to reflect the red wraps. I find that it's best to apply the stain when the machining is finished and the barrel is still mounted in the lathe. I lightly dip a soft cloth into my stain mix and apply it to the spinning barrel. The heat caused by the friction accelerates the absorption of the stain.

If you want a light-toned filler barrel, Dixie Gunworks in Union City, Tennessee, has what you need. The compound is called Chromium Trioxide; you mix it with water and swab it onto the barrel. When it's as dark as you want, neutralize it with a mixture of water and vinegar. After the barrel dries, whisk it with fine sandpaper before applying a finish.

I should add a few words of caution here. Chromium Trioxide is a hazardous chemical, and you need to be careful when handling and applying it. Always wear proper hand and eye protection.

Potassium Permanganate

In preparing to make our daughter's purple fly rod, I tried several combinations of stains and flaming. I eventually came up with a workable solution. I begin by flaming a culm of bamboo as per my usual method. Then I split the culm into strips.

Before I flatten the nodes, however, I sand off the bulk of the enamel. This is definitely out of sync with my normal procedures. I then swab on a solution of potassium permanganate and water and allow it to soak into the pores of the power fibers. After the solution has dried, I wash the strips with denatured alcohol to neutralize the chemical.

The strips are then prepared for heat treatment. I flatten the nodes and triangle the strips. After the strips are heat-treated, I dehydrate them and plane normally.

The test pieces showed a beautiful rich purple tinting. By the time the first edition of this book was printed, the rod was completed and my daughter was fishing with the colorful results.

Ammonia-Toning

To match the solid toning of impregnated or brown-toned rods, you can expose the roughly shaped blond sections to a strong ammonia atmosphere. This is done before heat-tempering. I've used ammonia hydroxide, which is normally the agent for developing blueprints. A strong household ammonia cleaner should work as well.

To make the bamboo react to the ammonia, you must also apply some heat. A good place to do the ammonia-toning is outside on a hot, clear day. The sun adds the heat, and the outdoor environment disperses the poisonous ammonia fumes.

The ammonia I buy is sold in 1-gallon jugs. To saturate a rod section with fumes, I first slide it into a piece of 1-inch clear vinyl tubing. I then bend one end of the tubing over the neck of the ammonia jug and fasten it in place with duct tape. The ammonia jug and the tubing are both set out in the bright sun.

Brown-toning takes a day or two of sunlight, depending on the coloration you require. Once you remove the rod section from the tubing, let it air out for a day or so before you take it inside.

Once again, you're working with dangerous materials. Complete this work outdoors, and take all normal precautions recommended by the manufacturer.

APPENDIX A: STEP-BY-STEP CHECKLIST

Select rod taper
- ☐ Length
- ☐ Line weight
- ☐ Action
- ☐ Number of pieces

Select appropriate culm
- ☐ Cut culm (if needed)
- ☐ Prepare nodes (lower half for butt or midsection, upper half for tips)
- ☐ Split culm in half
  - ☐ Flame halves (if desired)

- ☐ Split
  - ☐ Each half into thirds (6 total pieces)
  - ☐ Each third in half (12 total pieces)
  - ☐ Each sixth in half (24 total pieces)

Select
- ☐ 6 strips for butt from lower half of culm
- ☐ 6 strips for mid from lower half of culm
- ☐ 6 strips for first tip from upper half of culm
- ☐ 6 strips for second tip from upper half of culm (if needed)

Stagger strips
- ☐ Cut to working length
- ☐ Mark butt end with red marker

- ☐ Plane diaphragm area
  - ☐ Sharpen blade (if needed)

- ☐ Press nodes and sand node areas
  - ☐ Reflame (if needed)

- ☐ Plane initial 60-degree angle
  - ☐ Check accuracy of angles
  - ☐ Sharpen blade (if needed)

- ☐ Plane second 60-degree angle
  - ☐ Check accuracy of angles
  - ☐ Sharpen plane blade (if needed)

- ☐ Bind strips for heat treatment
  - ☐ Heat-treat
  - ☐ Let cool

- ☐ Determine taper dimensions
- ☐ Double-check

- ☐ Adjust final planing forms
- ☐ Double-check

- ☐ Initiate planing of tapered strips
  - ☐ Alternate sides
  - ☐ Alternate strips
  - ☐ Sharpen plane blade (if needed)

- [ ] Ensure that corners are sharp
    - [ ] Additional planing (if needed)

- [ ] Check angles of strips
    - [ ] Measure the 3 flat-to-point combinations
    - [ ] Correct angles (if needed)

- [ ] Deal with lifting nodes (if needed)
- [ ] Use scraper (if needed)

- [ ] Plane to within 0.005 inch of target dimensions
    - [ ] Additional planing (if needed)

- [ ] Scrape strips to target dimensions
    - [ ] Sharpen scraper blade (if needed)

- [ ] Bundle strips in staggered order
    - [ ] Bind with masking tape

- [ ] Check all seams' tightness at corners
    - [ ] Remake strips (if needed)

- [ ] Prepare all needed elements for gluing
    - [ ] Binder
        - [ ] New belt (if needed)
    - [ ] New toothbrush or glue spreader
    - [ ] Fresh newspaper

- [ ] Glue and bind
    - [ ] Spread and respread glue
    - [ ] Bind (string winding in both directions)

- [ ] Roll and straighten section
    - [ ] Roll section on newspaper
    - [ ] Check and recheck straightness
    - [ ] Hang to allow glue to cure

- [ ] Thermal-set (if needed)
    - [ ] Remove binding thread
    - [ ] Rebind with fresh thread
    - [ ] Thermal-set section (if needed)

- [ ] Clean up section
    - [ ] Remove binding thread
    - [ ] Sand section (removing glue residue and enamel haze)
    - [ ] Retone with Bic lighter (if needed)

Section complete
- [ ] Repeat for butt
- [ ] Repeat for mid (if needed)
- [ ] Repeat for first tip
- [ ] Repeat for second tip (if needed)

- [ ] Select correct ferrules
    - [ ] Prepare ferrules (crowns)

- [ ] Determine ferrule-seating dimensions
    - [ ] Total for more than one

- [ ] Determine exact section length

- [ ] Mount female ferrules

- [ ] Trim and fit tiptops

- [ ] Cut sections to exact length

- [ ] Mount male ferrules
    - [ ] Lap to fit female

- [ ] Determine spline of sections

- [ ] Assemble rod
    - [ ] Straighten (if needed)

☐ Handle
   ☐ Select cork
   ☐ Determine start location
   ☐ Ream (if needed), glue, and clamp cork
   ☐ Turn handle shape

Guides

☐ Select and prepare
☐ Determine location
☐ Wrap and tip
☐ Seal with finish
☐ Trim and sand

Finish

☐ Plug female ferrules
☐ Clean section(s)

☐ Apply finish
   ☐ Sand and clean between coats
☐ Remove ferrule plugs
   ☐ Polish finish from around ferrule opening

Reel seat

☐ Turn reel-seat filler
☐ Finish reel-seat filler
☐ Shim rod shaft with masking tape (if needed)
☐ Mount reel-seat components

☐ Test-cast rod

☐ Rod bag

☐ Rod tube

APPENDIX B: TOOL CHECKLIST

☐ Hacksaw
☐ Bamboo froe
☐ Hard rubber mallet
☐ Wooden mallet
☐ Paintbrush
☐ Mill file (8 inch)
☐ Sanding block
☐ Vise (Pony — altered)
☐ Heat gun with diffuser

Measuring instruments
☐ Dial caliper
☐ Depth gauge
   ☐ With Starrett 6632/6 point
☐ Center gauge
☐ Tape measure (12 foot)

Sharpening system
☐ Blade holder
☐ Blade-setting jig
☐ Coarse sharpening stone (300 to 500 grit)
☐ Fine sharpening stone (1,000 to 1,500 grit)
☐ Polishing stone (6,000 to 8,000 grit)
☐ Plastic tray (for water)

Plane
☐ 9½-style
☐ Hock blade

Forms
☐ First angle
☐ Second angle
☐ Final
☐ Binder or 1½-pound weight/pulley/string
☐ Heat-treating oven or similar device
☐ Cork handle grip
☐ Lathe (wood)
☐ Drill-mounted grinding wheel
☐ Thread tensioner (or thick book)
☐ Scalpel and #11 blades

Finish system
Inexpensive
☐ Piece of clear 4-mil plastic
☐ Pulley
☐ Fly reel

Expensive
☐ Permanent enclosure
☐ DCV gearmotor
☐ SCR control

APPENDIX C: TAPERS

This section contains the stress graphs and tapers for a variety of rods. Any one of the rods made from the tapers in this section would be an excellent choice for a beginner or an expert. If you'd like to design your own rod — or to make a rod with very specific characteristics — refer to Appendix G, which is a discussion of basic rod-design theory.

The Y-axis represents the f (b) (stress) value in inch-ounces while the X-axis gives the location of that value. The X-axis reads from 0 inch at the tip to a length that is equal to the action length of the fly rod. That point is normally located just above the handle, which explains why the graph length is normally 10 inches shorter than the total length of the fly rod. A general statement would be the greater the amplitude (highest value to lowest value), the faster the rod action. A reversed J-looking curve represents a rod with parabolic action.

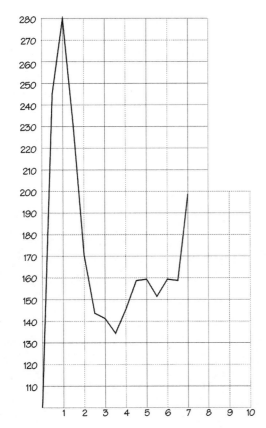

6'0"   DT #3
2-piece
Ferrule size ¹¹/₆₄

	TIP		BUTT
00	0.070	35	0.165
05	0.074	40	0.173
10	0.077	45	0.181
15	0.097	50	0.192
20	0.120	55	0.207
25	0.138	60	0.215
30	0.151	65	0.227
35	0.165	70	0.227
40	0.173	75	0.227

6'0"   DT #3
3-piece
Ferrule sizes ⁹/₆₄ and ¹³/₆₄

	TIP		MID		BUTT
00	0.070	20	0.120	45	0.185
05	0.074	25	0.139	50	0.197
10	0.077	30	0.154	55	0.213
15	0.097	35	0.170	60	0.223
20	0.120	40	0.178	65	0.235
25	0.139	45	0.185	70	0.235
		50	0.197	75	0.235

6'0"   DT #4
2-piece
Ferrule size ¹¹/₆₄

	TIP		BUTT
00	0.070	35	0.169
05	0.074	40	0.177
10	0.079	45	0.185
15	0.100	50	0.196
20	0.123	55	0.211
25	0.142	60	0.220
30	0.155	65	0.231
35	0.169	70	0.231
40	0.177	75	0.231

6'0"   DT #4
3-piece
Ferrule sizes ⁹/₆₄ and ¹³/₆₄

	TIP		MID		BUTT
00	0.070	20	0.123	45	0.189
05	0.074	25	0.144	50	0.201
10	0.079	30	0.159	55	0.218
15	0.100	35	0.175	60	0.228
20	0.123	40	0.183	65	0.241
25	0.144	45	0.189	70	0.241
		50	0.201	75	0.241

6'3" DT #2
2-piece
Ferrule size $^{11}/_{64}$

	TIP		BUTT
00	0.058	35	0.152
05	0.068	40	0.163
10	0.082	45	0.169
15	0.096	50	0.184
20	0.107	55	0.195
25	0.122	60	0.207
30	0.134	65	0.215
35	0.152	70	0.222
40	0.163	75	0.222

6'3" DT #2
3-piece
Ferrule sizes $^{8}/_{64}$ **and** $^{12}/_{64}$

	TIP		MID		BUTT
00	0.058	25	0.122	50	0.185
05	0.068	30	0.136	55	0.198
10	0.082	35	0.156	60	0.210
15	0.096	40	0.167	65	0.219
20	0.107	45	0.171	70	0.227
25	0.122	50	0.185	75	0.227

6'3" DT #3
2-piece
Ferrule size $^{12}/_{64}$

	TIP		BUTT
00	0.070	35	0.169
05	0.077	40	0.180
10	0.093	45	0.186
15	0.109	50	0.198
20	0.121	55	0.213
25	0.137	60	0.225
30	0.149	65	0.233
35	0.169	70	0.233
40	0.180	75	0.233

6'3" DT #3
3-piece
Ferrule sizes $^{9}/_{64}$ **and** $^{13}/_{64}$

	TIP		MID		BUTT
00	0.070	25	0.137	50	0.201
05	0.077	30	0.152	55	0.217
10	0.093	35	0.174	60	0.230
15	0.109	40	0.185	65	0.239
20	0.121	45	0.189	70	0.239

6'3" DT #4
2-piece
Ferrule size $^{12}/_{64}$

	TIP		BUTT
00	0.070	35	0.178
05	0.082	40	0.190
10	0.099	45	0.195
15	0.115	50	0.208
20	0.128	55	0.223
25	0.145	60	0.235
30	0.158	65	0.243
35	0.178	70	0.250
40	0.190	75	0.250

6'3" DT #4
3-piece
Ferrule sizes $^{9}/_{64}$ **and** $^{14}/_{64}$

	TIP		MID		BUTT
00	0.070	25	0.146	50	0.210
05	0.082	30	0.161	55	0.225
10	0.100	35	0.183	60	0.239
15	0.116	40	0.194	65	0.242
20	0.129	45	0.197	70	0.254

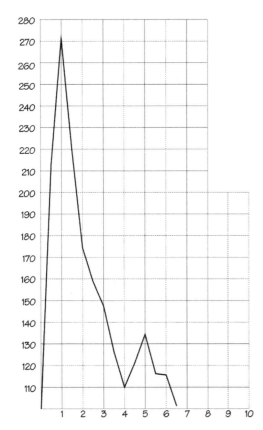

6'3" DT #2
2-piece
Ferrule size ¹⁰/₆₄

TIP		BUTT	
00	0.054	35	0.143
05	0.056	40	0.162
10	0.066	45	0.170
15	0.083	50	0.176
20	0.100	55	0.197
25	0.114	60	0.210
30	0.127	65	0.234
35	0.143	70	0.234
40	0.162	75	0.234

6'3" DT #2
3-piece
Ferrule sizes ⁸/₆₄ and ¹²/₆₄

TIP		MID		BUTT	
00	0.054	25	0.114	50	0.177
05	0.056	30	0.128	55	0.198
10	0.066	35	0.147	60	0.212
15	0.083	40	0.165	65	0.236
20	0.100	45	0.172	70	0.236
25	0.114	50	0.177	75	0.236

6'3" DT #3
2-piece
Ferrule size ¹¹/₆₄

TIP		BUTT	
00	0.061	35	0.158
05	0.063	40	0.178
10	0.074	45	0.186
15	0.092	50	0.192
20	0.112	55	0.214
25	0.126	60	0.228
30	0.140	65	0.253
35	0.158	70	0.253
40	0.178	75	0.253

6'3" DT #3
3-piece
Ferrule sizes ⁹/₆₄ and ¹³/₆₄

TIP		MID		BUTT	
00	0.061	25	0.126	50	0.193
05	0.063	30	0.142	55	0.216
10	0.074	35	0.161	60	0.230
15	0.092	40	0.182	65	0.256
20	0.112	45	0.188	70	0.256
25	0.126	50	0.193	75	0.256

6'3" DT #4
2-piece
Ferrule size ¹²/₆₄

TIP		BUTT	
00	0.066	35	0.168
05	0.068	40	0.190
10	0.080	45	0.198
15	0.099	50	0.204
20	0.120	55	0.227
25	0.135	60	0.241
30	0.149	65	0.267
35	0.168	70	0.267
40	0.190	75	0.267

6'3" DT #4
3-piece
Ferrule sizes ⁹/₆₄ and ¹⁴/₆₄

TIP		MID		BUTT	
00	0.066	25	0.135	50	0.206
05	0.068	30	0.152	55	0.230
10	0.080	35	0.172	60	0.245
15	0.099	40	0.194	65	0.272
20	0.120	45	0.200	70	0.272
25	0.135	50	0.206	75	0.272

6'6" DT #3
2-piece
Ferrule size 11/64

TIP		BUTT	
00	0.070	35	0.158
05	0.079	40	0.171
10	0.088	45	0.185
15	0.104	50	0.199
20	0.119	55	0.213
25	0.133	60	0.227
30	0.146	65	0.240
35	0.158	70	0.240
40	0.171	75	0.240
		78	0.240

6'6" DT #3
3-piece
Ferrule sizes 9/64 and 14/64

TIP		MID		BUTT	
00	0.070	25	0.133	50	0.201
05	0.079	30	0.148	55	0.215
10	0.088	35	0.162	60	0.230
15	0.104	40	0.176	65	0.245
20	0.119	45	0.188	70	0.245
25	0.133	50	0.201	75	0.245
30	0.148	55	0.215	78	0.245

6'6" DT #4
2-piece
Ferrule size 12/64

TIP		BUTT	
00	0.070	35	0.163
05	0.080	40	0.175
10	0.091	45	0.191
15	0.107	50	0.205
20	0.123	55	0.218
25	0.138	60	0.233
30	0.151	65	0.246
35	0.163	70	0.246
40	0.175	75	0.246
		78	0.246

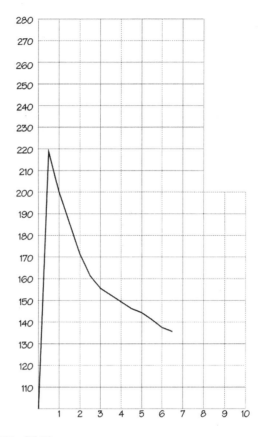

6'6" DT #4
3-piece
Ferrule sizes 9/64 and 14/64

TIP		MID		BUTT	
00	0.070	25	0.138	50	0.206
05	0.080	30	0.153	55	0.220
10	0.091	35	0.167	60	0.235
15	0.107	40	0.181	65	0.250
20	0.123	45	0.193	70	0.250
25	0.138	50	0.206	75	0.250
30	0.153	55	0.220	78	0.250

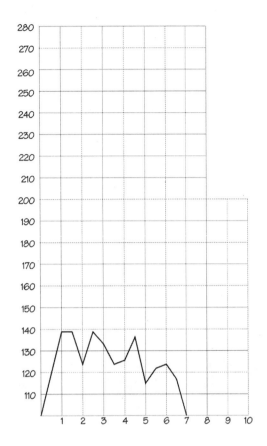

7′0″   DT #3/4
2-piece
Ferrule size $^{12}/_{64}$

	TIP		BUTT
00	0.074	40	0.182
05	0.087	45	0.190
10	0.100	50	0.216
15	0.116	55	0.226
20	0.135	60	0.238
25	0.142	65	0.256
30	0.156	70	0.286
35	0.172	75	0.286
40	0.182	80	0.286
45	0.190	85	0.286

7′0″   DT #3/4
3-piece
Ferrule sizes $^{10}/_{64}$ and $^{15}/_{64}$

	TIP		MID		BUTT
00	0.074	25	0.143	55	0.230
05	0.087	30	0.158	60	0.244
10	0.100	35	0.176	65	0.263
15	0.117	40	0.189	70	0.296
20	0.136	45	0.196	75	0.296
25	0.143	50	0.221	80	0.296
30	0.158	55	0.230	85	0.296
		60	0.244		

7'0" DT #2
2-piece
Ferrule size ¹¹/₆₄

	TIP		BUTT
00	0.059	40	0.164
05	0.061	45	0.184
10	0.072	50	0.193
15	0.090	55	0.199
20	0.108	60	0.221
25	0.121	65	0.235
30	0.135	70	0.248
35	0.148	75	0.274
40	0.164	80	0.274
45	0.184	84	0.274

7'0" DT #2
3-piece
Ferrule sizes ⁸/₆₄ and ¹³/₆₄

	TIP		MID		BUTT
00	0.059	25	0.121	55	0.198
05	0.061	30	0.135	60	0.221
10	0.072	35	0.150	65	0.235
15	0.090	40	0.168	70	0.250
20	0.108	45	0.187	75	0.276
25	0.121	50	0.193	80	0.276
30	0.135	55	0.198	84	0.276
		60	0.221		

7'0" DT #3
2-piece
Ferrule size ¹³/₆₄

	TIP		BUTT
00	0.066	40	0.182
05	0.068	45	0.202
10	0.080	50	0.209
15	0.099	55	0.213
20	0.119	60	0.237
25	0.133	65	0.251
30	0.148	70	0.266
35	0.163	75	0.293
40	0.182	80	0.293
45	0.202	84	0.293

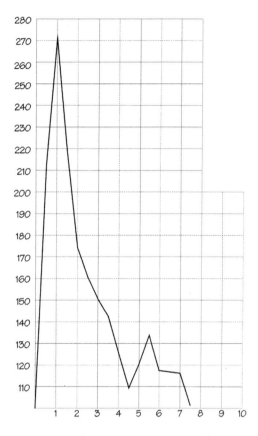

7'0" DT #3
3-piece
Ferrule sizes ⁹/₆₄ and ¹⁴/₆₄

	TIP		MID		BUTT
00	0.066	25	0.133	55	0.213
05	0.068	30	0.148	60	0.237
10	0.080	35	0.163	65	0.251
15	0.099	40	0.182	70	0.266
20	0.119	45	0.202	75	0.294
25	0.133	50	0.209	80	0.294
30	0.148	55	0.213	84	0.294
		60	0.237		

7'0"   DT #4
2-piece
Ferrule size $^{13}/_{64}$

TIP		BUTT	
00	0.068	40	0.184
05	0.070	45	0.206
10	0.082	50	0.214
15	0.102	55	0.220
20	0.123	60	0.244
25	0.137	65	0.258
30	0.152	70	0.272
35	0.166	75	0.300
40	0.184	80	0.300
45	0.206	85	0.300

7'0"   DT #4
3-piece
Ferrule sizes $^{10}/_{64}$ and $^{15}/_{64}$

TIP		MID		BUTT	
00	0.068	25	0.137	55	0.225
05	0.070	30	0.154	60	0.250
10	0.082	35	0.171	65	0.266
15	0.102	40	0.191	70	0.282
20	0.123	45	0.213	75	0.311
25	0.137	50	0.220	80	0.311
30	0.154	55	0.225	85	0.311
		60	0.250		

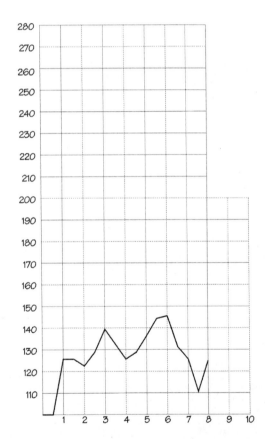

7'3"   DT #3/4
2-piece
Ferrule size $^{13}/_{64}$

TIP		BUTT	
00	0.074	40	0.183
05	0.090	45	0.194
10	0.103	50	0.204
15	0.120	55	0.214
20	0.135	60	0.226
25	0.146	65	0.247
30	0.154	70	0.264
35	0.168	75	0.288
40	0.183	80	0.290
45	0.194	85	0.290
		90	0.290

7'3"   DT #3/4
3-piece
Ferrule sizes $^{10}/_{64}$ and $^{15}/_{64}$

TIP		MID		BUTT	
00	0.074	25	0.147	55	0.217
05	0.090	30	0.156	60	0.229
10	0.103	35	0.172	65	0.252
15	0.121	40	0.189	70	0.271
20	0.136	45	0.200	75	0.299
25	0.147	50	0.208	80	0.299
30	0.156	55	0.217	85	0.299
		60	0.229	90	0.299

7′6″ DT #4
2-piece
Ferrule size ¹³/₆₄

	TIP		BUTT
00	0.070	45	0.203
05	0.081	50	0.214
10	0.094	55	0.225
15	0.115	60	0.237
20	0.134	65	0.246
25	0.146	70	0.257
30	0.155	75	0.268
35	0.170	80	0.275
40	0.192	85	0.275
45	0.203	90	0.275

7′6″ DT #4
3-piece
Ferrule sizes ¹⁰/₆₄ and ¹⁵/₆₄

	TIP		MID		BUTT
00	0.070	30	0.155	60	0.239
05	0.081	35	0.172	65	0.249
10	0.094	40	0.196	70	0.261
15	0.115	45	0.208	75	0.273
20	0.134	50	0.217	80	0.281
25	0.146	55	0.227	85	0.281
30	0.155	60	0.239	90	0.281

7′6″ DT #5
2-piece
Ferrule size ¹⁴/₆₄

	TIP		BUTT
00	0.070	45	0.210
05	0.085	50	0.221
10	0.098	55	0.233
15	0.119	60	0.245
20	0.139	65	0.255
25	0.151	70	0.266
30	0.160	75	0.277
35	0.176	80	0.284
40	0.199	85	0.284
45	0.210	90	0.284

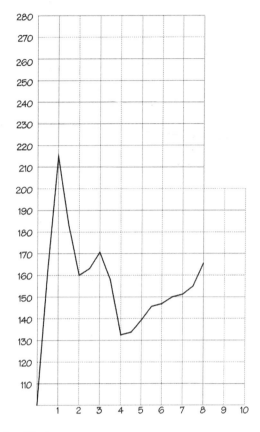

7′6″ DT #5
3-piece
Ferrule sizes ¹¹/₆₄ and ¹⁶/₆₄

	TIP		MID		BUTT
00	0.070	30	0.160	60	0.247
05	0.081	35	0.178	65	0.257
10	0.097	40	0.205	70	0.270
15	0.119	45	0.215	75	0.282
20	0.139	50	0.225	80	0.289
25	0.151	55	0.235	85	0.289
30	0.160	60	0.247	90	0.289

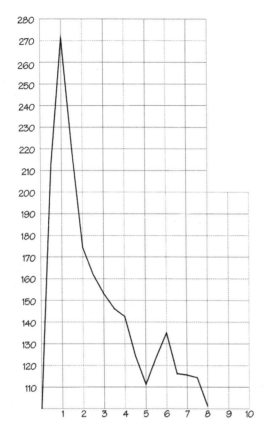

7′6″   DT #2
2-piece
Ferrule size ¹¹/₆₄

	TIP		BUTT
00	0.054	45	0.164
05	0.056	50	0.185
10	0.066	55	0.192
15	0.083	60	0.196
20	0.101	65	0.219
25	0.113	70	0.232
30	0.125	75	0.245
35	0.136	80	0.271
40	0.147	85	0.271
45	0.164	90	0.271

7′6″   DT #2
3-piece
Ferrule sizes ⁸/₆₄ and ¹³/₆₄

	TIP		MID		BUTT
00	0.054	30	0.125	60	0.197
05	0.056	35	0.138	65	0.219
10	0.066	40	0.150	70	0.233
15	0.083	45	0.167	75	0.247
20	0.101	50	0.187	80	0.273
25	0.113	55	0.193	85	0.273
30	0.125	60	0.197	90	0.273

7′6″   DT #3
2-piece
Ferrule size ¹²/₆₄

	TIP		BUTT
00	0.061	45	0.179
05	0.063	50	0.202
10	0.074	55	0.209
15	0.092	60	0.214
20	0.112	65	0.237
25	0.124	70	0.251
30	0.138	75	0.264
35	0.150	80	0.291
40	0.162	85	0.291
45	0.179	90	0.291

7′6″   DT #3
3-piece
Ferrule sizes ⁹/₆₄ and ¹⁴/₆₄

	TIP		MID		BUTT
00	0.061	30	0.138	60	0.215
05	0.063	35	0.152	65	0.238
10	0.074	40	0.165	70	0.253
15	0.092	45	0.183	75	0.267
20	0.112	50	0.204	80	0.295
25	0.124	55	0.210	85	0.295
30	0.138	60	0.215	90	0.295

7'6"   DT #4
2-piece
Ferrule size ¹³/₆₄

TIP		BUTT	
00	0.066	45	0.190
05	0.068	50	0.214
10	0.080	55	0.221
15	0.099	60	0.226
20	0.119	65	0.251
25	0.133	70	0.265
30	0.148	75	0.279
35	0.160	80	0.307
40	0.172	85	0.307
45	0.190	90	0.307

7'6"   DT #4
3-piece
Ferrule sizes ¹⁰/₆₄ and ¹⁵/₆₄

TIP		MID		BUTT	
00	0.066	30	0.148	60	0.227
05	0.068	35	0.162	65	0.252
10	0.080	40	0.175	70	0.267
15	0.099	45	0.195	75	0.281
20	0.119	50	0.217	80	0.310
25	0.133	55	0.223	85	0.310
30	0.148	60	0.227	90	0.310

7'6"   DT #4/5
2-piece
Ferrule size ¹⁴/₆₄

TIP		BUTT	
00	0.070	45	0.218
05	0.078	50	0.223
10	0.108	55	0.235
15	0.125	60	0.255
20	0.140	65	0.267
25	0.152	70	0.285
30	0.165	75	0.290
35	0.182	80	0.295
40	0.195	85	0.295
45	0.218	90	0.295

7'6"   DT #4/5
3-piece
Ferrule sizes ¹¹/₆₄ and ¹⁷/₆₄

TIP		MID		BUTT	
00	0.070	30	0.165	60	0.258
05	0.078	35	0.185	65	0.271
10	0.108	40	0.200	70	0.291
15	0.125	45	0.225	75	0.297
20	0.140	50	0.228	80	0.297
25	0.152	55	0.237	85	0.297
30	0.165	60	0.258	90	0.297

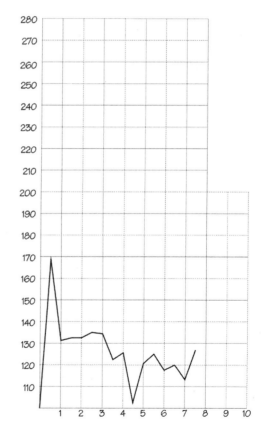

7'6"   DT #5
2-piece
Ferrule size ¹⁴/₆₄

	TIP		BUTT
00	0.070	45	0.218
05	0.095	50	0.232
10	0.118	55	0.240
15	0.135	60	0.248
20	0.148	65	0.262
25	0.163	70	0.280
30	0.180	75	0.295
35	0.197	80	0.300
40	0.211	85	0.300
45	0.218	90	0.300

7'6"   DT #5
3-piece
Ferrule sizes ¹²/₆₄ and ¹⁶/₆₄

	TIP		MID		BUTT
00	0.070	30	0.180	60	0.248
05	0.095	35	0.199	65	0.263
10	0.118	40	0.215	70	0.282
15	0.135	45	0.222	75	0.298
20	0.148	50	0.235	80	0.303
25	0.164	55	0.241	85	0.303
30	0.180	60	0.248	90	0.303

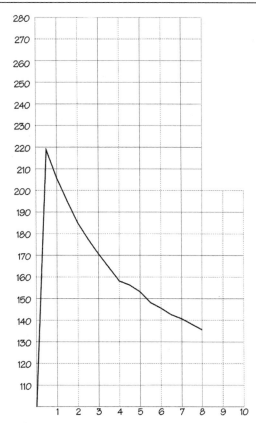

7'9"   DT #2/3
2-piece
Ferrule size ¹²/₆₄

	TIP		BUTT
00	0.062	45	0.164
05	0.064	50	0.177
10	0.083	55	0.191
15	0.097	60	0.203
20	0.109	65	0.216
25	0.121	70	0.228
30	0.131	75	0.241
35	0.142	80	0.254
40	0.153	85	0.288
45	0.164	90	0.288
50	0.177	95	0.288

7'9"   DT #4
2-piece
Ferrule size ¹³/₆₄

	TIP		BUTT
00	0.070	45	0.182
05	0.078	50	0.195
10	0.090	55	0.210
15	0.106	60	0.223
20	0.120	65	0.237
25	0.133	70	0.250
30	0.146	75	0.264
35	0.158	80	0.278
40	0.170	85	0.278
45	0.182	90	0.278
50	0.195	95	0.278

7'9"   DT #4
3-piece
Ferrule sizes ¹⁰/₆₄ and ¹⁵/₆₄

	TIP		MID		BUTT
00	0.070	30	0.146	60	0.226
05	0.078	35	0.169	65	0.240
10	0.090	40	0.174	70	0.255
15	0.106	45	0.187	75	0.270
20	0.120	50	0.199	80	0.285
25	0.136	55	0.213	85	0.285
30	0.146	60	0.226	90	0.285
35	0.169	65	0.240	95	0.285

8'0" DT #4
2-piece
Ferrule size 13/64

	TIP		BUTT
00	0.060	45	0.187
05	0.072	50	0.201
10	0.089	55	0.213
15	0.102	60	0.222
20	0.115	65	0.230
25	0.130	70	0.238
30	0.142	75	0.249
35	0.158	80	0.258
40	0.173	85	0.261
45	0.187	90	0.261
50	0.201	95	0.261
		96	0.261

8'0" DT #4
3-piece
Ferrule sizes 10/64 and 15/64

	TIP		MID		BUTT
00	0.060	35	0.160	60	0.222
05	0.072	40	0.176	65	0.230
10	0.089	45	0.191	70	0.238
15	0.102	50	0.204	75	0.249
20	0.115	55	0.214	80	0.258
25	0.130	60	0.222	85	0.262
30	0.142	65	0.230	90	0.262
35	0.160			95	0.262
				96	0.262

8'0" DT #5
2-piece
Ferrule size 14/64

	TIP		BUTT
00	0.070	45	0.204
05	0.080	50	0.218
10	0.098	55	0.230
15	0.113	60	0.238
20	0.126	65	0.247
25	0.143	70	0.255
30	0.155	75	0.266
35	0.173	80	0.274
40	0.189	85	0.278
45	0.204	90	0.278
50	0.218	95	0.278
		96	0.278

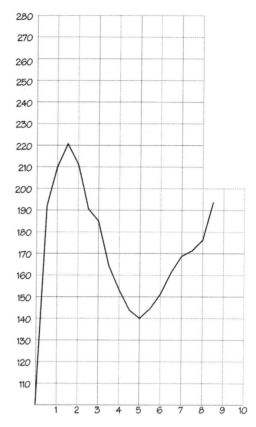

8'0" DT #5
3-piece
Ferrule sizes 11/64 and 16/64

	TIP		MID		BUTT
00	0.070	30	0.155	60	0.241
05	0.080	35	0.174	65	0.248
10	0.098	40	0.192	70	0.257
15	0.112	45	0.208	75	0.269
20	0.126	50	0.223	80	0.279
25	0.143	55	0.234	85	0.282
30	0.155	60	0.241	90	0.282
35	0.174	65	0.248	95	0.282
				96	0.282

8′0″   DT #6
2-piece
Ferrule size 15/64

TIP		BUTT	
00	0.074	45	0.225
05	0.089	50	0.239
10	0.109	55	0.251
15	0.125	60	0.260
20	0.140	65	0.268
25	0.158	70	0.278
30	0.172	75	0.287
35	0.191	80	0.297
40	0.208	85	0.300
45	0.225	90	0.300
50	0.239	95	0.300
		96	0.300

8′0″   DT #6
3-piece
Ferrule sizes 12/64 and 18/64

TIP		MID		BUTT	
00	0.074	30	0.172	60	0.262
05	0.089	35	0.193	65	0.270
10	0.110	40	0.211	70	0.280
15	0.125	45	0.229	75	0.291
20	0.140	50	0.244	80	0.301
25	0.159	55	0.255	85	0.305
30	0.172	60	0.262	90	0.305
35	0.193	65	0.270	95	0.305
				96	0.305

The Ballan Special

This particular rod design was requested by Bill Ballan, the famous reelmaker, when he was looking for a special three-piece 7-foot, 6-inch rod with a single butt section that could be assembled into a #3-weight or a #5-weight. The butt section is a #4-weight and the rest is assembled with either a #3- or #5-weight tip and midsection. As a #5-weight, the action of the rod is slowed by the lesser-weighted butt section, and as a #3-weight, the action is quickened by the overweighted butt.

To create the specifications, I used the Hexrod computer program, which is discussed in more detail in Appendix G, and which can be downloaded from my Web site at www.wcattanachrodco.com. The numbers for a #3- and a #5-weight rod taper (created from a common character curve) were plotted on the same graph. The butt dimensions were gleaned by calculations from an average of the two butts. Then, from the mid-end of the butt section, lines were drawn to join into each of the tip dimensions. Finally, to maintain a resemblance to the original design modified offsets were added at appropriate locations. The precise numbers were obtained from the graph, and the rod sections were constructed. In the time since I made this initial rod for Bill, I have applied the same technique to other rod designs.

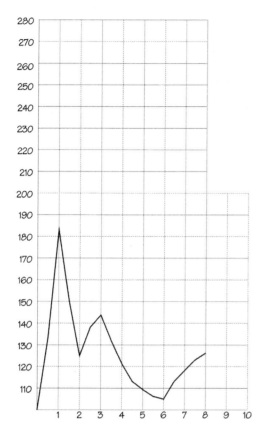

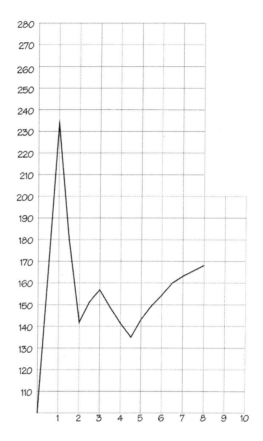

7'6" DT #3 & 5
(Bill Ballan Special)
3-piece
Ferrule sizes ⁹/₆₄ and ¹¹/₆₄ and ¹⁵/₆₄

First	#3	#5	Second	#3	#5	Third	
00	0.063	0.070	30	0.141	0.160	60	0.234
05	0.073	0.081	35	0.158	0.176	65	0.244
10	0.084	0.092	40	0.175	0.192	70	0.255
15	0.104	0.116	45	0.192	0.207	75	0.266
20	0.124	0.140	50	0.206	0.216	80	0.277
25	0.132	0.150	55	0.220	0.225	85	0.277
30	0.141	0.160	60	0.234	0.234	90	0.277

APPENDIX D:
DESIGNER COLORS

Ever since I first wrote about the idea of making our daughter a purple fly rod, I have had people ask me about color-toning of bamboo. For those who haven't heard the story, I made our son, Matt, a fly rod for Christmas the year he was 13. Lyndi, who is five years younger, let me know a short while later that when I made her fly rod, she wanted it to be purple. And I, like most dads, agreed to do it.

Well, she didn't have to wait until she was 13 to get her special rod. At the age of 11 she informed us that when we went up north to go fishing, she was going as well. So on the opening weekend of 1993 Lyndi was fishing the fabled North Branch of the Au Sable River with her 6-foot, 3-inch, three-piece, #4-weight purple bamboo fly rod. It also has a purpleheart reel-seat filler, and Ron Barch made a special tiger-striped maple Halcyon rod case that is — of course — also purple.

The truth is that the rod isn't exactly purple. It was only purple until I coated it with finish. It seems that the yellow tint of the polyurethane filtered the purple to a deep rich red. That's something I would've realized if I'd thought about it. Lyndi says it looks great.

(I'm not trying to start a trend of designer-colored fly rods here. However, color-toning can have some practical applications — especially if you flame- or brown-tone your fly rods.)

When I originally tried to tone bamboo I used chemicals, some of which were harsh. Then one day I was in a local art store and I got caught up in the myriad of new colored markers that the artists are using. It was then that I decided to switch from chemicals to water-based markers.

Because all the rods I make are flamed, I was also looking for a better way to touch up areas that I had sanded too much or that featured weak flaming. Before I started using colored markers, I had done these touch-ups with a bubble buster — an alcohol lamp with an intensifier nozzle. This was a little nerve-racking when I was trying to touch up glued tip sections — if I applied too much heat I could ruin the rod.

Now these touch-ups are easy and safe. Choosing one of several tones of brown, I simply wipe the marker across the weak area, wait for the color to dry, and then feather it in with a Q-Tip. If I'm not satisfied the first time, I simply wipe the color off the shaft and try again.

Once I'm satisfied with the area, I cover it with a light coating of tung oil to lock the color in place. I apply the oil by gently dabbing rather than spreading it with my finger or a cloth. The tung oil can and will lift the color from the rod shaft if you aren't careful. Lightly dabbing the tung oil into place keeps the added color from moving.

I don't need to use this trick often, but it certainly is a good one to know. It's handy if you go to Michigan and want a blue rod shaft with gold trim.

P.S. On that Fourth of July weekend Lyndi and I went fishing on several streams, and she landed her first solo trout with her purple rod. It was a 7-inch brook trout. Needless to say, we were both elated.

APPENDIX E: THE SOCIAL RODMAKER

As more and more people have gotten involved with bamboo rodmaking, the craft has become more social. It's not that it wasn't social in the past, just that there weren't enough people involved to create a crowd. Today there are several established get-togethers across North America, as well as others starting each year on a more local basis. Each seems to have its own character, but all of them blend shared information and good fun.

Corbett Lake, British Columbia

The Corbett Lake Workshop is a biennial event taking place on the last weekend of April on even-numbered years. It is the original event — always well organized and boasting attendees from around the world.

Catskills (Roscoe, New York)

Held at the Catskills Fly Fishing Center and Museum, this gathering has become very popular with rodmakers from the Northeast. It takes place on the weekend after Labor Day. Ken Gaucher and Robert Reid have acted as the organizers.

Grand River (Fergus, Ontario)

Held on the Memorial Day weekend, the Grand Gathering is just what its name suggests: a mix of well-presented demonstrations and excellent fishing. Ted Knott (905-304-0388) and several other rodmakers organize the event.

Grayrock (Grayling, Michigan)

Held officially the weekend after Father's Day, but unofficially anytime after the Father's Day weekend. It's supposed to coincide with the hex hatch. It features demonstrations, hands-on workshops, and "The Trout Bum BBQ."

Rodmakers (Internet e-mail repeater)

For more information about this and other Web sites of interest, contact the author at http://www.wcattanachrodco.com or check out http://www.canerod.com/rodmakers.

APPENDIX F: SOURCES

Please note that my list of sources is extremely selective and not comprehensive. And I hope I don't annoy those suppliers who aren't included. However, I only build a few rods each year, so I don't need a long list of supplies. In fact, some of my purchases will likely last a lifetime.

At the same time, I may have sources that would be helpful if you're serious about the craft of rodmaking. I would also be pleased to hear from other rodmakers about suggestions for future editions of this book.

General Rodmaking Supplies

Golden Witch Technologies
P.O. Box 159
Hopeland, PA 17533
717-738-7330
www.goldenwitch.com
Russ Gooding

Munro Rod Company
800-836-7558
www.munrorodco.com
Jon Lintvet

Sweet Water Rods
258 Main Street
Shoemakersville, PA 19555
610-562-8595
George Maurer

Adhesives

Nelson Paint
P.O. Box 907
Iron Mountain, MI 49801
906-774-5566
(URAC 185)

Nyatex
2112 Industrial
Howell, MI 48843
517-546-4046
Bill Hulbert
(Epoxy 10EH008/10E007)

Agate Stripping Guides

Daryll Whitehead
611 Northwest 48th Street
Seattle, WA 98107
206-781-0133

Bamboo

Charles H. Demarest Inc.
P.O. Box 238
Bloomingdale, NJ 07403
201-492-1414
Harold and Eileen Demarest

Binder

William Olsen
26121 Lawrence Road
Charlottesville, VA 22901
804-973-0896
(Beautiful Garrison-style brass binders)

Bubble Buster

Angler's Workshop
P.O. Box 1010
1350 Atlantic Avenue
Woodland, WA 98674
206-225-9445
Jim Britt

Cork

C & D Trading
P.O. Box 21072
Minneapolis, MN 55421
612-571-3832
Christ Kishish

Ferrules

Belvoirdale
P.O. Box 176
Wyncote, PA 19095-0176
215-886-7211
Grahame Maisey

Classic Sporting Enterprises
Roaring Brook Road
R.F.D. #3, Box 3
Barton, VT 05822
802-525-3623

Cortland-Rodon
P.O. Box 5588
Cortland, NY 13045
607-756-2851

REC Components
72 Shaker Road
Enfield, CT 06082
860-749-7977

Fingernail Bit

Cascade Tools Inc.
P.O. Box 3110
Bellingham, WA 98227-3110
800-235-0272
(Part C-1215)

Machinist Tools

Manhattan Supply Company
75 Maxess Road
Melville, NY 11747
800-645-7270

ENCO
5000 West Bloomingdale
Chicago, IL 60639
800-860-3400

Mica Strip Heaters

Grand Technologies
4513C Broadmoor
Grand Rapids, MI 49512
616-656-0866
Dan Schroeder

Mildrum Stripping Guides

REC Components
72 Shaker Road
Enfield, CT 06082
860-749-3476

Miscellaneous Rod Compnents

AER
6551 Clark Road
Bath, MI 48808
517-641-7277
Al Rohen
(Tax license required)

Nickel Silver

Corey Steel
P.O. Box 5605
Chicago, IL 60680
or
2800 South 61st Court
Cicero, IL 60804-3091
708-863-8000
800-323-2750

Threads

The Atlanta Thread Supply Company
695 Red Oak Road
Stockbridge, GA 30281
800-847-1001
(Glazed cotton 24/4 for tips, 16/4 for butts)

Hobby World
2851 Clyde Park
Wyoming, MI 49506
616-538-6130
(75-pound braided kite string for drive belts)

Three-Jaw Wood Lathe Chuck

Grizzly Imports, Inc.
P.O. Box 2069
Bellingham, WA 98227
800-541-5537

Plane Blades

The Japan Woodworker
1731 Clement Avenue
Alameda, CA 94501
800-537-7820

Hock Blades

Garrett Wade Company
161 Avenue of the Americas
New York, NY 10013
212-807-1757

Planing Forms

Frank Armbruster
18599 East Louisana
Aurora, CO 80017
303-745-1353
(Push-pull style)

Bellinger Reel Seats
2017 25th Street Southeast
Salem, OR 97302-1121
503-371-6151

Lon Blauvelt
15 Town Landing Road
Falmouth, ME 04105
207-781-5235
(Push-pull style)

Grindstone Angler
24 Mill Street North
P.O. Box 442
Waterdown, Ontario L0R 2H0
905-689-0880

Jeff Wagner
6549 Kingsdale Road
Parma Heights, OH 44130
440-845-4415

Reel Seats

Bellinger Reel Seats
2017 25th Street Southeast
Salem, OR 97302-1121
503-371-6151

REC Components
72 Shaker Road
Enfield, CT 06082
860-749-3476

Glen Struble Manufacturing Company
206 West View Drive
Roseburg, OR 97470
503-673-7977

Scrapers

Lie-Nielsen Toolworks
P.O. Box 9
Warren, ME 04864
207-273-2520
Tom Lie-Nielsen
(Reproduction 212)

The Japan Woodworker
1731 Clement Avenue
Alameda, CA 94501
800-537-7820
(Reproduction 212)

Snake Guides

Snake Brand
1006 Foothill Drive
Newberg, OR 97132
503-537-1908
Mike McCoy

Waterstones

The Japan Woodworker
1731 Clement Avenue
Alameda, CA 94501
800-537-7820
(King 1,000/6,000 combo)

APPENDIX G: THE CHARACTER OF A FLY ROD

The information contained here is for rodmakers who would like to better understand the physics involved in designing a rod from the ground up. It's also a good primer for the HEXROD computer program I wrote, which you can download from my Web site (www.wcattanachrodco.com). The HEXROD progrm is a powerful and flexible tool that you can use to extrapolate the stress curves of a given design or create a design from a given set of stress-curve characteristics.

The real credit for much of the research in rod design should go to Everett Garrison, whom I've mentioned several times in this book. In his *Master's Guide to Building a Bamboo Fly Rod* he presents a mathematical model for fly-rod design using stress curves. He refers to extreme fiber in bending, or f(b).

Garrison determined the moments (forces) created by the various weights of the line, bamboo, ferrules, guides, and finish at locations throughout the length of a fly rod. He then applied the character of an f(b) stress curve, which was a unique way of observing these elements. Instead of using a fixed figure, he chose to vary the value to either increase or decrease the flexure of the fly rod. His normal stress curve started with high values for the tip and gradually diminished the values through the length of the rod. This allotted the greatest flexure to the tip and gradually stiffened the rod into the butt.

To make Garrison's model less intimidating, I prefer to call these stress curves "character curves." Different fly rods cast with different characters. Stress curves simply reflect that character graphically. Expanding on this notion suggests that fly rods with different line weights can all have the same character — *if* their designs are all based on a common character curve. Granted, they may require different amounts of energy to cast properly, but they will still cast with the same character.

A New Era

Mr. Garrison developed his design ideas and mathematical principles in the late 1920s and early 1930s. During this period his only aids were paper, pencil, and slide rule. Today even the simplest calculators can help you with the required mathematics. What might have taken Garrison several days to complete can now be done in an evening. When I started working with software in the early 1970s, I saw Garrison's math as an ideal application for a computer. But even with a computer involved, you still need an understanding of both the mathematics and the complexities of a fly rod.

Because the planing forms Garrison used were adjusted at 5-inch intervals, the mathematics and graphs he developed have reflected this premise. He was unique in this respect; many other classic rodmakers worked in intervals of 6, 3, or even 1½ inches. For this reason I chose to write a computer program that would accept and work with information in 1-inch increments.

Expanding on Garrison's model, I felt that a ruler needed to be created. By a "ruler" I mean a standard that can be used to investigate or compare all rods. Unlike Garrison, I was looking for a bidirectional model. Not only would it calculate rod dimensions from stress curves, but it also had to calculate stress-curve information from existing fly-rod dimensions. In this way different fly-rod actions could be plotted and compared. Eventually, elements of different fly-rod designs could be blended to create new fly-rod tapers.

Action Length

Because you grip a fly rod with your hand, most rodmakers feel that the actual effect of a rod design ends at the cork grip. The techniques used in the design process are the same as those used for cantilevered beams. Consequently, the grip of the fly rod becomes the anchor point of the extended "beam." As a result, the action length — the part of the rod that reflects character — is the distance from the tiptop to the top of the cork grip.

The planing forms are set in 5-inch increments, so a figure for the action length that is divisible by 5 is always chosen. As an example, an 8-foot (96-inch) fly rod usually has a 7-inch cork grip and a 3½-inch reel seat. If the length of the grip and reel seat are subtracted from the overall length, the remainder is then the action length:

$$96 - 10\frac{1}{2} = 85\frac{1}{2}$$

In this case, a figure of 85 inches is used. In cases where a 5-inch increment does not fall close

to the end of the grip, you must decide whether to use an action length either ahead of the grip or buried under it.

Moments

A *moment* is defined as "a force attempting to cause rotation about a defined point." To be even more specific, the direction of force and the arm of leverage must be perpendicular. For example, look at tightening a nut with a wrench. Let's use these given factors: From the center of the nut to the center of the hand applying the force, the distance is 1 foot, or 12 inches. And the hand is applying a pressure of 1 pound, or 16 ounces. Then the moments of this example would be as follows:

```
L x P = M
1 foot x 1 pound = 1 foot pound
1 foot x 16 ounces = 16 foot ounces
12 inches x 1 pound = 12 inch pounds
12 inches x 16 ounces = 192 inch ounces
```

All of the above calculations and terms are equally correct. For my purposes, however, working with inch ounces will be the easiest method. I'll use inches to measure distance (L), and ounces to measure weight (P).

Impact Factor

Essentially this force is determined by the actual weight being hung off the tip of the fly rod — multiplied by a safety factor. The weight is actually that of the fly line being fished plus the weight of the tiptop itself, added together and expressed in ounces. This figure is then multiplied by 4, which is the safety factor.

Remember that Garrison's mathematics deal with static design, meaning that the elements are at rest. In real life a fly rod is a dynamic device; it sees motion and external forces other than those of just static weights. To visualize this concept, consider the fly line on the water surface. When the cast is started, not only is the weight of the fly line being lifted but also the surface drag applied by the water contact. The 4x multiplier was derived through similar tests that Garrison performed himself.

To better illustrate an impact factor, take a look back at the example I used to explain a moment (force). Remember the 1-pound force at the end of a 12-inch-long wrench? Of course, not all nuts loosen with just a steadily applied force. So you reach into the tool box for the hammer, which weighs 16 ounces. But you don't just position the hammer at the end of the wrench; usually you take a good swat at it. When the hammer "impacts" the wrench, the moments created far exceed that of the original static design.

Consider the difference between the two loads applied to the wrench as the safety factor. The designer of the wrench knew that the product was probably going to be misused in this fashion and built in a margin of safety.

Material Differences

Now also consider that there are variables involved in the material from which the wrench is constructed. It might be made of new steel or it might be recycled steel from that '63 Chevy you hauled to the junkyard. Each will have different structural properties. In wood construction, the soundness of the different types of wood is divided into the varying grades of lumber. Each grade has its limits with respect to defects, and those boards with excessive flaws fall into a lower structural grade. Through the grading process there can be less added safety factor, because the window of potential defects is narrowed.

In a sense, we need a grading process for the bamboo that will be used to make fly rods. Remember when you were choosing the "appropriate" culm? You were selecting a culm that had enough power-fiber depth to match or exceed the dimensions of your particular rod design. By being selective, you're narrowing the margin of possible variation from rod to rod. The flooring system in your house (for example) can be designed too solidly with no adverse effects. However, a #4-weight rod might become a #5-weight if you don't keep the tolerances of your materials and dimensions within specific limits.

Let me show you an example. At present, fly line is classified by the weight (in grains) of its first 30 feet. For a #4-weight fly line, this is 120 grains. A standard tiptop weighs about 8 grains. Because you'll be working in ounces, these figures need to be converted. There are 437 grains per ounce. The tip-impact factor would then be determined as follows:

$$Line = 120 \div 347 = 0.275 \text{ ounces}$$
$$Tiptop = 8 \div 437 = 0.018 \text{ ounces}$$
$$Total = 0.293 \text{ ounces}$$
$$Factor = \times 4$$
$$Tip\ impact = 1.172 \text{ ounces}$$

It's unlikely that you'd ever wish to design a rod that casts 30 feet, the distance at which all fly-line weights are standardized. So a simpler and still reasonably accurate method is to weigh the entire fly line. Then determine a weight per foot by dividing this total weight by the total length of the fly line. The resulting value will be weight per foot, which you can then multiply by the desired line length.

Tip Moments

Once you've determined the tip impact, you can calculate the moments created by the tip impact.

For an action length, imagine that you're designing a 7-foot, 6-inch (90-inch) rod. Together the normal handle and reel seat are 10 inches, so the action length of the 7-foot, 6-inch rod is 80 inches. And because the planing forms are set at 5-inch increments, the calculations of the tip impact would be as follows:

$$\text{Tip} \quad (1.172 \times 0) \quad = \quad 0.00$$
$$5'' \quad (1.172 \times 5) \quad = \quad 5.860$$
$$10'' \quad (1.172 \times 10) = 11.720$$
$$\bullet$$
$$\bullet$$
$$80'' \quad (1.172 \times 80) = 93.760$$

Line-in-Guide Moments

To account for the line as it passes down the rod, you need to determine the center of gravity for each location. You could also think of this as the balance point. For example, if the point under investigation is at a 5-inch location, then the center of gravity would be 2.5 inches, because the line is of uniform weight.

The line weight is always calculated for the appropriate line size. Looking back to our other line example, if 30 feet of #4-weight line weighs 120 grains, 1 inch weighs 0.334 grain or 0.0008 ounce. So the moments for the line on the rod would be as follows:

$$\text{Tip} \quad (0.0008 \times 0 \times 0 \times 4) \quad = \quad 0.0000$$
$$5'' \quad (0.0008 \times 5 \times 2.5 \times 4) \quad = \quad 0.100$$
$$10'' \quad (0.0008 \times 10 \times 5 \times 4) \quad = \quad 0.160$$
$$\bullet$$
$$\bullet$$
$$80'' \quad (0.0008 \times 80 \times 40 \times 4) = 10.240$$

Varnish and Guide Moments

Because of their diminished effect on the final results, Garrison calculated these values once and then used those figures as a standard for all future

rod designs. Even with the added power of a computer, it would be impractical to set up an algorithm to come any closer than the graphed values he calculated.

Ferrule Moments

The ferrule moments are calculated in the same fashion as the tip moments, except that there's no weight until the ferrules. In our example, if the 7-foot, 6-inch (90-inch) rod is a two-piece, the ferrules are located at 45 inches — so there would be no ferrule moments until that point. From experience, I know that a 7-foot, 6-inch two-piece rod requires a size $^{13}/_{64}$ ferrule, which weighs 118 grains or 0.271 ounce. Again, an impact factor is used (multiply by 4). Therefore the calculations would be as follows:

$$45'' \quad (0.271 \times 0 \times 4) \quad = 0.000$$
$$50'' \quad (0.271 \times 5 \times 4) \quad = 1.355$$
$$\bullet$$
$$\bullet$$
$$80'' \quad (0.271 \times 35 \times 4) = 9.485$$

Center of Gravity

For those instances when the ferrules are not on a 5-inch location, then your calculations must account for the center of gravity of their weight. Unlike the line that's off the rod, the ferrules are a part of the rod. So you'd use a length figured from the actual location to the one you're investigating.

Bamboo Moments

These are the most complex to calculate, but they're large and important enough to make calculation worthwhile. I won't go into all of the mathematics; I'll just try to explain the concept. As you move from the tip to the butt of the rod, the dimensions across the flats increase, and the mass increases. So you need to calculate the center of mass in order to find the location of the leverage arm and calculate the moments at each location.

When you begin, these values represent an imaginary rod. Then as the actual rod dimensions are derived, you can substitute the new values to bring the moments of the bamboo weight closer to their real-life values.

With all the individual moments calculated, their values are added together. This will give you the total moments for each location, from the tip to the end of the action length. Remember, however, that these totals are only temporary. As new dimensions are generated, the moments are recalculated because of the changes in the bamboo moments.

Dimensions

To determine the dimensions for your proposed fly-rod design, the total moments and the allowable stress values are combined in the following formula:

M = f(b)S where
M = moments
f(b) = permitted bending stress
S = section modulus (ln3)

Now, as I mentioned earlier, these dimensions are only temporary. To bring them closer to more accurate values, you recalculate the bamboo moments. You use the dimensions with the allowable stress values to get a second value, and then a third refiguring occurs.

All of these calculations, of course, raise a valid question. Would more cycles through the calculations actually yield more accurate dimensions? Remember that in practice you're working to be physically accurate only to the nearest 0.001 inch, and three derivations certainly yield these mathematical results.

Theory Versus Practice

On paper, Garrison's stress curve had a smooth flow, starting with a high value at the tip and gradually descending to lower values in the butt section. However, the calculated dimensions for the tip were not what Garrison used. He considered these numbers to be impracticably small, so he arbitrarily increased them. Then he blended the new tip dimensions into the natural slope of the dimensional graph.

Unfortunately, it is never mentioned in Garrison's writings what this did in relation to his stress curve. By adding material he consequently lowered the f(b) values at the tip. Instead of the 196000 value, in actuality the figure would be 51457.

Concerns

Wouldn't this significant difference affect a rod's character? It certainly set my own mind to wondering about simply rewriting the formula instead of solving dimensions using stress values. (Perhaps there's a clue in Garrison's text. In the passage that leads up to the mathematical explanation, we learn that Garrison may have used an 8-foot Payne in developing his stress curves.)

Whatever the explanation, I ended up with a computer program that is bidirectional with relation to stress values. And a similar program may launch you into discovering the theories and designs of rodmakers other than Garrison. All you need are the dimensions of a rod and the distance at which its casting strength is maximized.

I've made only one rod based on the Garrison tapers. Here again, I did it with my own preferences in mind. I started gathering dimensions (tapers) from different rods and swapping them with other makers. With each newly obtained taper, I ran the numbers through the HEXROD program to see what the character of the rod looked like from the point of view of stress curves. From this I narrowed down the different characters of rod tapers to those that I liked. Can I describe the action? Not really, but I can show you the character on a graph.

Tip	45883
05″	145740
10″	171041
15″	169797
20″	171094
25″	153944
30″	150051
35″	129181
40″	133008
45″	151417
50″	150430
55″	144962
60″	145942
65″	153009

A general description of this rod's character would be *parabolic*. But I seldom use this term, because to some makers it denotes a rod of slower action or character. Still, with a little imagination you can see the distinct reversed J of the curve. By almost everyone's definition, this is definitely a parabolic action. You have a softer tip, a rigid midsection, and a softer butt. On a graph it's clearly a reversed J.

Why Stresses, Not Dimensions?

I am often asked this question in discussions about rod tapers and alteration. As I mentioned earlier, an f(b) curve only represents a character. It merely relates to potential numbers when a tip-impact factor, number of sections, and similar elements are all applied. The character remains the same whether it's a #3-weight or a #4-weight, a two-piece or a three-piece.

If you were to look at the dimensions of these rods, however, you'd find little in common that you could alter with much success. Even if you compare two rods with the same number of pieces but different line weights, the general "slope" of the graphed dimensions will be different because of unique ferrule weights and bamboo weights.

	6′3″ #3/2	6′3″ #4/2	
Tip	0.065	0.070	0.005 dif
05″	0.077	0.082	
10″	0.093	0.100	
15″	0.108	0.116	
20″	0.120	0.128	
25″	0.137	0.146	
30″	0.150	0.160	
35″	0.169	0.179	
40″	0.180	0.191	
45″	0.185	0.196	
50″	0.198	0.209	
55″	0.213	0.224	
60″	0.225	0.236	
65″	0.233	0.244	0.011 dif

Things To Try

Over the years some of the best-casting rods I've produced had blended characters. By this I mean they were actually curve-averaged: Two distinct f(b) curves from two rods created an entirely new f(b) curve. The possibilities could, in theory, be endless, but there are certain limits to all workable combinations.

Rod design is not necessarily the mystery that some make it out to be. A good start might be to graph those tapers that you have cast and know the feel of. Then perhaps you might design a three-piece rod with the same character as a two-piece with which you're familiar. You could later move on to changing the line sizes of rods that you've made. You'll find that instead of just concentrating on which fly to pick when you're on the stream, you'll start to think more about the character of your rod and its part in your fly-fishing technique.

The Next Step

It may have been a presumption on my part, but I tried to advance the cause by simply rewriting Garrison's formula and beginning to solve for f(b)-given dimensions. In this way I could use his idea as a ruler to investigate other existing rods for their stress characteristics.

To determine a tip-impact factor (the weight of line hung off the rod tip), I cast a rod and used the distance at which it maximized as the value. This began to raise questions of how the energy was supposed to flow through a fly rod. Some of what I thought to be the best-casting rods had some of the most unusual stress curves.

Remember that a stress curve only defines the character of a rod. By recalculating different line weights and the number of sections, I've been able to make many different rods with the same characteristics.

A "Hinge"

As I suggested earlier, we each have our own fly-fishing styles. These are usually dictated by the waters we fish and the species we are pursuing. For more than thirty years I've chased trout in the streams of Michigan. So when newcomers to rodmaking ask me for advice, I recommend two things. The first is to be as knowledgeable as possible about rodmaking, almost a guru. And the second is to be learn all you can about the fishing style you've chosen. Following my own advice, I make only trout rods.

When I fish upstream, for example, I depend on two basic types of casts. The first is a roll cast, which I use to shotgun riffle waters. A good #4-weight rod should roll-cast 45 feet and transmit enough energy to turn over a 9-foot leader with a decent bug on it.

My second type of casting is the conventional targeted forward cast. But I practice it in a particular fashion. If I don't create action on the first cast, I expect that the rod will be able to deliver the fly back to the original position with only a simple backcast and delivery. In other words, my rod has to be able to load fast and shoot line — often up to 20 feet.

It's fairly simple to describe the rod action I prefer. The first break point is about a quarter of the length of the rod from the tip. A break point, or "hinge" as some call it, could be described as a point where the values shift from a smooth pathway. This gives a rod what's called a soft tip, and a soft tip allows you to cast the leader alone. After the break point, the rod loads normally and the effect of the soft tip gradually diminishes as line is added and the rod loads.

The second hinge is located at about three quarters of the rod length from the tip. This point adds a momentary pause in the transmission of energy in the rod. This break allows the line to form a better-developed loop when you roll-cast. The pause is needed in roll-casting because the surface tension of the line on the water has a tendency to slow the line's reaction. By moving this point away from your hand, more of the line will rise during the cast. The closer the break point to your hand, the more the line will fall during the cast. You've found the sweet spot when the line will cast level with the water surface.

If you look back at the character curve I listed earlier, you can actually see the break points, or hinges, to which I refer. The first is formed between the 10-inch and 20-inch points. The second hinge is located around the 45-inch point, which is 20 inches out from the hand. This is the hinge that allows the rod to roll-cast well.

Limitations

As precise and straightforward as some techniques may appear, there are limitations to computer-assisted fly-rod design. There are certainly times when human intervention is required, or rather desired — if the rules are too rigid, I feel that creativity is lost. After all, isn't it good to know that you can still color outside the lines?

One of the pitfalls of computer-assisted design is in lengthening or shortening a character curve. In these instances the distinct points of the base curve will be moved off the 5-inch increments and their impact on the character will be reduced. This is when intervention is needed. From the included curves, you can detect the specific areas that were stretched or shrunk. These less important areas were selected so that important hinges were left intact and remained at appropriate locations.

Step-Down Ferrules

Many of the classic rods were made with step-down ferrules. The term actually spells out how the ferrule works. Instead of the ferrule increasing to accommodate rod sections of the same dimension, the sections being joined are actually unequal in dimension by $\frac{1}{64}$ inch.

If you graph the character of these rods, you'll note severe spikes immediately before the ferrule. The character effect of these spikes is softened by the amount of material removed to mount this style of ferrule. If you intend to substitute a non-step-down ferrule in the rods constructed from these curves, the spikes in these character curves need to be smoothed out.

INDEX